Domestic Abuse
in the Novels of
African American Women

D1715553

Domestic Abuse in the Novels of African American Women

A Critical Study

HEATHER DUERRE HUMANN

McFarland & Company, Inc., Publishers

Jefferson, North Carolina

LIBRARY OF CONGRESS CATALOGUING-IN-PUBLICATION DATA

Humann, Heather Duerre, 1974– author.
    Domestic Abuse in the Novels of African American Women :
a Critical Study / Heather Duerre Humann.
        p.   cm.
    Includes bibliographical references and index.

    ISBN 978-0-7864-7956-6 (softcover : acid free paper) ∞
    ISBN 978-1-4766-1641-4 (ebook)

    1. American fiction—African American authors—History and
criticism.   2. Family violence in literature.   3. African Americans
in literature.   4. Spousal abuse—United States.   I. Title
    PS374.N4H86 2014
    813.009'896073—dc23   2014018132

BRITISH LIBRARY CATALOGUING DATA ARE AVAILABLE

Front cover image: serious woman
© Cheryl Casey/iStock/Thinkstock

Printed in the United States of America

McFarland & Company, Inc., Publishers
    Box 611, Jefferson, North Carolina 28640
        www.mcfarlandpub.com

I dedicate this book
to my wonderful children,
Ashley and James!

Acknowledgments

I am grateful to so many people for the support they provided to me at various stages of this project. I am indebted to Dr. Fred Whiting; to him, I will always be grateful for mentoring me during graduate school and for serving as my graduate advisor. He challenged me to think critically and taught me the power of revision, two valuable skills which aided me with this project. Thanks are also due to Dr. Yolanda Manora, Dr. Metka Zupancic, Dr. Albert Pionke, Dr. Tony Bolden, and the late Dr. Robert Young, for the professional encouragement and assistance they provided me during graduate school and the years since then. I remain grateful, as well, to Dr. Barbara McCaskill and Dr. Sujata Iyengar, both of whom encouraged my studies so many years ago. To my former students, I also owe my gratitude. I am especially indebted to those students who took my African American Literature course at the University of Alabama in 2010 and influenced my thinking about neo-slave narratives, Toni Morrison's fiction, and so many other things. I also would like to thank my friends (and running buddies), Stephanie Cobb, Kim West, and Bonnie Whitener.

Finally, I need to express my sincere and heartfelt thanks to my family for their encouragement. I especially appreciate the love and support of my grandmother, Alice Duerre, a retired schoolteacher. Words cannot express what I owe to my sweet husband, Madison Humann, and to our two wonderful children, Ashley and James. Thank you for being my inspiration and for always being there for me.

An earlier version of Chapter 3 appeared in *Revista Atenea* ISSN 0885–6079, Vol. XXXI, 1–2 Year 2011. An earlier version of Chapter 7 appeared in *Women's Studies: An Interdisciplinary Journal* as "Family Violence in *Love*" (43.2 [2013]: 1–18). I thank the editors for permission to reprint this material.

Table of Contents

Acknowledgments   vi
Introduction. What's Love Got to Do with It?   1

CHAPTER 1. Silence and Reclamation:
    Zora Neale Hurston's *Their Eyes Were Watching God*   19

CHAPTER 2. Dysfunctional Domesticity:
    Toni Morrison's *The Bluest Eye*   39

CHAPTER 3. Transformation and Testimony:
    Gayl Jones' *Corregidora*   51

CHAPTER 4. Voicing Violence: Alice Walker's
    The Color Purple   61

CHAPTER 5. Violent Spaces: Gloria Naylor's
    The Women of Brewster Place and *Linden Hills*   77

CHAPTER 6. Family Violence and Popular Fiction: Terry
    McMillan's *Mama* and *A Day Late and a Dollar Short*   99

CHAPTER 7. Family and the Legacy of Violence:
    Toni Morrison's *Love*   121

CHAPTER 8. Domestic Violence through a Science Fiction Lens:
    Octavia Butler's *Seed to Harvest*   135

Conclusion   165
Works Cited   169
Index   177

Introduction: *What's Love Got to Do with It?*

What do the 1993 film *What's Love Got to Do with It?*, Nikki Giovanni's poem "Woman," Ntozake Shange's poem "With No Immediate Cause," and musician Chris Brown's 2009 arrest for felony battery have in common? All are concerned with the problem of intraracial (within the same race) gender-based violence in the African American community. Domestic abuse has long been a hidden problem—and this is especially true in the African American community—but many black female artists, poets, and singers, have, over the past several decades, begun to weigh in on the issue of domestic abuse against black women and tried to map a better way. The high visibility of the Chris Brown case and the popularity of the Tina Turner film biopic open up a forum for public discussion and awareness of the issue of domestic abuse, but many African American female novelists have also been raising awareness about abused women through their literary works. Like films such as *What's Love Got to Do with It?* (which chronicles Tina and Ike Turner's abusive relationship) and the many songs and poems that confront the issue, much of the fiction written by African American female novelists sheds light on the complex—and once taboo—subject of domestic violence. These novels raise awareness about domestic violence by giving voice to the experiences of abused women and they also illustrate the myriad forces that conspire to keep hidden the problem of domestic abuse.

The aims of *Domestic Abuse in the Novels of African American Women* are threefold: to examine how African American female novelists portray domestic abuse and thus raise awareness about the complex problem, to outline how literary depictions of domestic violence are responsive to a variety of cultural and historical forces, and, finally, to explore the literary tradition of novels that deal with domestic abuse within the African Amer-

1

ican community—a tradition that was begun by Zora Neale Hurston in the 1930s and has since flourished and taken different forms, thanks to the diverse body of fiction created by more contemporary African American women writers. The literary works discussed in this book all reflect, question, and ultimately contribute to the ways in which contemporary American society shapes attitudes about, and responds to, the myriad problems related to domestic abuse. *Domestic Abuse in the Novels of African American Women* considers a diverse assortment of literary works: Zora Neale Hurston's literary masterpiece, *Their Eyes Were Watching God* (1937); Gayl Jones' blues novel, *Corregidora* (1975); Alice Walker's powerful epistolary novel, *The Color Purple* (1982); two timely novels written by Gloria Naylor, *The Women of Brewster Place* (1982) and *Linden Hills* (1985); Toni Morrison's classic, *The Bluest Eye* (1970), and her more recent novel, *Love* (2003); two of bestselling author Terry McMillan's novels, *Mama* (1987) and *A Day Late and a Dollar Short* (2002); and, finally, the books which make up Octavia Butler's epic science fiction series known as her *Patternmaster* (or sometimes *Patternist*) series, which was published in a single volume titled *Seed to Harvest* (2007). Octavia Butler's first published novel, *Patternmaster* (1976) was the first book in this series to appear. From 1977 until 1984, she published four additional novels in the series: *Mind of My Mind* (1977), *Survivor* (1978), *Wild Seed* (1980) and *Clay's Ark* (1984). Butler later expressed a dislike for the novel *Survivor,* so she declined to bring it back into print. Consequently, *Survivor* is not included in *Seed to Harvest.*

Looking at this selection of books reveals how African American women writers from different eras have confronted domestic violence through their literary depictions. Examining these authors' literary treatment of domestic abuse also demonstrates that domestic violence has a history and that its history has changed dramatically—and within a relatively short period of time.

As part of its project, this book also seeks to address an underexplored dynamic: the relationship between the abuse of individual women and the larger structure of oppression that African American women face. This book illustrates the connection between these two (albeit sometimes seemingly distinct) problems. The principal arena where these two problems meet and come to a head is in the domestic sphere and within the family structure. Though not always acknowledged by common perceptions of it, the family, as a social structure, actually belongs to the private sphere and public sphere alike. The problems and limitations that individual women encounter within their homes relate to, overlap with, and in some ways mirror the broader social problems that women face as a group. Moreover, there is a link between societal expectations and views about females and the way individual women are treated by their families. This connection has the potential to affect various aspects of women's lives and experiences, but a particularly difficult and dangerous outcome of this link is that the problem of domestic violence against women—a problem that is always both personal and political—is perpetuated within our society because of how we, as a society, situate the family within our culture. Our society relies upon the various political and economic functions of the family to maintain the larger sociopolitical structure, yet insists on viewing much of what happens within the domestic sphere, and within the family structure, as a private matter. The supposedly private nature of the home thus conspires to cover up and justify incidents of domestic abuse.

This book explores the relationship between the personal and the political with respect to the issue of domestic violence by offering literary analyses of the fiction of Zora Neale Hurston, Gayl Jones, Toni Morrison, Alice Walker, Gloria Naylor, Terry McMillan, and Octavia Butler. This project considers how these authors portray domestic abuse and investigates how their literary depictions of domestic violence are responsive to a variety of cultural and historical forces. One facet of this book's central argument is that there has been a significant transformation in terms of how society has viewed domestic violence since Hurston so profoundly confronted the issue in her 1937 novel. Since the publication of *Their Eyes Were Watching God,* there have been further shifts in terms of societal attitudes about the problems. Indeed, even between the late 1960s, when Morrison was busy writing *The Bluest Eye,* through the beginning of the 21st century when she published *Love,* cultural attitudes have transformed widely with respect to domestic abuse—and these changes can traced by examining the novels produced during this period. The 1930s represents a time period when domestic issue was seen as a nonissue. Indeed, a major criticism of *Their Eyes Were Watching God*—and Hurston as a writer, in general—is that her fiction was too domestic and utterly apolitical (as if politics and the domestic sphere were mutually exclusive). Many critics dismissed this novel precisely because it deals with the politics of the domestic sphere and, moreover, Hurston's contemporary reviewers and critics ignored the numerous and rampant incidents of domestic violence, which not only make up so much of the action of the novel but which also prove pivotal to the development of the novel's protagonist.

If *Their Eyes Were Watching God* reflects an era when domestic abuse was treated as a nonissue, the time span that begins with 1960s and continues to the 1980s constitutes a period characterized by denial of the problem of domestic violence, a denial that is reflected in much of the fiction of that time. Literary representations of domestic abuse in the late 20th and early 21st centuries show a period that signals a shift to an imperfect recognition of the problem. By using several literary works as examples, this book traces the relationship between society's changing attitudes about domestic violence and the way particular authors not only address the issue, but also complicate our understanding of it. The different authors and texts considered all share a common trait in that they all raise awareness about the issue of domestic abuse, yet they differ from one another with respect to how they engage with the problem.

Addressing domestic abuse not only means engaging with a controversial topic, but it also means dealing with a concept that is very much in flux because of how the term has grown over time to include a wide range of offenses, some of which would not have been characterized as problematic, let alone abusive, in the past. Discussing domestic violence means having to rely on labels that are altogether insufficient to describe it and the myriad problems associated with it—terms such as "domestic abuse," "domestic violence," and "intimate abuse," which are too broad and too vague to sufficiently address the variety and range of offenses subsumed under those labels. Writing about domestic abuse also means considering its history and addressing how American society and our medical, psychological, and legal communities have, alternately, dealt with, tried to deal with, and failed to deal with the host of problems associated with it. These issues, which would be necessary to discuss in any examination of domestic violence, are especially crucial to this project, which seeks to highlight how contemporary African American female authors' portrayals of domestic abuse respond both directly and indirectly to a variety of cultural and historical forces including medical, psychological, and legal discourses/debates, the nation's political leanings, racial and socioeconomic issues, and attitudes about human rights, including women's and civil rights.

Significantly, the authors addressed in this project not only reflect but also oftentimes contribute to these complex and interrelated forces. Zora Neale Hurston, Gayl Jones, Toni Morrison, Alice Walker, Gloria Naylor, Terry McMillan, and Octavia Butler complicate our understanding of domestic abuse in several ways. In their literary works, these writers depict characters who commit an assortment of offensive behaviors that all could be labeled as domestic abuse. These behaviors range from yelling, taunting, and threatening, to slapping, pinching, kicking, punching, and beating. In the novels in question here, females are—sometimes figuratively, other times literally—locked up in their homes. They are also forced into marriages, made to undergo abortions, used as breeders against their will, and subject to a range of sexual abuse including child molestation, statutory rape, child rape, and rape; both arson and multiple murders figure into the novels in question. Though the offenses depicted in these novels run the gamut, two common threads bind them together: they all occur within the home, and their perpetrators, witnesses, accomplices, and victims are intimately acquainted with one another. By including a range of offenses in their novels, these authors not only highlight what the term domestic violence has grown to include, but they also identify behaviors as domestic abuse that had not hitherto been considered as such. Yet another way Hurston, Jones, Morrison, Walker, Naylor, McMillan, and Butler engage with the issue is by showing how the supposedly "private" nature of the domestic sphere works to hide incidents of domestic abuse and leads to the problem's being minimized. These authors' portrayals also work to show the relationship between the larger structure of women's oppression and the mistreatment and abuse women face in the home. Through these types of depictions these writers not only raise awareness about the problem, but they also reveal its political nature. They offer pointed critiques of society, by implicating the broader sociopolitical structure in justifying and covering up—and therefore perpetuating—the problem of violence in the home. Their representations of violence in the home work to underscore how even over a short period of time, society's perspectives about domestic abuse have changed and continue to change.

By writing about domestic abuse, the authors considered in this book all raise awareness about the problem, yet the publication of their novels—novels which, of course, all center on domestic violence—also coincides with a heightened awareness of the problem in the medical and legal communities, as well as with more media attention being paid to the problem. Far from offering a static picture of women's abuse and oppression, the characters and scenarios within these literary works demonstrate how ideas about women and the family have evolved over time. As the problem of domestic violence surfaces in these novels, so, too, do related concerns, including the bagginess of the term and the inadequacy in the way our society has dealt with the problem. Therefore, as part of this Introduction, it is crucial to discuss some points related to my concerns about domestic violence—including how the family has been theorized historically and the etymology, connotations, and the complexity of the term domestic violence.

The Family as Public/Private

Just as Marx recognized, the family performs various crucial economic and political functions including the reproduction of a labor supply and the sustenance of current and future workers. Far from simply being a "private matter," sexual reproduction has a specific political and economic dimension—reproduction guarantees a steady supply of future workers that can one day be exploited for profit as part of the system of capitalism. In fact, "reproduction and kinship are themselves integrally related to the social relations of production and the state," a point scholar Rosalind Petchesky asserts as she discusses the intersection of labor, social class, and the domestic sphere (377). As Petchesky and others have argued, production plays a critical role by ensuring that there will be an ever ready pool of labor supply. Maintaining gender-specific roles within the family—both inside and outside the home—is absolutely necessary to the continuation of the current economic and sociopolitical system, as well. The various kinds of duties that women typically perform inside of the home—the countless hours women spend cooking, cleaning, bearing and rearing children, and caring for their spouses, among other tasks—is almost always unpaid labor and, as such, helps to maintain an exploitative system. It is not an accident, nor can it be attributed solely to biology, that women have ended up performing these jobs.

A trend that began in the 19th century and then intensified in the early part of the 20th century was the reorganization of labor during the industrial revolution, which caused many men to begin spending their daytime hours outside of the home, in the workplace. The mass exodus of men from the home to the workplace during working hours encouraged the widespread beliefs that household chores were so-called women's work and the domestic sphere was the proper realm for women, and, as well as other factors, has contributed to how women are viewed by 20th and 21st century societies.

Though issues related to women and the labor they have historically performed, and often still perform, have been—and remain—extremely complicated because of race and social class (not to mention other historically specific factors) feminists tend to agree that the work women do without receiving credit or payment is clearly one way women have been, and still are, exploited. Women who work outside of the home have other issues relating to exploitation to contend with, as well. These include discrimination, sexual harassment, and unequal pay, not to mention the myriad complexities that arise for the many working women who frequently take on the same responsibilities inside of their homes that their contemporaries who do not work outside of the home do.

Of course, race, too, plays a major role in terms of societal views about—and expectations of—women. A key example of a feminist who addresses the constellation of concerns related to race, economics, and gender is Angela Davis, a scholar who discusses women and the labor they perform in her book *Women, Race, and Class.* In that study, Davis addresses the complexity of the issues that dictate women's behavior. Although society plays a large role in determining what acceptable behavior is for women, it is often an individual woman's family who puts pressure on her to conform to society's expectations. Family, then, not only serves as a basic economic unit within the system of patriarchal capitalism, but it also has the distinct political function of helping to maintain its status quo. Although today many of us recognize that the family clearly has a distinct political function, the household and the family structure have been traditionally understood to be part of the private sphere.

Significantly, private and public spheres have historically—even going back to antiquity—been considered distinct and separate from one another. As Anita Allen explains, the Greeks "distinguished the 'public' sphere of the *polis,* or city-state, from the 'private' sphere of the *oikos,* or household"; the Romans similarly differentiated "*res publicae,* concerns of the community, from *res privatae,* concerns of individuals and families"; and, post–Enlightenment Western thought still recognizes the "classical premise that social life ought to be organized into public and private spheres" as well as the "premise that the private sphere consists chiefly of the home, the family, and apolitical intimate association" (461). She describes how this distinction has traditionally existed and how it has been traditionally understood:

> The public realm was the sector in which free males, whose property and economic status conveyed citizenship, participated in collective governance. By contrast, the private realm was the mundane sector of economic and biological survival. Wives, children, slaves, and servants populated the private sphere, living as subordinate ancillaries to male caretakers [Allen, 461].

The notion that the public and the private occupy two separate spheres had—and still has—a significant impact on how we think about a catalog of concerns including those relating to the family, privacy, equality, economics, and gender roles, to name just a few. Further, the idea that the public and the private constituted, and at least by some people's estimation still constitute, two distinct spheres privileged, and still privileges, certain classes of individuals and roles over others. Another effect of maintaining a distinction between the public and private realms is that, under the guise of protecting privacy, certain negative behaviors, including violence against women, are able to persist, even when they are clearly threatening or harmful. This is because they occur outside of the scope of what is considered public. Even today, in the 21st century, much of what happens in the home is seen by many as a private affair.

Although the distinction between private and public realms obscures and helps to minimize how large a problem domestic violence truly is—by, among other things, successfully covering up instances of it and treating it like a private matter—the split between private and public spheres is not the only factor contributing to this problem. Though domestic abuse is seen as an aberration by society (one that threatens the private sphere), it is actually a product of its organization. Domestic violence, and more broadly, violence against women are social practices that have arisen under the conditions of capitalism and male dominance. Importantly, however, what constitutes domestic violence and society's perceptions of, and reactions to, the whole host of problems associated with it are unstable concepts. In many regards the family replicates in a microcosm the anxieties and expectations of society at large, and as society's image of the family changes, so, too, do our perceptions of domestic violence. This serves to further suggest that domestic violence is very much a concept in flux.

Domestic Violence Is Both Personal and Political

Critical to understanding domestic violence—and its causes and consequences—is recognizing that domestic violence and all violence against women, for that matter, is foremost a political issue. In fact, as Lisa H. Schwartzman argues, violence against women—including rape and domestic violence—is fundamentally both a feminist and political issue, not merely a personal problem for the individual (or individuals) victimized. Though undoubtedly individuals so often tend to see their own abuse as personal and frequently feel ashamed about it, as if they are somehow part of the problem or as if their abusers' behaviors would change if they somehow altered their behavior, it is important to recognize that this perception itself is a product of the larger sociopolitical system. Indeed, shame and self-recrimination are the mechanisms by which the ideological status quo is maintained. The roots of domestic violence are more sinister, complicated, and systematic than something we could simply attribute to individual human interactions. If domestic violence is both a personal problem—for the woman or women suffering because of it—and a political problem, one that affects women as a group and society as a whole, recognizing it as such will help to show the reasons why it is so prevalent and will help to uncover how domestic violence is part of a socially constructed system of abuse of women.

Domestic Violence: A Problematic Term

I have thus far been calling, and for the sake of clarity will continue to refer to, acts of violence against women and children by those close to them as domestic violence or domestic abuse, because these are the terms commonly used, but it is necessary to point out the inadequacy of this type of phrasing. My dissatisfaction with the terms domestic violence and domestic abuse is similar to the one that critics of the term sexual harassment frequently cite: these terms are both too broad and too vague. Domestic violence and domestic abuse are catch-all phrases that describe any number of problematic behaviors that range from emotional abuse like mocking, insults, and other types of putdowns, to various types of physical abuse such as punching, pinching, and kicking, but these terms can also refer to even graver offenses such as rape, maiming, attempted murder, and murder. The fact that these terms are used to describe such a wide range of abusive behaviors points to an inadequacy in both the way our society expresses and deals with an entire catalog of problems associated with abuse perpetrated against women by those close to them. The fact that we have failed to come up with a better way to describe this type of systematic violence against women is both frustrating and fitting, for it points to the larger problem of a culture of violence against women and a society that attempts to minimize the impact of violence against women. Using euphemisms or a catch-all phrase like domestic violence might even worsen the problem by either soft-pedaling the issue or further confusing it since domestic violence can mean so many different things and can describe the most minor insults as well as the most egregious physical harm—and even worse.

This concern over labeling that arises when talking about domestic violence is a function of the malleability of all such terms. Akin to the argument about the concept of child abuse made by Ian Hacking in his article "The Making and Molding of Child Abuse," I am contending here that our concept of what constitutes domestic violence is not only too broad, but also historically variable. Hacking persuasively argued that child abuse "is not one fixed thing" and claimed that "since 1962 the class of acts falling under 'child abuse' has changed every few years" (259). Similarly, what society counts as domestic violence has changed over time.

Looking at the history of the term domestic violence further illuminates the myriad problems surrounding the issue. The *OED* does not have an individual listing for the term domestic violence; the entry for "domestic violence" is a subcategory within the entry "domestic." More disturbing, perhaps, is the lack of history reported for the term domestic violence in the *OED* entry, and that there is hardly any mention of the issue of domestic violence in all but the most recent books that discuss the family and theorizations of the family—indeed, both the term itself and references to the types of problems associated with domestic violence are conspicuously missing from many discussions and theorizations of the family. It's difficult to find discussions about domestic abuse in books about the family that were published before the 1990s. In fact, the term domestic violence and its synonyms—domestic abuse, spousal abuse, wife beating, etcetera—are seldom, if ever, mentioned in books on the family and theorizations of the family from even the 1970s and 1980s. Sadly and tellingly, many of these books' indices have no mention whatsoever of the term domestic violence (or affiliated terms).

Domestic violence is a prevalent problem, but it has for so long merited so very little attention in books from a wide range of academic disciplines, including sociology, history, psychology, and the law, as well as those intended for a more general audience, all of which at least purport to address the family in society and contemporary theorizations of the family. Taken together, these observations suggest several possibilities: domestic violence is an aberration, and thus, has no place in a functioning, stable family; domestic violence is a private matter, something to be dealt with inside the family; and domestic violence is a taboo subject, something not to be addressed or even mentioned. If the possibilities mentioned here seem a bit contradictory, it is not accidental; each of the three possibilities echoes a popular societal attitude about domestic violence. If these three explanations do not fit all that well together, it is because views on what constitutes domestic violence, how much of a problem it is, and what—if anything— can and should be done about it vary greatly. It is worth noting, too, that all of these explanations share a common drawback: the same discourses that sanction them are themselves part of the system that allows if not encourages the problem. Indeed, domestic violence works as a regulatory mechanism that must remain unacknowledged in order to produce these contradictions.

So, how do we address, or even sort through, the various, overlapping implications of, and questions surrounding, these explanations? If, for example, domestic violence is truly an aberration, then how do we account for its prevalence? Also, since domestic violence has traditionally been viewed as a private matter, then what, if anything, can (and should) society do about it in terms of protecting those it affects? Finally, if domestic violence is, and remains, such a taboo subject, then how can we hope to eradicate or at least minimize the problem if we cannot even talk about it openly? What becomes most evident by the multitude of questions raised here is that more examination is needed of the complex set of problems associated with domestic violence.

If domestic abuse has been a neglected subject in general, the effects that domestic violence has had on black women have been particularly underexplored. Writing back in 1989, Darlene Clark Hine pointed out, "One of the most remarked upon but least analyzed themes in Black women's history deals with Black women's sexual vulnerability and powerlessness as victims of rape and domestic violence" (912). These remarks were true in the 1980s and they still remain true today. Indeed, even in the 21st century, there remains a notable lack in terms of the history of the all too common problem of domestic abuse and how it has impacted women of color over time. Where there does seem to be attention paid to the issues of domestic abuse and intra-racial violence is in novels. As Hine notes, the "themes of rape and sexual vulnerability have received considerable attention" in the literary works of "Black women novelists" (192). Not only are novels replete with examples of domestic abuse, but significantly these creative works also serve as a leading indicator of society's growing awareness of the problem of domestic violence and other types of violence against women.

Domestic Violence, Society, the Media and the Law

The manner in which domestic violence has been dealt with by the psychological, medical, and legal communities further highlights that it is very much a concept in flux. It was not until the late 1970s that the problem of domestic violence began to garner any real attention, which coincides with the time in which Battered Woman Syndrome (BWS) was first proposed. Dr. Lenore Walker, a clinical psychologist, coined the term "Battered Woman Syndrome." (Various sources credit her including Joe Wheeler Dixon's "An Essay on Battered Woman Syndrome" and Roth and Cole's "Battered Woman Syndrome." See Walker's 1979 book *The Battered Woman* for her description of BWS.) Since then, this syndrome has become a recognized disorder, and it is now included in both the current and previous editions of the handbook of the American Psychiatric Association (the *DSM-IV* and *DSM-V*). Recognizing that there may be a pathology associated with domestic violence suggests a degree of awareness about, and concern for, this problem, but there is also a danger of pathologizing the perpetrators and victims of this type of abuse, because it denies victims' agency at the same time as it reduces the perpetrators' responsibility, and thus, culpability.

Questions such as these grow even more complex when considering how domestic violence was dealt with in previous decades. For example, in the 1980s, as the 1988 case of *The State of Kansas vs. Peggy Stewart* illustrates in detail, there was little agreement between the courts and the medical and psychological communities in terms of victims' rights to defend themselves against abusers. The Peggy Stewart case, which centers on a woman who fatally shot her abusive husband while he was asleep in the family home, as well as the way the legal system approached Stewart's case, underscores the degree of ambivalence there was toward victims of domestic abuse at that time. It also suggests society's complex perspective about the private sphere. Though Peggy Stewart was found "not guilty" by reason of self-defense, the verdict was appealed on the grounds that, because her husband was asleep when she killed him, there was no immediate danger to her when she acted. This case highlights society's tension about the seriousness of domestic violence and the wide range of opinions about how and to what lengths victims of domestic violence should go to defend themselves from their abusers. It also shows that there is a growing awareness of, and correspondent problems with, legally complex issues pertaining to domestic violence cases including considering what legally constitutes an "immediate" versus an "enduring" threat and how this question relates to the actions and psychological state of victims of domestic violence who stand up to their attackers.

When looking at the 1990s—a point in time less than ten years after the Peggy Stewart case—it is easy to see that domestic violence remains prevalent, but that attitudes about it have begun to shift in a rather short period of time. To be sure, the 1990s brought a degree of heightened awareness of the issue. In 1995, for example, the U.S. Department of Justice founded the Violence against Women Office; in 1996, a National Domestic Violence Hotline was founded. The hotline is still around today. Yet, despite the fact that there was some progress made in the 1990s, even in the 21st century, there remain conflicting opinions about how victims of domestic violence who defend themselves should be dealt with.

An excellent example of this can be seen in two Missouri cases which made the headlines in 2009. Two women who had been imprisoned for their roles in killing their abusive husbands had their sentences commuted yet were not officially paroled or released until three years later. Both husbands were abusive and were killed in the 1980s. Former Missouri Governor Bob Holden commuted the two women's sentences in 2004, but the parole board refused to release the women until 2007 because they feared that releasing them "would depreciate the seriousness of their crimes." This case suggests there is still a significant degree of ambivalence about domestic violence in the 21st century and specifically, that only so much has changed since the 1980s when there was so much disagreement over to what lengths abused women could defend themselves.

Literary Representations of Domestic Abuse

The various literary works examined in this book—*Their Eyes Were Watching God, Corregidora, The Women of Brewster Place, Linden Hills, The Color Purple, The Bluest Eye, Mama, A Day Late and a Dollar Short, Love,* and *Seed to Harvest*—all reveal, probe into, and contribute to the ways in which contemporary American society shapes attitudes about, and responds to, the multitude of problems related to domestic abuse at the same time as they give voice to oppressed and abused women. Individually, these works of fiction illuminate the different causes and consequences of domestic abuse and show the problem from a range of vantage points—

indeed, the perspectives of perpetrators, accomplices, victims, and witnesses alike are represented at different points. One effect is that they show how broader social ills not only trickle down to the home, but are also made manifest within the home and family structure. Another outcome is these novels reveal how the private nature of the domestic sphere both covers up incidents of domestic abuse and works to label the crimes and misdeeds that occur there as "private" matters. These novels also highlight how there is a range of offenses subsumed under the catch-all phrase domestic abuse.

America in the 1930s was very much a patriarchal society. During that era, African American females were oppressed in the home at the same time as they faced racial discrimination and economic injustice. If a woman faced abuse in her home, who would she turn to? Where would she go if she left the home? Zora Neale Hurston's *Their Eyes Were Watching God* (1937) was written in the midst of an era that had yet to even address racism and gender oppression. Moreover, the 1930s were lean and desperate times economically, which not only could lead to abuse, but could even further limit a woman's choice if she faced violence in the home. Two of the other novels that I address—Toni Morrison's *The Bluest Eye* (1971) and Gayl Jones' *Corregidora* (1975)—were published in the 1970s, a time when there were virtually no resources available to help abused women. Although domestic violence is an issue that cuts across lines of race, ethnicity, and social class, women belonging to the underclass and women of color were (and still are) particularly at risk of being victimized in the home. Law enforcement was not merely ill-equipped to deal with the problem, but they seemed to be in denial that the problem even existed. In the 1970s, domestic violence had yet to become the subject of heated political debates. The medical and psychological communities had not yet paid any real attention to the issue, either. Contributing to these problems, during this decade women, and particularly African American women, were plagued with discrimination and oppression in most every aspect of their lives. To be sure, both the Civil Rights movement and the women's movement had begun, but many of the gains that many of us now take for granted in the 21st century had not yet been achieved by feminists or human rights workers in the 1970s.

Terry McMillan's novel *Mama* (1987), Alice Walker's *The Color Purple* (1982), and Gloria Naylor's *The Women of Brewster Place* (1982) and *Linden Hills* (1985) were all published in the 1980s, and they therefore reveal domestic abuse to be a largely hidden problem. The so-called private nature of the domestic sphere, where the majority of the abuse depicted in these novels occurs, covers up the problem of family violence at the same time as their settings discourage involvement by law enforcement or other members of the community. In *Mama,* McMillan's depiction of violence in the home shows how domestic abuse has become normalized, rather than being seen as a problem. Additionally, McMillan demonstrates, through this novel, how the cycle of poverty and violence work together to oppress women and prevent them from achieving the American dream. In *The Color Purple,* Walker paints domestic abuse as commonplace and an inherent part of patriarchy. Naylor's *The Women of Brewster Place* and *Linden Hills* (like McMillan's novel *Mama*) clearly operate as broader social indictments of women's treatment and the larger sociopolitical and economic conditions in contemporary America. Naylor highlights, too, through her literary representations of domestic abuse its regulatory function—that is, how domestic tyranny can function as a way to create order in the home.

Terry McMillan's *A Day Late and a Dollar Short* (2002) and Toni Morrison's *Love* (2003) offer 21st century perspectives about the problem of domestic abuse. Through the use of multiple narrative voices, McMillan explores the many dilemmas that the large and dysfunctional Price family must confront. In her novel *Love,* Morrison presents a retrospective glance of the system-wide problems that foster the oppression and abuse of women. Through her depictions of the novel's characters and the problems they face, Morrison critiques marriage and family life in 20th century America. In this representation of a dysfunctional family, Morrison shows how the home can be a sinister place. Ultimately, though, she offers a degree of hope and reconciliation for two of the novel's main characters, Christine and Heed, when they stop blaming each other for the abuse and oppression suffered by each woman.

The science fiction novels that make up Octavia Butler's *Seed to Harvest* (2007) trace the troubling, complicated, and centuries-long relationship between two supernatural beings, Doro, an African man who survives by transferring his consciousness from one body to another, and Anyanwu, a shape-shifter; the series also shows the consequences of their violent union by the way Butler describes the fierce and volatile new world created by their descendants. Butler's series opens up possibilities not traditionally afforded to more traditional literary genres because she considers the treatment of domestic abuse through the lens of science fiction literature.

Although the different literary works examined in this book all deal with domestic abuse—and though these books all give voice to the domestic violence experienced by women of color—the other concerns addressed in each literary work vary to a degree. Published in 1937, Hurston's *Their Eyes Were Watching God* provides a glimpse of how domestic violence was viewed during an earlier era, and at the same time, it shows how a female from that time period makes strides to regain her voice amidst those who seek to silence her. In Morrison's *The Bluest Eye* (1971), a novel she began writing in 1962, her characters highlight the hidden and secretive nature of violence that occurs within the home, a point that the book's narrator, Claudia MacTeer, makes clear very early in the text when she begins her account of the story with the phrase "quiet as it's kept" (Morrison, 6). *Corregidora,* by Gayl Jones, centers on Ursa Corregidora dealing with the abuse she faced personally at the same time as she tries to come to terms with the legacy the Corregidora women (that is, the women in her family) pass down to Ursa, a legacy that also transmits trauma transgenerationally (through the matrilineal line).

Products of the 1980s, Gloria Naylor's novels *The Women of Brewster Place* (1982) and *Linden Hills* (1985) and Terry McMillan's *Mama* (1987) all raise awareness about domestic abuse by showing how the problem is hidden because the private nature of the domestic sphere works to cover up the problem at the same time as the setting discourages involvement by law enforcement or other members of the community. Naylor's novels demonstrate, as well, the relationship between women's literal—meaning physical and geographic—and figurative places in society. McMillan's novel *Mama,* through her protagonist Mildred Peacock, a feisty survivor who tries to keep her family together in an economically depressed town, also shows the relationship between setting and the oppression women face. Thus, all three of these novels stress the roles environment and geography play in shaping women's lives.

Alice Walker's *The Color Purple* highlights the precarious place of women in the patriarchal south through the depictions of the horrific abuse the novel's protagonist (Celie) suffers at the hands of her stepfather and husband. Though the novel remains troubling, Walker ends on a rather hopeful note by showing Celie reuniting with her children (who were taken from her), reconciling with much of her family, and ultimately regaining her voice, which had for so long been silenced.

Toni Morrison's *Love* shows how far-reaching the effects of abuse can be, for Bill Cosey, the man the novel centers on and the perpetrator and cause of much of the violence depicted in the novel, continues to exert his influence from beyond the grave. Terry McMillan's *A Day Late and a Dollar Short* shows a multigenerational family dealing with a range of contemporary problems including abuse and its aftermath. Using the lens of science fiction, Octavia Butler's *Seed to Harvest* traces the centuries-long history of abuse faced by women of African descent and eventually, provides a forward-looking perspective on the problem of domestic abuse. Thus, in this respect, Butler's series provides both a retrospective and (ultimately) prospective view on how domestic abuse affects African American women.

In the chapters that follow, I provide literary analyses of novels by Hurston, Morrison, Jones, Walker, Naylor, McMillan, and Butler, paying particular attention to these authors' treatment of the problem of intraracial (within the same race) gender-based violence in the African American community. Because the tradition of giving voice to domestic violence within the African American community began with Zora Neale Hurston, I first address her treatment of domestic abuse in *Their Eyes Were Watching God.* I do so both to examine it for its own sake and to consider as well how Hurston, through writing this novel, introduces the rich and diverse literary tradition of novels that follow in its footsteps by confronting the widespread problem of domestic abuse. After looking at Hurston's novel from the 1930s, *Domestic Abuse in the Novels of African American Women* provides literary analyses of the novels from the more recent decades in order to look at the shift that occurs over time in terms of societal attitudes about the problem of domestic abuse, a shift that these novels make visible.

CHAPTER 1

Silence and Reclamation: Zora Neale Hurston's *Their Eyes Were Watching God*

One of the aims of *Domestic Abuse in the Novels of African American Women* is to explore the rich and varied literary tradition of novels that deal with domestic abuse within the African American community. This tradition began with Zora Neale Hurston (1891–1960) in the 1920s and 1930s, and, since then, it has flourished and taken different forms because of the diverse body of fiction created by more contemporary African American women writers. Zora Neale Hurston is not merely important to African American literature, but she, as María Frías Rudolphi emphasizes in her essay "Marriage Doesn't Make Love: Zora Neale Hurston's *Their Eyes Were Watching God*," is a writer "canonized as the 'literary ancestor' of provocative writers" like Toni Morrison, Alice Walker, Gloria Naylor and others, who follow in her tradition (37). Because the tradition of giving voice to domestic violence within the African American community began with Zora Neale Hurston, it is important to devote a chapter of this book to her treatment of domestic abuse in *Their Eyes Were Watching God* (1937), not only to examine Hurston's novel for its own sake, but also since it spawned such a rich and diverse tradition of novels which follow in its footsteps by confronting the widespread problem of domestic abuse.

An anthropologist and noted author, Zora Neale Hurston was a fixture of the Harlem Renaissance before writing her masterpiece, *Their Eyes Were Watching God*, a novel that was greeted with mixed reviews. A book with a complicated reception and publication history, *Their Eyes Were Watching God* was met with controversy early on. Alain Locke, who was an important voice of the Harlem Renaissance, wrote an early review of the book that suggested that *Their Eyes Were Watching God* was out of step with the more serious literary trends of the Harlem Renaissance. Richard Wright was even harsher in his criticism of the novel, blasting it in the magazine *New Masses* by proclaiming it contained "no theme, no message, no thought" (Wright, 25). As Mark Spilka emphasizes, Wright dismisses Hurston's novel without any acknowledgment of "male abusiveness in black marriages" (8). Other reviewers, including Sterling Brown, similarly dismissed *Their Eyes Were Watching God,* seeing it as "worthless because it seemed to ignore the political and social realities of the time" (James, 230). Many contemporary black reviewers also criticized the novel for being too sentimental, a feature of the novel that many contemporary white reviewers (paradoxically) seemed drawn to. By and large, their reviews offered more praise for Hurston's novel than did the black reviewers' of that time period.

Though the novel was much discussed in the years following its initial publication, Hurston's work slid into obscurity for decades, due to a number of cultural and political reasons. It was not until the 1970s when, thanks in large part to Alice Walker, *Their Eyes Were Watching God* again became popular reading—and a mainstay in high school and college literature courses. The mixed reactions to the novel that emerged at the time of its initial publication, coupled with the fact that the book nearly dropped off the radar only to be revived when, in 1975, Alice Walker published her now seminal article "In Search of Zora Neale Hurston" in the March 1975 issue of *Ms.* Magazine, adds to the sense that *Their Eyes Were Watching God* was, and remains, a provocative and potentially polarizing text. Indeed, some critics, such as Philip Goldstein, have gone as far as to say that *Their Eyes Were Watching God* is an inherently "problematic text" (125). Though much of the scholarship that emerged in the late 20th and early 21st centuries praises *Their Eyes Were Watching God* as Hurston's masterpiece (and celebrates the novel as an early example of feminist literature written by an African American author), the same type of criticism that plagued Hurston's novel in the 1930s persists. For example, Hazel Carby indicts the book for not having a political message, thus echoing the type of criticism that Locke, Wright, Brown, and others levied against Hurston. Carby was especially critical of the characters Hurston created in *Their Eyes.* She went as far as to say that the novel depicts "a folk who are outside of history" (Carby, 77).

Their Eyes Were Watching God: Janie's Story

Their Eyes Were Watching God centers on Janie Crawford, an African American woman, who, after returning to the town of Eatonville, Florida, from a long absence, tells the story of her life and journey via an extended flashback to her close friend, Pheoby. Janie shares her story with Pheoby because the two women are close friends, but she also does so in order for Pheoby to relay Janie's story to the prying townspeople who have been gossiping about her in her two-year-long absence. Janie's life has four major periods, her childhood being the first and the latter three corresponding to her three marriages to three very different men. Though the novel describes these distinct periods in Janie's life, throughout most of the novel (and throughout the majority of Janie's life), there is a constant: Janie is silenced and controlled by those close to her. Her grandmother forces young Janie into a loveless marriage with the much older landowning Logan Killicks, her second husband "Jody" (Joe Starks) oppresses her throughout their marriage and physically abuses her, and her third husband, "Tea Cake" (Vergible Woods), savagely beats her and later, in a very dramatic scene, when he's driven mad by rabies and threatens Janie's life, he leaves her no choice but for her to defend herself using lethal force.

Published in 1937, this novel offers a glimpse of the types of challenges faced by black women who, like Janie Crawford, confronted racism and discrimination in a patriarchal society at the same time as their own families sought to control them and force them into silence and submission. By tracing Janie's journey, complete with the abuse and oppression she faced, *Their Eyes Were Watching God* also provides 21st century readers a vivid snapshot of how domestic violence was viewed during an earlier era. Ultimately, because Janie survives and eventually triumphs, the novel serves to document how a female from that time period can make strides to regain her voice amidst those who seek to silence her.

Domestic Violence as a Theme

There is a large and rich body of criticism on Hurston's *Their Eyes Were Watching God,* but a surprisingly small portion of this scholarship addresses domestic abuse, though it is a recurring theme in the novel. A great deal of the scholarship written about this book focuses, instead, on the novel's narrative structure and on Hurston's use of language. Throughout the novel, Hurston indeed utilizes an interesting narrative structure, dividing the presentation of the story between literary narration and idiomatic discourse in order to tell the story of Janie's search for identity, love, and self-fulfillment. Tim Peoples provides a clear, yet succinct, analysis of the novel's narrative structure in his recent article, "Meditation and Artistry in *The Bluest Eye* by Toni Morrison and *Their Eyes Were Watching God* by Zora Neale Hurston." As he explains it,

> the novel's organization follows two models that operate simultaneously, but for different effects. The sequential organization (1) begins with Janie telling her story, (2) continues with her story, and (3) ends with Janie bringing the story to a close. The chronological organization (1) begins with Janie's life with Nanny and her marriage to Logan Killicks, (2) continues with her marriage to Joe Starks and her residence in Eatonville, and (3) ends with Janie's marriage to Tea Cake and her return to Eatonville to tell her story to Pheoby [Peoples, 187].

Presented in the dialect of the times, rich in local color, and full of examples of the black oral tradition, *Their Eyes Were Watching God* has also been frequently praised for Hurston's unique use of language. Critics are correct to commend Hurston for her control of language, but they generally overlook the fact that, in *Their Eyes Were Watching God,* language functions, as well, as a main source of Janie's emerging identity and eventual empowerment.

There is also a significant amount of critical discussion about Janie's path toward self-discovery—and this makes sense because, on one level at least, the novel *is* about its protagonist, Janie Crawford, and her search for identity. This aspect of the novel has been explored in much detail by a variety of scholars and critics including Mary Helen Washington, Elizabeth Jane Harrison, Henry Louis Gates, Jr., Claire Crabtree, and others. Washington discusses Janie's search for her identity in the Foreword to the Harper Perennial Edition of *Their Eyes Were Watching God;* there, she suggests that the book is about "a woman on a quest for her identity" (Washington, xi). She finds Janie remarkable, largely because she reads her as "powerful, articulate, self-reliant, and radically different" from any of her literary predecessors (Washington, xi). In her essay, "Re-Visioning the Southern Land," Harrison not only argues that the novel is about Janie's "heroic quest for identity," but proposes that this facet of the novel overshadows all others, including what she sees as a "beautiful romance between Janie and Tea Cake" (294). Gates, in the "Afterword" to *Their Eyes Were Watching God,* refers to the major action of the novel as "the charting of

Janie Crawford's fulfillment as an autonomous imagination" (197). Similarly, Claire Crabtree, who addresses the novel in her article "The Confluence of Folklore, Feminism and Black Self- Determination in Zora Neale Hurston's *Their Eyes Were Watching God*," sees Janie's quest as central to the book. She asserts that, through Janie, Hurston explores the twin themes of feminism and black self-determination.

Though, as numerous critics have argued, Janie's quest does make up a central part of the novel, analyzing *Their Eyes* solely with this in mind neglects to address another crucial facet of the novel: the domestic violence angle. Without a doubt, and despite the volume of scholarship that exists on this novel, Hurston's treatment of domestic abuse in *Their Eyes Were Watching God* has been underexplored. *Domestic Abuse in the Novels of African American Women* seeks to fill in the gap in terms of addressing this important facet of the novel. In *Their Eyes Were Watching God*, domestic violence is the elephant in the room. In the context of the book, the other characters react to the abuse Janie faces by usually ignoring it and/or refusing to address it as a problem. In one instance, a character is praised for raising his fists against her (when Tea Cake beats Janie, he actually becomes the envy of the townspeople—as does Janie, due to her response to his beating of her and for playing the role of victim so well!). It is not only the novel's characters who frequently fail to react appropriately to the abuse Janie faces; these violent incidents are all too often either ignored or remain unaddressed by the novel's critics, as well.

It is important to examine the many incidents of domestic violence that occur in this novel for the same reasons that domestic abuse merits attention in general: to raise awareness about the issue, to show how the problem is often a hidden one, and to connect African American women's oppression and abuse within the home with a broader, system-wide exploitation of African American women (and women, in general) in a patriarchal society. Domestic violence is a pattern of coercive control in an intimate relationship, which may be characterized by isolating and controlling behaviors, manipulation and/or intimidation in order to create an atmosphere of fear, and other forms of abuse. In *Their Eyes Were Watching God*, Janie is plagued by this same pattern of control and abuse. Throughout so much of her life, Janie's grandmother and all three of her husbands use manipulation and physical force to make her submit to their desires.

When discussing domestic violence, it is critical to remember that abusive behavior can take many forms and might be different in every relationship. This, too, proves to be true in the case of Janie, who encounters

different types of abusers in the forms of her grandmother and three husbands. Nonetheless, Janie Crawford confronts a form of domestic abuse
with each. Janie leaves her grandmother's home when she is forced to marry
Logan Killicks and live on his farm, she flees marriage with the older and
controlling Logan for the promises made to her by Jody, a savvy entrepreneur and business owner with political aspirations, and ultimately she ends
up with the younger, free-spirited Tea Cake; yet in each relationship she
faces abuse and oppression. Janie's situation shows that domestic violence
is widespread, and it reveals the level to which abusive behavior was condoned by 1930s society. Addressing Hurston's treatment of domestic abuse
in this novel uncovers for readers the mostly tolerant attitude about domestic abuse that prevailed in 1930s America, yet there is another reason why
it is important to investigate the treatment of domestic violence in *Their
Eyes Were Watching God:* this type of analysis reveals another significant
layer to Hurston's novel. Consequently, considering the domestic violence
angle of *Their Eyes Were Watching God* enriches, rather than takes away
from, readings of the novel that focus on Janie's path to self-fulfillment.

Janie's Childhood

Janie Crawford's story begins (chronologically, at least) with her relating some key scenes from her childhood. The two most pivotal of these
events connect with Janie's early stages of self-discovery. The first takes
place when she is six years old and she becomes aware of her racial identity.
Janie, who has been raised by her grandmother, Nanny, grows up with a
white family, the Washburns. Janie frequently plays with the Washburns'
children, who treat her well. In fact, she thinks she is white (like them)
until she sees a photograph of all the children and realizes she is black. The
second occurs when she is sixteen years old and experiences her first romantic crush—and her first kiss. In the scenes which feature a teenaged Janie,
the text conflates her awakening sexual desire with her search for self. Janie
finds herself spending a lot of time in her grandmother's yard watching a
blossoming pear tree, a tree which seems to call her "to come and gaze"
(Hurston, 10). The tree "stirred her tremendously," and, after gazing at it,
she has a revelation: "she wanted to struggle with life but it seemed to elude
her" (Hurston, 10–11). Such musings are (for a time, at least) cut short
when her grandmother, Nanny, catches her with a neighborhood boy,
whom she disapproves of. What, in another situation, could have been

merely an innocent first kiss turns out to be much more pivotal for Janie due to her grandmother's overreaction.

When Nanny sees "Janie letting Johnny Taylor kiss her over the gatepost," she goes crazy (Hurston, 10). Nanny, fearing that Johnny Taylor will use Janie and then discard her as worthless, decides that she must intervene. Her own worldview was forged by a variety of tragic circumstances, all of which conspire together and cause Nanny to believe that marrying her young granddaughter off to a sixty-something-year-old man is the best course of action. Nanny suffered life under the system of slavery. Under this exploitative system, she was sexually abused by her white master (she became pregnant by him), physically abused by the master's wife, and denied a traditional family life. Her own daughter Leafy (herself a product of rape) was violently raped by a black schoolteacher, which resulted in her becoming pregnant with Janie (whom she later abandons). Nanny's own experiences of being sexually exploited and abused, combined with her feelings of helplessness with respect to her own daughter's sexual abuse, make her suspicious of men's motives. She comes to believe that marriage is the only respectable and safe path for the young Janie, who she fears will otherwise become a "mule" to some man. Eschewing more romantic notions of love for her belief that a good marriage is really about financial security and upward mobility, she forces Janie into marriage with their neighbor, Logan Killicks.

Though some critics, such as Sharon Lynette Jones, mistakenly read the marriage between Logan and Janie as consensual—Jones calls it a "marriage of consent"—the fact remains that Janie really had no choice in this matter (187). Her protestations against the marriage are initially ignored by her grandmother. When Janie remains staunch in her refusal to marry the much older Logan, a man she says looks "like some ole skullhead in de grave yard," her grandmother becomes enraged at her seeming unwillingness to "marry off decent" (Hurston, 13). After having been on the receiving end of violence for so much of her life, Nanny becomes physically abusive herself and proceeds to hit Janie violently when she refuses to comply with her demand: "She slapped the girl's face violently, and forced her head back so that their eyes met in struggle" (Hurston, 14). Thus, the victim of so much abuse under the system of slavery becomes an abuser herself by perpetrating domestic violence against her young granddaughter. This interaction between Nanny and Janie is significant, because it highlights for readers the long-term consequences, as well as cyclical nature, of violence. Nanny's own life was shaped by so much violence, and, sadly, she passes this legacy on to young Janie by abusing the girl. In the case of Nanny, the system of slavery introduced violence into her life. Though she was "freed," slavery left its mark not only on her, but also on Leafy and Janie (since Nanny passes this legacy of violence on to her descendants).

Though Nanny is clearly abusive in her treatment toward Janie, Hurston does not depict her as a simple, two-dimensional villain in the novel; on the contrary, *Their Eyes Were Watching God* presents her as rather sympathetic. By providing an account of Nanny's life—and revealing how her personal history is full of so many trials and such devastating violence, which she endured and witnessed during slavery and the Reconstruction era—Hurston explains (though does not excuse) her behavior. In her own mind, Nanny sees marriage as a form of "protection" for Janie and will use any means necessary—including violence—to make sure that Janie goes along with her plan (Hurston, 15). After hitting Janie, and in an attempt to justify her decision (and also wanting to explain what she wants to protect Janie from), Nanny tells Janie the story of their family tree that is embedded with slavery, rape, and other forms of violence. By passing down this story, Nanny is not only revealing to Janie their shared family history, but she is also keeping the legacy of slavery and abuse alive. Indeed, she transmits the trauma she and Janie's mother faced to Janie through this account of their family history. After hearing these details, facing abuse at the hands of her grandmother, realizing that her grandmother is resolute in her demand, and (very likely) fearing that she has no place else to go, Janie eventually gives in to a marriage that she does not want.

Janie's Married Life

Janie's hopes for a romantic union dwindle when the realities of marriage to Logan Killicks set in. About two months into her marriage to Logan, Janie, feeling miserable and unfulfilled, visits her grandmother seeking advice. Not only does Nanny see Janie's protests as trivial—both her complaint that her marriage to Logan is loveless and her criticism of Logan for being old and unattractive fall on deaf ears—but Nanny also blames Janie for not appreciating the financial security and respectability that marriage to the much older Logan affords. She reminds Janie that, thanks to being married to the well-off Logan, she "got a house bought and paid for and sixty acres uh land right on de big road," which Nanny thinks Janie ought to be grateful for (Hurston, 23). It's important to remember that Nanny's perspective on Janie's expectations of marriage is based on her own early experiences of life under the institution of slavery. Since Nanny herself was denied a traditional marriage (and the respectability that comes along with it), she is puzzled why Janie doesn't appreciate the respectability that being married to Logan Killicks affords her. Also, in Nanny's experience, owning land is a privilege reserved for whites, so a black man who owns it is immediately worthy of love. She tells Janie that Logan is her protection, and then she sends Janie "along with a stern mien" (Hurston, 24). Janie remains dissatisfied being married to Logan, in part because their relationship does not conform to her idealized image of romantic love, but there are other factors at play, as well. Logan's treatment of Janie has worsened over time (and it continues to worsen), which also contributes to Janie's eventual decision to leave him.

Logan, initially enamored with the girl, soon takes Janie for granted. His true intentions, that he wants a domestic helper rather than a lover or partner, become clear. He begins to feel that Janie does not do enough work around the farm and he, like Nanny, comes to believe that Janie is ungrateful for the relative comfort and security that being married to him provides. Péter Gaál Szabo discusses some of these marital problems in his essay, "Transparent Space and the Production of the Female Body in Zora Neale Hurston's *Their Eyes Were Watching God* and *Jonah's Gourd Vine.*" There, he argues that Janie's marriage to Logan Killicks "turns out to be a material treatise, an undesired *job* with clearly defined gender roles emplaced in definite spheres of the house" (Szabo). It is when Logan no longer feels as captivated by Janie as he once did that he really begins to treat her poorly, at first criticizing her for not doing enough around the house and farm, and later, trying to find ways to control and manipulate her into conforming to his idea of an ideal mate. He starts bossing Janie around and acting as if her role is to simply do work for him; at one point, he orders her to do hard labor while he ventures out to buy a mule.

During his absence, Janie first encounters the man who will become her second husband, Joe "Jody" Starks. While working in the field (at Killicks' behest), she spies a handsome man walking down the road near the family farm. Janie brings him some water and the two get to talking. Jody makes a real impression on Janie because of his "cityfied, stylish" dress, seeming sophistication, and apparent self-confidence (Hurston, 27). Jody is immediately attracted to Janie's beauty, and he flatters her. He acts astonished that "a pretty doll-baby" like Janie is "behind a plow," and tells her that she was "made to sit on de front porch and Rock," not to toil away in the fields (Hurston, 29). The couple begins meeting up with each other from that time. Joe dazzles Janie with his aspirations and his vision of the future, telling her that he wants to be famous. He also promises to treat Janie like a "lady," assuring her that his intention is to "make a wife" out of her, if she will consent and run away with him (Hurston, 29).

While Janie mulls over the decision of whether or not to elope with Starks, her relationship with Logan Killicks continues to deteriorate. At one point, he insists that her place is wherever he says it is; he tells her, "You ain't got no particular place. It's wherever Ah need Yuh" (Hurston, 31). He also says many derogatory things about Janie's family, especially Janie's mother (Leafy), who gained a bad reputation in those parts. When Janie tells Logan that she is considering leaving him, Logan further insults her and they quarrel. This argument culminates with Logan threatening to kill Janie with an axe, a threat which convinces Janie that she needs a change of scenery. Running away with Jody Starks provides her such an opportunity, so she meets up with him, the two head to Green Cove Springs, and they get married.

Before turning to discuss Janie's relationship with Jody Starks, it is worth emphasizing that her marriage to Logan Killicks represents a pattern all too commonly found in abusive relationships. Domestic abuse is not only about physical assault. Batterers oftentimes use different kinds of psychological (or other nonviolent) tactics to gain power and control in the relationship, and this is the case with Logan, who prior to resorting to physical violence and threatening Janie's life, employs other techniques in an attempt to silence and control Janie, such as constantly criticizing her and treating her like a servant (both of which are behaviors regularly found in abusive relationships). He is also guilty of emotional abuse and uses stereotypically abusive tactics such as making degrading remarks about her (Logan frequently insults Janie) and her family (recall that Logan is highly critical of Janie's mother, Leafy, and puts Janie down because of Leafy's bad reputation). As a rule, domestic violence is about power and control over another person, so when Logan's insults and manipulation fail to bring him his desired results (Janie's silence and compliance), he adopts another strategy: threatening Janie's life. To be clear, Janie and readers of the text have good reason to take Logan's threat to Janie's life seriously. Prior threats to kill are considered one of the strongest risk factors linked to domestic violence–related homicide. This risk increases with the specificity of the threat made (in other words, the risk is greater if the abuser is very specific about plans or intended methods), so Logan's unambiguous threat to use an "axe" to kill Janie makes her risk of peril at his hands even greater.

Although when Janie flees the abusive and controlling Logan she is full of high hopes for a romantic life with the ambitious and good-looking Jody Starks, a suitor who turned on the charm to woo her, this marriage, too, ends up being rife with problems, since he puts a stranglehold on her life. Starks arrives in Eatonville to find the town's residents devoid of ambition, so he arranges to buy more land from the neighboring landowner, a decision which turns him a nice profit in no time: "Janie was astonished to see that the money Jody had spent for the land came back to him so fast. Ten new families bought lots and moved to town" (Hurston, 41). Starks hires local residents to build a general store for him to own, and he is relentless in drumming up business for the store. Although Janie remains impressed with Jody's ambition and business acumen, she soon realizes that her wants her as a trophy wife. His behavior becomes increasingly controlling as he starts telling her how to dress and behave, both of which are telltale signs of an abusive relationship. For example, on the night of the general store's grand opening, Jody "told Janie to dress up and stand in the store all that evening. Everybody was coming sort of fixed up, and he didn't mean for nobody else's wife to rank with her" (Hurston, 41). Jody's motives here are clear: he believes that the image of a perfect wife will reinforce his powerful position in town. Indeed, Janie causes quite a stir in the store when the townspeople see her dressed to the nines in "silken ruffles" (Hurston, 41). Her fancy store-bought dresses are quite a contrast to the "percale and calico" worn by the other women (Hurston, 41).

Awestruck by Starks, the people of the town appoint him mayor. He has Janie run the general store, but he forbids her from participating in the substantial social life that occurs on the store's front porch, which demonstrates that, as is the case with many abusive men, Starks wants to limit Janie's social activities. As a justification for his refusal to let her socialize with the other townspeople, he explains to her that in her new role as the mayor's wife, she must resist such activities for the sake of appearances. The women of the town are reluctant to socialize with Janie anyway, feeling that she is of a higher status than they. Janie, who "began to feel the impact of awe and envy against her," quickly realizes that the "wife of the Mayor was not just another woman as she supposed," and she grows lonely (Hurston, 46).

Jody's treatment of Janie worsens as time passes. Not only does he succeed in isolating her, but he also frequently criticizes her, which the townspeople notice. For instance, one local man witnesses how Starks "gits on her ever now and then when she make little mistakes round de store" (Hurston, 49). Another townsperson comments on how Janie "don't talk much" and speculates that this is a result of the way Jody "rears and pitches" when Janie makes a mistake in the store. Observations such as these reinforce the sense that Jody's control over Janie is related to language. He uses his domineering voice to belittle Janie while at the same time forcing her to remain silent. Although Jody Starks differs from Logan Killicks in terms of personality, looks, and profession, both men similarly seek to control Janie—and both resort to manipulation and put-downs to force her into silence and submission. In addition to verbally berating Janie, Jody becomes increasingly controlling in other ways. No longer satisfied with telling her how to dress, he also starts to tell her how to groom, forcing her to hide her hair "tied up lak some ole 'oman round the store" (Hurston, 49).

The townspeople notice Jody's maltreatment of Janie, but they do nothing to intervene. The town's residents defer to Starks in all sorts of matters, in part because of his position as a store owner and Eatonville's mayor, but there is "something else," too, that made "men give way before him. He had a bow-down command in his face" (Hurston, 47). Though Jody has, perhaps, earned some respect in Eatonville because of his successes as an entrepreneur and politician, he has also turned into a man whom others fear: "there was something about Joe Starks that cowed the town" (Hurston, 47).

Though the text provides a range of possible explanations for why the townspeople refuse to intervene on behalf of Janie when Jody's mistreatment of her grows worse, it is worth pointing out that this type of reaction in the face of domestic abuse is all-too-common and symptomatic of a larger problem: the unwillingness of outsiders to speak up on behalf of victims of domestic abuse. Indeed, society's lack of understanding about the dynamics of domestic violence is one of the greatest obstacles a domestic violence victim faces. All too often, outsiders are reluctant to speak up for victims of domestic abuse because they feel like they should not get involved in what they see as a private family matter. Remaining quiet about abuse, however, helps to perpetuate it, a point that Deborah M. Horvitz makes clear in *Literary Trauma: Sadism, Memory and Sexual Violence in American Women's Fiction,* her book-long examination of literary representations of physical and sexual violence. She argues that "silence is *not* a neutral act; rather, it is a politically regressive one that passively permits the continuation of violence" (Horvitz, 4).

The relationship between Starks and Janie continues to sour, and the abuse she faces takes a real toll on her. Just like Logan Killicks before him, Joe Starks constantly orders Janie around. When she calls him on this behavior, telling him, "You sho loves to tell me what to do," he retorts that it's "'cause you need tellin'" (Hurston, 71). Though Janie "fought back with her tongue as best she could," she comes to realize that "it didn't do her any good. It just made Joe do more" (Hurston, 71). The effect of Joe's control is apparent, for Janie, who was once vital, is now under his thumb where "we can see only momentarily sparkles of the woman she once was" (Rudolphi, 40). Janie understands that her husband "wanted her submission and he'd keep on fighting until he felt he had it" (Hurston, 71). Janie's last ember of love for Joe Starks seems to go out when, one evening, the dinner she prepared wasn't to his liking, causing him to hit "her face in the kitchen" (Hurston, 71). At this moment, her "image of Jody tumbled down and shattered," and she never looked at him the same way again (Hurston, 72).

Even though Janie ceases to love Jody, whose abuse of her has grown worse over time, she does not leave him. Her situation in Eatonville shows how difficult it can be for a woman to get out of an abusive relationship, especially during that time period and especially for a woman like Janie, who has neither family nor friends to turn to for help. In fact, it is not until Starks, whose health had been declining for some time, passes away that Janie is really free of him. In this sense, *Their Eyes Were Watching God* presents a rather disheartening view of domestic abuse by suggesting, through the portrayal of Joe and Janie's marriage, that sometimes the only way out of a violent relationship is through the death of the abuser.

After the death of Jody Starks, Janie releases her hair, a physical feature that Starks and so many other men found attractive, from the head rag he forced her to wear. This gesture demonstrates Janie reasserting her identity as a desirable woman. With Jody no longer around to silence Janie, she is free, and she can now present herself to the world on her own terms. Although Janie re-covers her hair in a kerchief long enough to satisfy the community of mourners at Jody's funeral, she burns her head rags immediately thereafter, thus symbolically freeing herself from the chains those head rags came to represent.

Janie, now a wealthy widow, realizes that she is still considered beautiful, and she finds herself with an abundance of suitors, all of whom she rebuffs until she meets the handsome and younger "Tea Cake" (Vergible Woods), a drifter with no financial means who surprises and delights her with his easygoing personality. On first glance, Tea Cake is drastically different from both Logan Killicks and Joe Starks. Janie finds his manner of courting her—joking around with her, teaching her how to play checkers, and taking her hunting and fishing—quite refreshing. The townspeople, however, strongly object to the relationship between the two: "It was after the picnic that the town began to notice things and got mad. Tea Cake and Mrs. Mayor Starks!" (Hurston, 110). Folks in Eatonville also notice that she has "quit attending church" and has started to wear "high heel slippers and a ten dollar hat!" (Hurston, 110). Janie's actions anger the townspeople because they expect her to behave just as she did when Joe Starks was alive. In addition to disapproving of Janie and Tea Cake's relationship, the townsfolk also question his motives in courting the well-to-do widow. Indeed, even her friend Pheoby warns Janie about Tea Cake, reminding her that there is an age gap between them and cautioning her that he might make a fool of her.

Janie, however, insisting that they are in love (and ignoring her friend Pheoby's warning), leaves Eatonville for Jacksonville to meet up with her new beau. Janie arrives in Jacksonville to an eagerly awaiting Tea Cake, who hauls "her off to a preacher's house first thing," so the two can get married right away (Hurston, 116). Much of the scholarship written on *Their Eyes Were Watching God* ranks Tea Cake as the "best" of Janie's three husbands, citing the fact that he is the only man who truly loves and respects her, and praising him for giving her the chance to enjoy life. To many critics, Tea Cake seems to be the quintessential romantic hero, and one scholar, Anastasia Carol Curwood, even goes as far as to say that the relationship between Janie and Tea Cake represents "the most eloquent expression of an ideal of romantic love" within "a fictionalized account" (141). To be sure, many of the novel's critics view the marriage between Janie and Tea Cake in a mostly positive light.

To be fair, Janie's marriage to Tea Cake is arguably more egalitarian than her previous ones. For instance, Tea Cake and Janie speak freely with one another (this, of course, was not the case in either of her other marriages, since both Logan Killicks and Joe Starks tried to silence her). He also encourages her to participate in a number of activities (such as hunting, fishing, and game-playing), and he enjoys it when Janie socializes (something Joe Starks forbade). Even considering these positive attributes to the marriage—and despite the fact that there is real chemistry between the two— Tea Cake is far from an ideal mate and their marriage is far from perfect.

Early in their marriage, he steals "two hundred dollars" of Janie's money and gambles it away (Hurston, 118). Tea Cake is also very controlling. For instance, he, like Starks before him, selects Janie's clothing. In fact, in so many matters, Tea Cake makes most of the couple's decisions. Although Janie now has enough money to provide a comfortable living for both of them, Tea Cake insists that they live the type of lifestyle he is more accustomed to. While on the surface, Tea Cake might appear noble for this, this decision (which is *his* decision) forces Janie to adhere to a lower standard of living—and he makes this decision, perhaps, simply for the sake of his masculine pride. He also puts her in harm's way by his association with criminals, most of whom he's met through his gambling habit. It is his idea to move to the Everglades and, later, his decision to try to ride out a hurricane which endangers them both.

Jealousy also threatens their relationship—and it takes different forms. While living and working in the Everglades, Janie "learned what it felt like to be jealous for the first time," when she catches Tea Cake flirting with a younger woman named Nunkie (Hurston, 136). Tea Cake sees his relationship with Janie threatened as well, when he realizes that a woman named Mrs. Turner has been trying to break up their marriage in order to set Janie up with her brother. Mrs. Turner's attempt to woo Janie on behalf of her brother proves to be a catalyst in the disintegration of Janie and Tea Cake's marriage, because, in response to Mrs. Turner's meddling, Tea Cake (like Joe Starks, before him) resorts to violence in order to control Janie. When Mrs. Turner brings her brother to town to introduce him to Janie, it results in Tea Cake's whipping Janie to show Mrs. Turner's brother that he has full control over his wife. Though Tea Cake deserves the blame for his physical abuse of Janie, the particulars of this scene are worth highlighting because they point to Tea Cake's motive. Tea Cake, the passage makes clear, "whipped Janie. Not because her behavior justified his jealousy, but it relieved that awful fear inside him. Being able to whip her reassured him in possession. No brutal beating at all. He just slapped her around a bit to show he was boss" (Hurston, 140). Thus, as this passage makes clear, Tea Cake physically abuses Janie to exert control over her and to demonstrate his level of control to others.

Instead of disapproving of Tea Cake's assault of Janie, their friends seem impressed by it. Several people remark that he is lucky to have a woman with fair enough skin to show signs of a beating. Tea Cake himself feels a significant amount of pride, as well, in "having been able to mark her with his fists," a point that Tom McGlamery makes in his book *Protest and the Body in Melville, Dos Passos, and Hurston* (106). Stuart Burrows also discusses this scene in order to address Tea Cake's abusive behavior. In his article "'You Heard Her, You Ain't Blind': Seeing What's Said in *Their Eyes Were Watching God*," he notes how the "marks left on her skin by Tea Cake's beatings" serve as another way for Tea Cake "to make visible his power over Janie to the rest of the community because her light skin retains the marks of physical abuse" (Burrows, 448). Tea Cake's behavior in the aftermath of his beating of Janie also garners community approval. Both men and women in the community are jealous about the way the Woodses act so lovingly toward each other after his striking her.

Tea Cake's jealousy and violent behavior hit new extremes when, after the two are stranded by a hurricane and Tea Cake contracts rabies, he goes crazy and tries to kill Janie, leaving her no choice but to defend her own life. When a storm hits the Everglades, Tea Cake insists that he and Janie stay put and ride it out. In the chaos of the storm, which turns out to be more devastating than was predicted, a rabid dog attacks the couple and ends up biting Tea Cake. Janie summons a doctor, but there is little that he can do. Janie comes to understand that Tea Cake is "liable tuh die" and that he will more than likely "suffer somethin' awful befo' he goes" (Hurston, 177). Janie decides to stay with Tea Cake and tend to him, but his behavior becomes increasingly erratic. For instance, at one point, he becomes paranoid about Janie's whereabouts and questions why she tried to "slip off" from him (Hurston, 180). Janie tells him that he is acting "jealous 'thout me givin' cause" (Hurston, 180). As his behavior grows increasingly unpredictable, Janie becomes very frightened of Tea Cake and starts to wonder if he would really hurt her or if he just wants to "scare her" (Hurston, 182).

When Janie moves out of the bedroom they share to sleep in another room, Tea Cake becomes enraged. He asks, "Janie, how come you can't sleep in the same bed wid me no mo?'" (Hurston, 183). Janie tries to reassure him by reminding him, "De doctah told you tuh sleep be yo'self," but Tea Cake, fueled by jealousy and madness, will not be placated. He ends up charging at Janie with a gun (Hurston, 183). Tea Cake tries to shoot Janie with his pistol, which "snapped once," missing her (Hurston, 183). Realizing that the bullet missed, Tea Cake takes aim at her again. Seeing that he intends to shoot her, Janie raises her rifle and ends up shooting him with it in self-defense. Janie's act of defending herself ends her violent confrontation with Tea Cake, but the matter is far from resolved.

Domestic Violence and the Courtroom

After Janie kills Tea Cake in self-defense, she is charged with murder and must defend herself in court. The courtroom scene remains one of the most debated scenes in the novel, and for good reason: it illustrates some of the problems that victims of domestic abuse face. The fact that Janie ends up in court shows that society and law enforcement failed her on a number of levels. Had there been someone to intervene on Janie's behalf, perhaps Tea Cake's madness, jealousy, and abuse—all of which culminated in the scene where Janie was forced to defend herself—would have been kept in check. Instead, a variety of circumstances (a society that condoned, if not encouraged, Tea Cake's abuse of Janie and the fateful hurricane—to name just two) conspired to isolate Janie and put her life in danger. Also, the fact that she ended up in court shows that law enforcement did not readily believe her account. Had they felt her shooting of Tea Cake was unequivocally self-defense (or had they thought that her shooting was justified), she would not have been made a defendant in the first place.

On its most basic level, the courtroom scene points out what little representation the criminal justice system offered abused women who killed their partners in self- defense. The courtroom scene is not just about how law enforcement failed Janie (and women like her), though. This scene also provides Hurston an opportunity to have Janie speak for herself. Maureen McKnight discusses the trial scene in her article "Discerning Nostalgia in Zora Neale Hurston's *Their Eyes Were Watching God.*" She describes how the jury "listened intently and been greatly persuaded by Janie's account" (McKnight, 109). It is important that Janie speaks for herself in this scene, for it shows that Janie, despite being silenced for so long, can express herself and stand her ground. Though law enforcement did not listen to Janie, and though so many community members failed her, as well, the jury finally hears her.

Just like her abusers' control was connected to their use of language, Janie's emerging sense of self remains linked to her use of language and her power to testify—both in the courtroom scene and throughout the long story she relates to Pheoby about her life and experiences (recall that the entirety of the novel consists of the conversation between these two women). For these reasons, Hurston's choice of Janie as narrator is crucial. By positioning Janie as the novel's narrator and by beginning the novel by showing a middle-aged Janie Crawford returning home, Hurston allows Janie to speak for herself. By allowing Janie to tell her story to Pheoby, a friend and confidant (and a woman who is sympathetic to Janie's experiences), Hurston gives voice to Janie's experiences and allows her to be heard and understood. In his essay, "Zora Neale Hurston and the Speakerly Text," Henry Louis Gates describes Pheoby as "an ideal listener" to Janie's story (145).

Describing Janie, Maureen McKnight notes that, at this point in the novel, she is "forty-ish, thrice married, financially secure, and confidently independent. In other words, she has come into her own" (88). By positioning a middle-aged Janie as narrator, Hurston presents a more mature Janie who has (finally) reclaimed her voice. So long victimized and silenced, this older Janie can finally speak for herself, which marks a significant point on her journey toward self-actualization, which she achieves only after confronting the abuse and oppression that plagued her for so long. Janie not only has survived three abusive marriages, but she eventually triumphs by telling her story. Though Janie regains her voice after being silenced and controlled for so long, her triumph comes at a steep cost. Not only does she lose Tea Cake, a man she loved (despite his faults), but she was forced to resort to the use of lethal force in order to save her own life. Thus, the novel provides a disheartening message about what it takes to end domestic abuse, since for Janie it takes Tea Cake's death (not to mention an understanding and sympathetic jury) for her to finally achieve freedom and autonomy. What's even more discouraging is that another message that *Their Eyes Were Watching God* sends about domestic violence is that, far too often, a victim of abuse can *only* escape by literally running away (as Janie did from Logan Killicks) or through the death of her abuser (such as what happened with Joe Starks and Tea Cake Woods).

One problem with this novel, then, is that it fails to address strategies for dealing with domestic violence, beyond running away from or killing off the abusive partner. Janie leaves Logan to run away with Jody Starks, Jody dies, and Janie kills Tea Cake in self-defense. In none of these relationships did the abuse Janie faced end because it was confronted by law enforcement or others in the community (nor did she, or her husbands, ever try to seek help from the medical or psychological communities). Instead, Hurston depicts Janie escaping abuse and oppression by running away (from Killicks); she further suggests that sometimes the only way out of a violent relationship is through the death of the abuser (which is what happens in the cases of Jody and Tea Cake).

Janie's story therefore shows that, in the 1930s, a woman had little hope of either law enforcement involvement or community support if she found herself confronting domestic abuse. If a 21st century audience is uneasy with this message, or with the way *Their Eyes Were Watching God* ends, it is for good reason. This failure, however, is not Hurston's. Rather, the novel's inability to provide a better resolution for Janie's predicament reflects the larger societal problems that plagued America during Hurston's lifetime. In other words, our uneasiness about the book's resolution reflects our discomfort with the way domestic abuse was viewed by 1930s society. In *Their Eyes Were Watching God,* Hurston depicts a society that was not merely ill-equipped to deal with domestic abuse, but one that typically treated the problem as a nonissue. Hurston's protagonist, Janie Crawford, negotiates the best she can within this given set of conditions.

Their Eyes Were Watching God: A Problematic Novel?

Their Eyes Were Watching God remains a complicated—and in some ways problematic—text, but the novel succeeds in giving voice to Janie, a woman who struggles with her identity at the same time as she faces abuse from those close to her. Through Janie, Hurston succeeds in highlighting the complex set of circumstances that conspire to oppress women—and all too often lead to women's abuse—that existed in 1930s America, a time rife with racial discrimination and gender oppression. Hurston's novel reflects an America that had not even begun to come to terms with the issue of domestic violence, let alone one equipped to adequately deal with it. Though this novel offers rather disheartening views of society's understanding of and attitudes about domestic abuse, Hurston raises awareness about the issue through its protagonist Janie and the problems she faces.

Not only does Zora Neale Hurston offer a snapshot of her era's attitudes about domestic violence, but Janie's struggles also foreshadow the challenges that women in decades to come will encounter. Moreover, *Their Eyes Were Watching God* anticipates the abundance of novels that appear in the late 20th and early 21st centuries by African American women writers who address domestic abuse (and thereby continue to raise awareness about the issue). Today, Zora Neale Hurston's legacy lives on, not only through her extant works, which have taken their rightful place in the literary canon, but also through more contemporary writers like Toni Morrison, Gayl Jones, Gloria Naylor, and Octavia Butler, all of whom revisit many of the same themes that Hurston addresses in her masterpiece, *Their Eyes Were Watching God*, including the important but so often neglected theme of domestic violence.

CHAPTER 2

Dysfunctional Domesticity: Toni Morrison's *The Bluest Eye*

In *The Bluest Eye,* a novel that Toni Morrison began writing in the 1960s, she highlights the hidden and secretive nature of much of the violence that occurs within the home. This is a point that the book's narrator, Claudia MacTeer, makes clear when she begins her account of Pecola's story with the phrase "quiet as it's kept" (Morrison, 6). By starting her narration in this manner, Claudia highlights how domestic violence was seen as shameful and secretive. In *The Bluest Eye* (as well as in *Love,* which is the focus of a later chapter of this book), Morrison also depicts violence in the home as one ill effect of patriarchal capitalism and a product of a racist and classist society. Another point emphasized in this novel is that broader social problems trickle down to, and are made manifest within, the family structure and domestic sphere.

Morrison and Her Critique of the Family

Toni Morrison (born Chloe Wofford) was born in Ohio in 1931. Morrison studied at Howard University and at Cornell before working as a textbook editor and, later, at Random House, where she edited books by (now-famous) authors such as Toni Cade Bambara, Angela Davis, and Gayl Jones. During her time at Random House, Morrison also began writing fiction, at first informally. Her first novel, *The Bluest Eye,* was published in 1970. *The Bluest Eye* tells the story of Pecola Breedlove, a young girl who faces horrendous emotional, physical, and sexual abuse in her home at the same time as she is forced to confront a racist and sexist society which seeks to marginalize her since she does not fit into a racist idea of beauty.

In *The Bluest Eye,* Morrison depicts the family structure as highly dysfunctional in a variety of ways. Her depiction of the Breedlove family works as part of her overarching critique of the family, which is a recurring theme of her literary works. Beyond using her fiction to indict the nuclear family as flawed, she has also gone on record in interviews as criticizing the family structure by suggesting that it simply doesn't work in our society. For example, in one such interview, Morrison remarked that the "little nuclear family is a paradigm that just doesn't work. It doesn't work for white people or for black people" (*Conversations*, 260). She has also publicly stated that racism has negatively scarred American society to a much greater degree than is widely acknowledged by the American public. The wide-reaching effects of racism, as well as society's attitudes about racial difference, can been seen in our country's literature as well as history, a point which Morrison emphasizes in *Playing in the Dark: Whiteness and the Literary Imagination,* where she asserts that "the literature of the United States, like its history, represents commentary on the transformations of biological, ideological, and metaphysical concepts of racial difference" (65). It only makes sense that these concerns would emerge in Morrison's fiction, as well. Indeed, both *The Bluest Eye* and *Love* (which will get more in-depth treatment in a later chapter of this book) show the relationship between social ills—including racism—and the dysfunctional nature of the family structure.

In *The Bluest Eye,* the marriage between Cholly and Pauline Breedlove (Pecola's parents) is unhealthy, unfulfilling, and abusive. Cholly is an alcoholic, and Pauline, a neglectful and sometimes abusive mother, largely abandons her own family in order to spend time with the Fisher family, a white family she works for. Thus, Pecola suffers because of her treatment by society at large, as well as at the hands of those in her family. Although Morrison depicts characters such as Pecola's parents, Cholly and Pauline, as part of the problem, she makes it clear that society, too, is to blame for many problems that manifest in the home and family structure. Even when she depicts characters who perpetrate acts that are perverse and sometimes horrendously violent, Morrison refuses to simply condemn them for their actions. Rather than vilifying these characters, she eschews simple two-dimensional representations of them and, instead, humanizes them to the degree that makes readers understand (even if we do not sympathize with) their plights and perspectives. By fleshing out the characters who commit terrible acts, Morrison forces her readers to closely examine the roles played by both society and individual pathology, for she (perhaps more so than any of the other authors discussed in *Domestic Abuse in the Novels of African American*

Women) seems to be at odds with traditional explanations for the prevalence of domestic abuse.

Stereotypes and Society

Speaking about *The Bluest Eye,* Gurleen Grewal contends that "the novel goes well beyond replicating stereotypes," for this novel, "in confronting stereotypes goes to the heart of the matter: to the race-based class structure of American society that generates its own pathologies" (118). As Grewal's remarks suggest, Morrison seems intent on interrogating the "race-based class structure" of the United States in *The Bluest Eye* in order to highlight its destructive nature. Indeed, throughout the novel, Morrison implicates society at large—which she portrays as both directly and indirectly responsible for Pecola's dilemmas—as well as Pecola's family for her precarious situation.

Though Pecola's home life is the antithesis of idyllic, her problems do not stop when she leaves the domestic sphere. As Marc C. Conner emphasizes in his book *The Aesthetics of Toni Morrison: Speaking the Unspeakable,* "not only does the community fail to aid her in her distress," but in the end they are shown to be complicit in Pecola's destruction (57). Rather than coming to Pecola's rescue, society is to blame, in part, for the tragic details of her life. Just as Deborah Cadman asserts, "the dangerous and terrifying conditions of Pecola's household are also present in the community beyond her 'yard'" (71). Morrison, by narrating a series of encounters where Pecola comes face-to-face with racism in some of its most insidious forms, stresses the degree to which a racist and sexist society is to blame for her situation.

The teachers at her school do not like her and other children relentlessly tease her. She is looked down upon by others in her neighborhood. A prime example of this can be seen in the case of Mr. Yacobowski, the storekeeper, who undoubtedly contributes to Pecola's sense of alienation and marginalization. When the two briefly interact at his store, his revulsion toward her is unmistakable—and it has a profound effect on her. His feelings about her are made abundantly clear in the passage that follows, which shows Pecola entering his store to buy Mary Janes, her favorite candy:

> She looks up at him and sees the vacuum where curiosity ought to lodge. And something more. The total absence of human recognition—the glazed separateness. She does not know what keeps his glance suspended. Perhaps because he is grown, or a man, and she is a little girl. But she has seen inter-

est, disgust, even anger in grown male eyes. Yet this vacuum is not new to her. It has an edge; somewhere in the bottom lid is distaste. She has seen it lurking in the eyes of all white people. So. The distaste must be for her, her blackness [Morrison, 49].

This unfortunate encounter only further reinforces for Pecola what she has already come to believe is true. She has learned that, based upon racist and racialized notions of beauty, she does not measure up. Pecola feels self-loathing because she has been rejected and de-valued by society.

Far from serving as a refuge from a world which devalues her, her family, instead, further diminishes her. Her mother is physically abusive of her, and the horrors she is subjected to come to their fruition when her father, Cholly, violently rapes her. The combination of the Breedloves' extreme poverty, their refusal, or perhaps inability, to resist an oppressive racist ideology, and the abject conditions under which they are forced to live contribute to the way they devalue Pecola. The violence against Pecola, like so much of the violence perpetrated against women, occurs alongside—and, in part, is allowed by—economic dependence and a material lack, yet, Morrison takes care to show, too, that racism plays a key role in Pecola's suffering. The Breedlove family has bought into racist ideology; they firmly believe they are "ugly" (Morrison, 39). As Claudia MacTeer explains, the Breedloves' ugliness came from their conviction, a point made clear in the following passage:

It was as though some mysterious all-knowing master had given each one a cloak of ugliness to wear, and they had each accepted it without question. The master had said, "You are ugly people." They had looked about themselves and saw nothing to contradict the statement; saw, in fact, support for it leaning at them from every billboard, every movie, every glance. "Yes," they had said. "You are right." And they took the ugliness in their hands, threw it as a mantle over them, and went about the world with it [Morrison, 39].

The Breedlove family have unquestioningly accepted society's notions of beauty and have used that as a measuring stick to deem themselves unworthy—and it is this same judgment that contributes to young Pecola's suffering.

Pecola wants to be everything she is not; her desires manifest themselves in her longing for Mary Janes and her craving to drink milk out of a Shirley Temple cup. Her infatuation with these cultural symbols of beauty can be traced back to her mother, who is similarly invested in them. Unhappy with her lot in life, Pauline Breedlove, Pecola's mother, tries escape, first by going to movies and later by abandoning her family by turning her attention to the Fishers, the white family she works for as a domestic. She likes going to the cinema because there "in the dark her memory was refreshed, and she succumbed to her earlier dreams. Along with the idea of romantic love, she was introduced to another—physical beauty" (Morrison, 122). The Hollywood icons of the 1940s are the supposed ideal of American beauty, and they capture Pauline's attention.

Morrison identifies the danger in Pauline's blind acceptance of Hollywood's notion of beauty later in this same passage; she declares that love and physical beauty are "probably the most destructive ideas in the history of human thought. Both originated in envy, thrived in insecurity, and ended in disillusion" (Morrison, 122). Working for the Fisher family has much the same appeal for Pauline that going to the movies once did. In their home, she fits in. She relishes the cleanness and relative luxury of their home with its fine kitchen, fully stocked pantry, and plush white towels, all of which she prefers to her own home and its contents. The Fishers give Pauline a nickname ("Polly"), which she likes, and they think of her as the "ideal servant" (Morrison, 128). Pauline's allegiance to the Fishers at the expense of her own family causes her to neglect her own household, which, in turn, makes the Breedlove home fall further into disarray.

The fact that Pauline values the Fishers and their young daughter more than her own family becomes abundantly clear to Pecola when she, along with her friends Claudia and Frieda MacTeer, visit Mrs. Breedlove at work. During this episode, Pecola sees a blueberry pie that her mother has just baked. While trying to inspect it, she accidentally drops it, causing it to fall on "the floor, splattering blackish blueberries everywhere. Most of the juice splashed on Pecola's legs, and the burn must have been painful, for she cried out and began hopping about just as Mrs. Breedlove entered" the kitchen (Morrison, 108–109). Despite the fact that Pecola is not only embarrassed by the spill but also clearly injured by the burn on her legs, Pauline immediately responds by knocking "her to the floor"; she then "yanked her up by the arm, slapped her again, and in a voice thin with anger, abused Pecola directly and Frieda and me by implication" (Morrison, 109).

Pauline's preference for the Fisher's little daughter, whom she (adding insult to injury for poor Pecola) consoles only moments after beating Pecola in the above referenced scene, sends a clear message to Pecola that Mrs. Breedlove deems the white family—and especially their little daughter— as more valuable than her. Mrs. Breedlove's preference for the little white

Fisher girl over her own daughter shows how she has internalized society's racism to the point that she devalues her own child because of it. As Barbara Frey Waxman asserts in her essay "Girls into Women: Culture, Nature, and Self-Loathing in Toni Morrison's *The Bluest Eye*" (1970), Pauline Breedlove's "distaste for her pathetic daughter suggests her embrace of the Master Narrative" (48). This realization further contributes to Pecola's desire for blue eyes. For, as Margaret Delashmit points out in her essay "*The Bluest Eye: An Indictment*," when "Pauline embraces the white family she works for, especially the little white girl with blue eyes, to the extent that she neglects her own family, blue eyes become for Pecola a metaphor for her mother's love" (14). Pecola's mother is unable and unwilling to give her the attention she needs and she thus clearly plays a part in Pecola's victimization, yet it is arguably her father's violent assault of her that leads to her total psychic breakdown near the novel's end.

"Reading" Cholly Breedlove

As Karla Alwes argues in her article "'The Evil of Fulfillment': Women and Violence in *The Bluest Eye*," Cholly Breedlove "does not exclude Pecola from his life or ignore her very existence," but rather "his attention destroys her" (93). Cholly perpetrates an almost unimaginably horrific act on his young, vulnerable daughter, but Morrison takes care to paint him as more than just a monster. We learn through his back story about formative experiences that contributed to his violent behavior and skewed view of the world. One such experience is tied to his first sexual encounter. As a teenager, Cholly had sneaked away from his Aunt Jimmy's funeral with an adolescent girl named Darlene. The experience begins pleasantly for both Cholly and Darlene, but soon turns tragic when they are interrupted by two white men, hunters with flashlights. Spying the partially disrobed couple in an embrace, they force Cholly to perform in front of them. Rather than directing his anger at the white hunters who are deliberately humiliating him and Darlene for their own perverse entertainment, Cholly redirects his rage onto Darlene, who is lying there helpless before an unwelcome audience. Cholly admits that "he hated her" at that moment (Morrison, 148).

Thus, because of this violent encounter, at a young age Cholly Breedlove, as George Potter puts it, "begins to funnel his racial frustrations—brought on by a lack of power and ability to direct his own life—

toward sexualized violence" (47). The humiliation of this encounter lasts even after the men leave. Cholly admits that the prying eyes of the white men and their intrusive flashlight "wormed its way into his guts and turned the sweet taste of muscadine into rotten fetid bile" (Morrison, 148). The scene is telling, for it works to both explain and foreshadow Cholly's violent behavior later in life because it conflates brutality, sexuality, and humiliation for Cholly at a tender age—and at a time when he is especially vulnerable since his Aunt Jimmy, who raised him and cared for him, has just died. We thereby learn through this passage that one of Cholly's formative experiences involved sexual violence, humiliation, and powerlessness.

Only adding to his feelings of frustration and alienation, Cholly learns as he tries to make his way in the world that, for reasons intricately tied to his race and social class (as well as to the specific realities about his family) there is no real place for him in early 20th century society. Abandoned by his mother, who literally tried to throw him away when he was a baby and abandoned (at least from Cholly's perspective) again by his Aunt Jimmy when she died (she cared for him while she was alive, but her death effectively orphans him a second time), he goes seeking his father with the hope that he will find an identity through a relationship with him. This, too, proves to be a devastating experience for Cholly, who is humiliated (yet again!) and sent away by the man he believes to be his father. Society has nothing to offer Cholly, either. As an uneducated African American male without family connections living in the early decades of the 20th century, he has very limited choices. The best he can hope for is to eke out a living any way he can. The culmination of these experiences and the realization that there are little or no opportunities for him in American society lead to Cholly's turning to alcohol to escape his lot in life.

Though Cholly's sexual assault of Pecola is atrocious and there is no justification for it, Morrison does provide an explanation for his behavior by describing the events that lead up to it and by showing us how Cholly has been systematically humiliated and excluded from both his family and society at large. Jennifer Gillan points to the long-lasting repercussions of Cholly's negative experiences in her article "Focusing on the Wrong Front: Historical Displacement, the Maginot Line, and *The Bluest Eye*"; she underscores how the "history of Cholly Breedlove suggests his demoralization over his exclusion from full citizenship" (292). It is only acknowledging the combination and complexity of his life experiences that allows him to come across as more than just a monster. As Kimberly Drake explains in her essay "Rape and Resignation: Silencing the Victim in the Novels of

Morrison and Wright," really "'looking' at Cholly involves seeing his full complexity, examining the interrelations between his experience under oppression, his psychology, and his actions. Cholly becomes simple (or 'flat') only to readers who refuse to look at him, who attempt to judge him either innocent or guilty and dismiss him based on this judgment" (63).

Rather than showing Cholly's attack on Pecola through her point of view, Morrison allows the reader to glimpse what he is thinking as he spies her in the home's kitchen, doing the dishes and "scratching the back of her calf with her toe" (Morrison, 162). As he watches her, he is reminded of when he first met his wife Pauline because of the way Pecola is holding her foot; at the same time, he feels taken aback by her demeanor and that she looks so "whipped" (Morrison, 161). As he stands in the kitchen watching her, Morrison describes the "sequence of emotions" he felt: "revulsion, guilt, pity, then love" (Morrison, 161). Full of "guilt and impotence," he is overcome with a desire to "break her neck—but tenderly" (Morrison, 161). Borne out of these feelings of "hatred mixed with tenderness," Cholly rapes Pecola and then flees the house (Morrison, 162–163). Filtering these events through Cholly's eyes in no way excuses his behavior, nor does it make Pecola any less sympathetic or any less a victim. It does, however, serve to humanize Cholly and show how his depraved behavior has its roots in broader social ills, including racism, poverty, and lack of opportunity. Thus, this scene shows the relationship between violence in the home and larger social problems, which works as part of Morrison's indictments of both the nuclear family and 1940s American society. Not only are Cholly's and Pecola's fates intimately connected with the material circumstances of their lives, but indeed, in *The Bluest Eye,* as Potter emphasizes, "all the characters are inextricably tied to their social circumstances, to say nothing of the impression left by memory and history" (43).

Toward the end of *The Bluest Eye,* Morrison writes, "Love is never any better than the lover. Wicked people love wickedly, violent people love violently, weak people love weakly, stupid people love stupidly" (Morrison, 206). This statement helps to explain the destructive nature of Pecola's family (it is also one of the novel's messages), which extends to how Cholly and Pauline treat each other. They have an abusive relationship consisting of violent outbreaks described as "violent breaks in routine that were themselves routine" that "relieved the tiresomeness of poverty" (Morrison, 41). Not only has the cycle of abuse in their marriage become routine, it has also become formalized, as the following passage from the novel illustrates:

> Cholly and Mrs. Breedlove fought each other with a darkly brutal formalism that was paralleled only by their lovemaking. Tacitly they had agreed not to kill each other. He fought her the way a coward fights a man—with feet, the palms of his hands, and teeth. She, in turn, fought back in a purely feminine way, with frying pans and pokers, and occasionally a flatiron would sail toward his head. They did not talk, groan, or curse during these beatings. There was only the muted sound of falling things, and flesh on surprised flesh [Morrison, 43].

As this scene suggests, violence has become such a part of the Breedloves' relationship that rules have been—albeit tacitly—set as to how they conduct themselves. Moreover, that their fighting has taken some of the qualities of their lovemaking points to the sexualized nature of their violence and the further conflation of sexuality, violence, and home life for the Breedloves. Pecola's home life has, as the novel's end makes abundantly clear, succeeded in destroying her. Phyllis Klotman sums it up nicely: "Cholly's perverse love is in the end the only love she experiences. But it is not a love that nurtures growth. Even the child she bears him dies" (125). Without unconditional love and acceptance, Pecola is unable to come to terms with what she has been through and she sinks into madness.

Yet, for all the wrongs they perpetrate, Pecola's marginalization cannot be blamed solely on her parents, for, as Morrison makes clear through her narrative, society, too, must bear responsibility for Pecola's tragic fate. Klotman points to this fact when she argues, "Just as her father and mother ironically nurture death, so does the society contribute to Pecola's psychic Death" (Klotman, 125). The fact the novel closes with "the evil of fulfillment"—that is, Pecola's staunch and unwavering belief that Soaphead Church has transformed her eyes to blue—reiterates how society, to the end, has been complicit in Pecola's destruction. As Karla Alwes contends:

> Pecola's mad belief that she has attained blue eyes at the novel's end pointedly underscores the fact that violence in *The Bluest Eye* is not solely the result of a drunken father or a misanthropic soothsayer. Morrison makes very clear what she believes to be the primary source of the victimization of women, especially black women. It is a different, perhaps more brutal, type of rape because it penetrates and infects the women with a paralyzing disease whose chief symptom is self-hatred [96–97].

For Pecola, then, it is the combination of her abusive family and a racist society that devalues her that is ultimately to blame for her fate. Not only does Morrison rely on the novel's content to emphasize how both her family and society are responsible for Pecola's fate, but she also relies on the structure of *The Bluest Eye* to drive that message home. Indeed, form and content work side by side to illustrate Morrison's critiques of both the nuclear family and mid-century American society.

The Bluest Eye: A Coming-of-Age Story

The Bluest Eye is (and has frequently been described as) a female bildungsroman. Though the novel certainly has many qualities of a traditional bildungsroman, Morrison provides a new spin on this traditional genre through her use of the primer form in the novel via the "Dick and Jane" preface and prologue (the "Dick and Jane" primer was popular in the 1940s and 1950s). Including the "Dick and Jane" story is imaginative, but it also makes sense in terms of the sociopolitical messages Morrison wants to convey. This inclusion is also in keeping with the bildungsroman form (since a bildungsroman is traditionally understood as a novel of formation, and education, of course, plays a key role in an individual's formation). Klotman, who discusses the importance of the novel's form, emphasizes the connection between the primer form and education. She notes, "The novel opens with three versions of the 'Dick and Jane' reader so prevalent in the public schools at the time (the 1940s) of the novel. Morrison uses this technique to juxtapose the fictions of the white educational process with the realities of life for many black children" (Klotman, 123).

The schools, of course, as Louis Althusser emphasized, are an apparatus of ideology; following this line of reasoning, the "Dick and Jane" primers thus operated historically as part of ideology—it normalized the nuclear family and it depicted a stereotypical and supposed ideal of family life. By using the primer form, Morrison is able to contrast the dysfunctional Breedlove family with this supposed ideal to illustrate the problems Pecola faces and to simultaneously question hegemonic notions about 20th-century family life. Morrison thus reveals how these so-called values promulgated by mid–20th-century America were in fact often detrimental because of how they excluded and devalued anyone who fell outside society's prescribed boundaries. Importantly, Morrison does not just borrow the "Dick and Jack primer" as it originally appeared; she actually includes three different versions of the "Dick and Jane" narrative—the original and two revisions—in order to point to not only the forces that Pecola must contend with, but also to further emphasize the wide chasm between not only the Breedloves and the supposed ideal, but also the vast differences between them and some of their neighbors, who are similarly marginalized but manage to resist ideology and provide their children with a counter-narrative to the prevailing discourse—and hence, offer them a sense of self that has been denied to Pecola. Klotman illustrates how these three different versions function symbolically in the novel. She explains:

> These three versions are symbolic of the lifestyles the author explores in the novel either directly or by implication. The first is clearly that of the alien white world (represented by the Fisher family) which impinges upon the lives of the black children and their families while at the same time excluding them. The second is the lifestyle of the two black MacTeer children, Claudia and Frieda, shaped by poor but loving parents trying desperately to survive poverty, the Northern cold and Northern style of racism they encounter in Ohio. The Breedloves' lives, however, are like the third—the distorted run-on-version of "Dick and Jane," and their child Pecola lives in a misshapen world which finally destroys her [Klotman, 123].

As these remarks by Klotman highlight, Morrison's generic choices go a long way toward explaining the deeper messages of this novel. Thus, together, the form and content of *The Bluest Eye* reveal Morrison's sociopolitical messages including that the domestic sphere is fertile ground for violence and that, rather than existing and operating separately, the larger social problems that plague 20th-century American society—including sexism, racism, and poverty—are tied directly to the objectification, commodification, and violation of women by those close to them.

CHAPTER 3

Transformation and Testimony: Gayl Jones' *Corregidora*

Born in Kentucky in 1949, Gayl Jones has written in genres such as poetry, short stories, and critical essays, but she is best known for her novels *Corregidora* (1975), *Eva's Man* (1976), and *The Healing* (1998). Much of Jones' fiction explores the theme of contradictory, coexisting emotions—specifically the contradictory emotions of love and hate. This dimension of her fiction is something that Jones has addressed at length, including during an interview with Claudia Tate from *Black Women Writers at Work*, where Jones states, "I was and continue to be interested in contradictory emotions that coexist. I think people can hold two different emotions simultaneously" (Tate, 95).

The pull between love and hate propels much of the narrative of Gayl Jones' blues novel *Corregidora* (1975), which centers on the experiences of Ursa Corregidora, a female blues singer who is physically abused. At the same time that the novel explores the contradictory emotions its protagonist Ursa feels, *Corregidora* simultaneously reflects and responds to the practice of attempting to control and silence black female bodies. Indeed, *Corregidora* highlights the degree to which the black female body operates as a site of ideological conflict in mid-twentieth-century America, a dynamic with roots that, as this narrative makes clear, extend back to slavery. This chapter examines representations of and resistance to the black female body as both object and commodity (two ways of defining the black female body that take agency away from the woman in question and, instead, shift the power to those who would use and abuse her) in *Corregidora* by considering how others, and Ursa herself, use her body to define—and confine—her.

In *Corregidora*, those who seek to lay claim to Ursa's body have different, and sometimes competing, agendas. A common theme nonetheless binds them together: the desire to adapt and appropriate her body for their own purposes—purposes which are political in nature and that exist in direct response to the ideological forces of 1940s America at the same time as they link up indirectly with the legacy of slavery that Ursa and the other Corregidora women continue to suffer from and bear witness to. Considering the various functions attributed to the black female body in this literary context—and within its historical context—allows me to situate my observations regarding black sexual politics and ideology in *Corregidora* within the larger debate about the roles race, class, and gender play with respect to the commodifying and policing of female sexuality. This type of analysis will also permit me to trace the cycle of violence and exploitation that, as this novel highlights, begins with slavery and ends with late capitalism.

Corregidora and the Cycle of Violence

The cycle of violence that the Corregidora women bear witness to and suffer from begins with slavery. Their namesake, old man Corregidora, was a "Portuguese seaman turned plantation owner," who sired both Ursa's mother and grandmother (Jones, 10). By enslaving Ursa's great-grandmother, her "Great Gram," repeatedly sexually violating her, and forcing her into prostitution, he lays claim to her body in a number of different ways. He objectifies her for his own sexual desires. He commodifies her sexuality, as well, by selling her body to other men for profit: "He would take me hisself first and said he was breaking me in. Then he started bringing other men and they would give me money and I had to give it over to him" (Jones, 11). This account highlights that old man Corregidora had a personal motive—his own perverse pleasure—as well as a profit incentive to exploit and abuse Great Gram, incentives further underscored by his nicknames for her: "A good little piece. My best. Dorita. Little gold piece" (Jones, 10). He benefits on yet another level from his repeated sexual violation of her, since it results in her bearing him a child whom he legally has ownership rights to and can potentially garner a profit from. Thus, he further commodifies her by exploiting her reproductive labor by laying claim to its product—the child she bears—a practice common in slavery.

In the decades since *Corregidora* was first published, numerous scholars, including Angela Davis, Deborah Gray White, and Hortense J. Spillers, have discussed this practice as part of their overall examinations of the experiences of female slaves. For instance, in *Women, Race, and Class* Davis notes how the legal system was adapted during slavery times to reward the sexual abuse of female slaves by slave owners. The legislation of that era "adopted the principle of partus sequitur ventrem—the child follows the condition of the mother. These were the dictates of the slaveowners who fathered not a few slave children themselves" (Davis, 12). White explains in her book *Ar'n't I a Woman? Female Slaves in the Plantation South* that "once slaveholders realized that the reproductive function of the female slave could yield a profit, the manipulation of procreative sexual relations became an integral part of the sexual exploitation of female slaves" (White, 68). In her essay "Mama's Baby, Papa's Maybe" Spillers highlights that "under the conditions of captivity, the offspring of the female does not 'belong' to the Mother, nor is s/he 'related' to the 'owner,' though the latter 'possesses' it, and in the African-American instance, often fathered it, and, as often, without whatever benefit of patrimony" (Spillers, 269).

Thus, it is under abusive and oppressive conditions just like those Davis, White, and Spillers describe that old man Corregidora sires Ursa's grandmother and mother. The legacy the Corregidora women pass on to Ursa is a transgenerational transmission of trauma stemming from the physical, sexual, emotional, and economic abuses inflicted on them by him under the system of slavery. He is not only her ancestor, but functions in the text as well as "the symbolic progenitor of evil within Ursa's limited world" (Tate, 140). Indeed, Ursa's foremothers have actively worked to keep his memory alive: "Four generations of Corregidora women, beginning with her great-grandmother, refuse to let his memory die with time. They pay homage to him by promulgating his sins in ritualized oral expression, passed down from generation to generation of female children" (Tate, 140). The mandate that the Corregidora women must "make generations" is passed down the matrilineal Corregidora line by Ursa's Great Gram (Jones, 101). She believes that by continuing the line, she will preserve the evidence of the atrocities old man Corregidora committed as a "slave-breeder and whoremonger" (Jones, 8–9). Great Gram stresses to Ursa that by recounting these stories, she is "leaving evidence" and tells Ursa that "you got to leave evidence too" (Jones, 14). Because old man Corregidora, along with other slave owners, destroyed records in an attempt to cover up these crimes, the Corregidora women must pass on the history of these atrocities orally and continue to bear witness to what happened: "They burned all the documents, Ursa [...] we got to keep what we need to bear witness" (Jones, 72). Indeed, this edict has been issued in direct response to, and as a way to counter, the slave owners who attempted to hide their crimes. As Stephanie Li points out in her essay "Love and the Trauma of Resistance in Gayl Jones' *Corregidora*," "by instructing Ursa to make generations to preserve the memory of their sexual abuse, Great Gram and Gram convert the female body into a form of documentation" (132).

Great Gram's pronouncement, as Deborah Horvitz observes, means, indeed, that the Corregidora "women's bodies are again used as the site of history's inscription" (Horvitz, 46). To a degree, Great Gram's charge represents a project of reclamation. Her mandate refigures the body as a potential path to testimony—"bearing witness"—and healing. Yet, these efforts to redefine the female body and, specifically, the maternal body, remain problematic for a number of reasons. Horvitz emphasizes one result of Great Gram's charge: "their commodification is continued by the women themselves, not for money this time, but for history" (Horvitz, 46–47). As Li remarks, this mandate works also to transform the female body into a tool and thus reduces women to a physical function. She explains:

> Once objectified as lucrative "pussy" within the slave economy, the Corregidora women now privilege the womb as the primary site of female value. In both conceptions, women are reduced to a physical function and alienated from any notion of personal desire or sexual pleasure. By shifting attention from the reproductive to the purely sexual, Great Gram and Gram stress the creative potential of women. However, they appropriate the female body as a tool rather than claim it as a means of asserting personal agency [Li, 133].

By using their bodies to "make generations" and "bear witness" to the horrors committed under slavery, the Corregidora women reappropriate for themselves what was once used for others' purposes, but in their attempt at reclamation they find themselves unable to define their bodies in any ways other than the one laid out for them by Great Gram.

Not only does Great Gram traumatize them by retelling her stories to them time and again—and thus makes them relive the abuses she suffered—but her charge to "make generations" also transforms their sexual relations into rote encounters carried out with the purpose of procreation, not pleasure, in mind. Ursa's mother confides in Ursa that she was drawn to Martin because she saw him, not as a life-partner, but as a way to help her fulfill Great Gram's charge. To Ursa, she admits "I didn't want no man" (Jones, 114). She discloses her reasons for having sexual relations with Martin: "It was like my whole body knew it wanted you, and knew it would have you" (Jones, 114). Mama has obeyed the edict laid out for her, but it costs her dearly. She is unable to relate to Martin or any man in any way other than sexually, yet sexual fulfillment is closed off to her, too, since, for her, sex is strictly about procreation, a way to "make generations." Horvitz highlights how the tragic Corregidora family history affects Ursa's mother's relationships, as well Ursa's own relationship, with men when she declares that "Mama's sexual life, like her own, has been ruined by slavery" (Horvitz, 40). As Li explains,

> Mama is the first of the Corregidora women not to experience the horrors of physical enslavement and the perverse cruelties of Corregidora. Instead she endures the destructive consequences of her foremothers' demand to make generations. Raised upon stories that present men as domineering rapists who commodify and abuse women, Mama fears men even as she is drawn to Martin so that she can fulfill the mandate of her foremothers [Li, 133].

For Mama, the desire to fulfill Great Gram's charge is so strong and so all-consuming that it eclipses any other longings she might have.

A Project of Reclamation?

Mama's attempt to reclaim her body by fulfilling Great Gram's mandate does represent a shift from how Gram and Great Gram's maternal bodies were used/abused under the system of slavery (and, in the case of the Corregidora women, by a blood relative), yet Mama's reappropriation of her body remains clouded nonetheless by historical practices, including the practice during slavery of forcing women to serve as breeders. Additionally, her so-called desires may be tainted by the very system she seeks to subvert. As Butler emphasizes, "the female body that seeks to express itself is a construct produced by the very law it is supposed to undermine" (Butler 93). Despite Mama's belief that "making generations" is an act of subversion, she participates, to a degree, within a system and society that wants to define her by her reproductive abilities. Thus, she conforms to society's prescribed role for her at the same time as she tries to redefine herself by/through her body's functions. Butler explains this dilemma; the female body, she stresses, "freed from the shackles of the paternal law may well prove to be yet another incarnation of that law, posing as subversive but operating in the service of that law's self-amplification and proliferation" (Butler 936).

Ursa's current dilemma, like her mother's, has its roots in the myriad forms of abuse her foremothers suffered under the system of slavery. When a violent confrontation with her drunken husband, Mutt Thomas, causes her to miscarry and forces her to undergo an emergency hysterectomy, she must come to terms with her inability to fulfill the mandate laid out for her by her Great Gram. For Ursa, this proves quite difficult. The desire to "make generations" has been deeply ingrained in her, as a conversation she has with Tadpole, the man who will become her second husband, makes clear:

> "What do you want, Ursa?"
> I looked at him with a slight smile that left quickly. "What do you mean?"
> "What I said. What do you want?"
> I smiled again. "What all of us Corregidora women want. Have been taught to want. To make generations" [Jones, 22].

Ursa's foremothers have indoctrinated her into their belief system so much so that she has internalized their desires as her own. She wants, as she puts it, "what all of us Corregidora women want," and now that she is unable to "make generations," she must find another way to define herself. This already difficult task proves even more complicated for Ursa because she must do it amidst individuals and a society which seeks to define—and confine—her in ways that fit their agendas.

Far from operating separately from the system which exploited her foremothers, the conditions under which Ursa is oppressed and defined link up in a very real way to the legacy of slavery. In fact, Ursa is figuratively confined by the same forces that literally enslaved her foremothers. As Griffiths emphasizes, "the legacy of Corregidora's plantation follows her, and she seems enslaved to others and owned by their desires" (Griffiths, 357). Ursa must, then, not only reconcile the voices of her foremothers, who have sought to control her destiny with their mandate to "make generations," but on an almost daily basis, she also must confront others who seek to objectify her and lay claim to her body. This is, of course, the case with Mutt Thomas, whose relationship with Ursa is often described in terms that suggest ownership. What sets Mutt off and leads him to assault Ursa that fateful night at Happy's Café, where he shoves her down the flight of stairs causing her to miscarry and also lose her womb, is that men at this club, where she is singing, "mess with they eyes" at her, which Mutt not only heartily dislikes but also resents since he sees their gaze as an infringement on his proprietary rights over Ursa (3).

Thus, it is a conflict over her body, and who can lay claim to it, that is responsible for her accident and inability to "make generations." At another point, Mutt demands of her, "Are you mine, Ursa, or theirs?" (Jones, 45). Tellingly, Mutt's question assumes that someone must have ownership rights over Ursa—in his view, she must either belong to the Corregidora line, and thus be "theirs," or she must belong to him. He does not allow the possibility that Ursa, perhaps, is her own agent, a self-determining individual. Rather, he feels she must belong to—and thus answer to—someone else. Later in the novel, Ursa recalls how Mutt liked to claim exclusive rights to her body and her sexuality: "Talking about his pussy. Asking me to let him see his pussy" (Jones, 46).

Mutt, however, is not alone in wanting Ursa to conform to his own desires and agenda, a point Jennifer Griffiths highlights. She explains,

> in every interaction, Ursa must see herself as an object of someone else's desire or as a sexual threat to other women. In both the public space of the nightclub, the fair, and the town streets and in the private spaces in which she seeks refuge and recovery, Ursa's body exists as a spectacle, revealing a legacy that she has internalized and the outside world has confirmed [Griffiths, 356].

Ursa is an object of sexual desire for Cat, whose advance Ursa spurns, and for her second husband Tadpole McCormick, the club owner who assumes ownership rights over her, as well. Though he does not physically abuse Ursa like Mutt did, he is emotionally abusive—he, as well, is a very controlling presence in her life, wanting a say in what she eats, how much she sleeps, and how long she performs on stage at a time. When Tadpole puts Ursa on stage at his club to sing, he commodifies her, both because he makes money through her talents and by the way he exploits her physical attractiveness and desirability as a way to fill up seats in his club.

Singing the Blues

Indeed, it is when Ursa sings the blues on stage that it becomes most obvious that her body is caught between conflicting narratives. Ursa represents a cash profit to Tadpole when she performs at his club. He profits financially from her talents as a blues singer and thus appropriates her bodily functions, her voice and her presence on stage, for his own purposes. This is true, as well, of the owner of the Spider, another nightclub where Ursa performs. He suggests as much when he repeatedly tells her that his club's popularity is due, in large part, to her singing: "I knew when I seen you, get you here and we'd be doing good business. Something powerful about you" (Jones, 93). Ursa, thus, is clearly commodified on the job by those who earn money from her singing. She, however, is also objectified when she performs the blues, a point Mutt makes clear in his jealous rants about how men "mess" with her when she is on stage (Jones, 3). Mutt paraphrases these men's desires, asserting that when they see her perform they can think of nothing but "that woman's standing up there. That good-lookin woman standin right up there" (Jones, 84).

Though Mutt's anxieties and accusations stem, in part, from his jealous nature and his desire to possess Ursa, his observations about how men objectify Ursa when they see her on stage nonetheless ring true. Ursa is sexually defined on the job; remember, for instance, that part of her allure as a singer is, of course, her physical attractiveness and stage presence. The tendency to sexually define women on the job is a widespread practice, which numerous feminist scholars make clear. In her study *Sexual Harassment of Working Women* Catharine A. MacKinnon posits that men "'consume' women's sexuality on the job," and women must "accommodate this fact as part of their work" (22). MacKinnon is careful to point out the pervasiveness of this practice. She explains that women must confront this tendency regardless of the type(s) of work they perform. Thus, as she emphasizes, a woman "need not be a secretary or hold a 'woman's job' to be sexually defined on the job" (MacKinnon, 19). Adrienne Rich, who in her essay "Compulsory Heterosexuality and Lesbian Existence" also examines the practice of sexually defining women on the job, points out how "women in the workplace are at the mercy of sex as power in a vicious circle" (21). Indeed, working women have had to learn to accept a degree of powerlessness with respect to this practice. For women, it has been and remains part of the price of holding a job in a male-dominated society. Rich explains:

> The fact is that the workplace, among other social institutions, is a place where women have learned to accept male violation of their psychic and physical boundaries as the price of survival; where women have been educated—no less than by romantic literature or by pornography—to perceive themselves as sexual prey [Rich, 22].

In Ursa's position as a female blues singer, she must confront her sexualization on the job—and the fact that when she performs the blues at these clubs she is "sexual prey" to the men in the audience.

Yet, for Ursa, singing the blues is also a form of expression which represents her attempt at recovery and reclamation. She emphasizes these reasons for performing the blues when she says, "I didn't just sing to be supported [...] I sang because it was something I had to do" (Jones, 3).

Singing the blues connects Ursa with an ideological framework that is specifically African American. As Angela Davis observes in *Blues Legacies and Black Feminism,* both the "historical context within which the blues developed" and the subject matter of blues songs reveal "an ideological framework that was specifically African-American" (4). At the same time, for Ursa, singing the blues is a type of personal narrative. As K. M. Langellier highlights in her essay "Voiceless Bodies, Bodiless Voices," a personal narrative functions as "a story of the body told through the body which makes cultural conflict concrete" (208). This is indeed the case for Ursa Corregidora, a woman who uses her singing to give voice to her own experiences of abuse as well as to pass on the story of her ancestors and the struggles and violence they faced. As Langellier explains, for many performers, a personal narrative represents a "performative struggle over personal and social identity rather than the act of a self with a fixed, unified, stable or final essence" (208). This, too, remains the case for Ursa, who reencounters her and her foremothers' struggles as a way to confront them as she performs her blues songs.

Singing, for Ursa, then is a process rather than a final product. It is by singing the blues that Ursa thus confronts the very forces that attempt to confine and define her as she also reflects them. By performing blues songs, Ursa is finally able to reconcile the legacy of pain she has inherited from old man Corregidora and her foremothers with her personal struggles in mid-twentieth-century America. In her essay "The Role of the Blues in Gayl Jones' *Corregidora,*" Donia Allen explains that "by digging around in the past and connecting it to her own life, Ursa is able, finally, to move beyond it" (261).

Ursa's Testimony

Thus, for Ursa, her (once abused) body functions, also, as a path to testimony; by singing the blues, Ursa connects to the spiritual. Through her ritual of singing, she is finally able to "bear witness" to the atrocities committed during slavery as well as to testify to her own abuse and personal struggles. By telling her story and the stories of her foremothers, Ursa's singing operates as means of recovery and reclamation. Through her voice, Ursa's body functions as an instrument to counter the various cultural and historical forces that seek to oppress and contain her. Though the path of "making generations" to "bear witness" to old man Corregidora's crimes is closed off to Ursa because of her miscarriage and subsequent hysterectomy and because she is therefore unable to literally fulfill that mandate, she is nonetheless able to obey and honor the spirit of this command through her blues songs. By extension, Gayl Jones is able, through her novel *Corregidora,* to give voice to the experiences of abused women and show how they, by reclaiming their own voice, can move beyond the cycle of abuse rather than remaining trapped by it.

CHAPTER 4

Voicing Violence:
Alice Walker's *The Color Purple*

Set in the rural south, Alice Walker's seminal novel *The Color Purple* (1982) tells the story of Celie, a poor African American woman who faces terrible violence at the hands of her stepfather and husband. The novel shows Celie's long path toward self-discovery in the face of oppressive circumstances. Though Celie remains the focus of the novel, in *The Color Purple* Walker also chronicles the lives of other African American women in the southeastern United States in the early and middle parts of the 20th century. Through the novel's female characters such as Celie, Sofia, and Shug, Walker highlights the precarious position of African American women in society at the same time as she calls attention to the problem of intraracial violence through the dilemmas Celie and others face. The novel thus addresses numerous issues related to the abuse, exploitation, and oppression of black women.

Alice Walker and *The Color Purple*

Born in Georgia in 1944, Alice Walker is a prolific and award-winning author as well as an activist. Over her decades-long writing career, Walker has published a number of novels, short story collections, children's books, essays, and poetry collections. Her many well-known works include *The Third Life of Grange Copeland* (1970), *In Love and Trouble: Stories of Black Women* (1973), *Meridian* (1976), *The Temple of My Familiar* (1989), *Possessing the Secret of Joy* (1992), *The Way Forward Is with a Broken Heart* (2000), *Absolute Trust in the Goodness of the Earth* (2003), and *A Poem Traveled Down My Arm: Poems And Drawings* (2003), among others. Walker, however, is perhaps best known for her 1982 epistolary novel, *The*

Color Purple, which was awarded the 1983 Pulitzer Prize in fiction and the National Book Award. The novel was later adapted into a film (Stephen Spielberg's 1985 film by the same name) and a musical.

The Color Purple, set in rural Georgia and, later, Tennessee, spans roughly thirty years of the protagonist Celie's life. The events of the novel begin just after the turn of the century, when Celie is fourteen years old. She has been raped and impregnated by Alphonso, a man she believes to be her father (he is actually, as Celie later learns, her stepfather). After violently assaulting Celie, Alphonso threatens her, telling her, "You better not never tell nobody but God" (Walker, 11). Thus, through this disturbing introduction to Celie's life, Walker sets the stage for many of the novel's major themes at the same time as she initiates the journal entries that Celie writes and addresses as letters to God.

The horrendous abuse Celie suffers at the hands of her stepfather, Alphonso, and later, her husband, makes up much of the novel, so a major theme of *The Color Purple* is domestic abuse. Yet, the novel also depicts Celie's transformation from victim to survivor. Walker portrays Celie as a woman who, over time, finds the ability to regain her voice and ultimately reclaim her agency, so *The Color Purple* is also a novel about hope in the face of adversity because of the way Celie eventually triumphs and comes into her own, despite the abuse, oppression, and many obstacles she faces.

It is not incidental that Alphonso's violent sexual assault and attempt to silence the young girl end up prompting Celie to find her voice through writing. For Celie, the "horror of this experience is evident," but it also becomes apparent that this violence is "the catalyst for Celie's search for voice," a point Martha J. Cutter emphasizes in her article "Philomela Speaks: Alice Walker's Revisioning of Rape Archetypes in *The Color Purple*" (166). Catherine E. Lewis makes a similar contention in her article "Serving, Quilting, Knitting: Handicraft and Freedom in *The Color Purple* and *A Women's Story,*" where she argues that "the impetus for Celie's writing is her rape by Alphonso" (239). As Lewis points out, "Alice Walker presents the book as the result of Celie's silence, confusion, and frustration" (239).

Celie has to find a way to deal with the trauma of the repeated sexual abuse she suffers at the hands of Alphonso, so she begins to write in order to make sense of what is happening to her, as well to document the violence she's forced to endure. Commenting on Alphonso's attempt to silence Celie by telling her to reveal to no one except "God" what he's done to her, Lewis further asserts that "Celie takes Alphonso's idea literally, and as tensions rise in the family, Celie records herself. When she marries Albert, she continues to write" (239). Indeed, to survive her abusive marriage to Albert, she continues to turn to her writing as a way to cope. For Celie, however, the act of writing becomes not only a coping mechanism but it later proves to be an essential means toward self-discovery. Writing gives her the opportunity to express her feelings of shame, humiliation, and pain while charting her growing awareness of American society. To be sure, throughout the novel, Walker emphasizes that this ability to express her thoughts and feelings is crucial to Celie's developing a sense of self.

At first, Celie is unable to resist those who seek to violate and silence her. Prompted by Alphonso's warning to remain quiet about his abuse of her, Celie initially feels that the only way to persevere is to remain silent. Not only has Celie been forced into silence by her abusive stepfather but she's been rendered invisible by society at large. As Rasul A. Mowatt, Bryana H. French, and Dominique A. Malebranche argue in their essay "Black/Female/Body Hypervisibility and Invisibility," a sense of "invisibility is a fundamental aspect of being Black in a White-dominated society"(645). Thus, Walker initially presents Celie, who is abused and objectified by Alphonso, as entirely passive and lacking the power to assert herself through actions or words. Her letters to God, in which she starts to reveal her story and the terrible abuse she's suffered, become her only outlet. Yet, because Celie is so young and not yet accustomed to describing her experiences, her narrative begins as rather jumbled despite her efforts. Tellingly, as Celie matures and her ability to make sense of what's she endured increases, her ability to clearly communicate the horrors she's lived also grows. Celie's act of writing, then, operates as a means for her to not only come to terms with what's happened to her, but her chronicling of her life also functions as a way for readers of the novel to witness her transformation as she gains a voice and agency, both of which Alphonso and others have taken pains to deprive her of.

For Celie, finding her voice remains one of her central challenges, and for Celie this is an especially difficult task since she must contend with abusive family relationships at the same time as she negotiates a society which devalues and seeks to oppress her. As part of his discussion of the novel in his article "Celie in the Looking Glass: The Desire for Selfhood in *The Color Purple*," Daniel W. Ross highlights that "finding the courage to speak is a major theme of *The Color Purple*" (69). Throughout the novel, readers are able to bear witness as Celie, little by little, recovers her own history, sexuality, spirituality, and voice.

Because of the types of struggles Celie faces, she comes to represent the many women who encounter similar challenges in their own lives. The novel, then, traces Celie's individual liberation and portrays her reality during the post-reconstruction era at the same time as Walker uses her to connect to—and reclaim—the past, which is important for African American women; indeed, through Celie, Walker is able to articulate "a personal and historical transition for the Black woman and her community" (Floyd-Thomas and Gillman, 530).

Beyond documenting the abuse Celie suffers and her ultimate ability to overcome it, *The Color Purple,* however, is also "the study of the changing roles of women" in society (Lewis, 237). In this sense, too, the novel is not just about Celie but it functions, instead, as a testimony to "the struggles and spirits of women who must make spaces for themselves in patriarchal societies" (Lewis, 237). One of these women is Shug Avery, a blues singer and sometime mistress of Albert (Celie's husband). Shug becomes Celie's friend and confidant—and eventually her lover—and, through her nurturing and guidance, she helps Celie grow into an independent woman. Another woman who plays an important role in the novel is Sofia, Harpo's wife. Physically imposing and assertive, Sofia befriends Celie. Sofia fights back when abused and she refuses to submit to whites, so she serves as an example for Celie through her steadfast perseverance in the face of hardship. Nevertheless, Sofia endures much suffering during her life, as well, so she also serves as a reminder of the costs of resistance and the difficulties of confronting gender oppression and institutional racism.

The Color Purple: **The Controversy**

Since the time of its initial publication, *The Color Purple* has sparked a great deal of controversy. Both the 1982 novel and the 1985 film instigated heated debates about black cultural representation and the effects Walker's portrayals of her characters have had on the image of black people in the United States. A number of black male critics complained that the novel reaffirmed old racist stereotypes about black men and black families—and about pathology in black communities. For example, the novelist Ishmael Reed has been outspoken about *The Color Purple* since the time of its debut; he suggested that Walker depicts her characters' lives as unnecessarily harsh and brutal. In 1985, a very vocal critic, Tony Brown (the host of the television program *Tony Brown's Journal*) described the film *The Color Purple* as "the most racist depiction of black men since *The Birth of a*

Nation" as well as the "most anti–Black family film of the modern film era." Reed and Brown's reactions are not atypical, for as Ronda Racha Penrice points out in her article "*The Color Purple* 25 Years Later: From Controversy to Classic," many black male critics have "claimed that *The Color Purple* was an assault on the black male image." Jacqueline Bobo echoes a similar sentiment in her article "Sifting through the Controversy: Reading *The Color Purple*," where she states that the novel has "been the subject of intense opposition since the arrival" of the book in 1982, largely due to the "negative portrait" she presents of society and "black men in particular" (332).

The taboo subject matter of the book has sparked controversy, as well. Indeed, in the decades since the book's initial publication, *The Color Purple* has remained one of the most challenged novels of the 20th and 21st centuries. As Pepper Worthington discusses in "Writing a Rationale for a Controversial Common Reading Book: Alice Walker's *The Color Purple*," the book has been the focus of controversy for several reasons, including its subject matter: "The subject matter of *The Color Purple* includes incest, rape, wife-beating, adultery, hints of lesbianism, drugs, alcoholism, African tribal customs, and murder" (Worthington, 48).

All of this debate has also resulted in *The Color Purple*'s having been banned several times since its initial publication. In the 1980s, many high schools across the country banned the book for its controversial subject matter. For example, in 1984 it was decided that an Oakland, California, high school honors class was not "intellectually mature enough to study the work," due to some explicit scenes and its subject matter (Baldassarro). In 1986, the book was removed from the shelves of a Newport News, Virginia, school library because of "its profanity and sexual references" (the novel, however was "made accessible" to "students over 18, or who had written permission from a parent") (Baldassarro). Even in recent years, the novel has been banned. For example, in 2010 the novel was banned for offensive language, being sexually explicit, and unsuited to age group. In 2009, the book was challenged in Burke County schools in Morgantown, North Carolina, by parents concerned about the homosexuality, rape, and incest portrayed in the book.

Even so, *The Color Purple* has always had its avid supporters, not only among black women, but also among others who have lauded the novel as a feminist fable. Critics have often praised Walker's straightforward depiction of taboo subjects in the novel and her clear rendering of folk idiom and dialect through Celie's written voice. For example, Mel Watkins, a contemporary reviewer of the novel, describes *The Color Purple* in the *New York Times Book Review* as "indelibly affecting" and asserts that Walker's narrative style encourages readers to have an "intimate identification with the heroine." Similarly, Peter S. Prescott, another of the novel's contemporary reviewers, praises Walker by calling *The Color Purple* "an American novel of permanent importance" (67). In her review of the novel, Dinitia Smith went as far as to suggest that Walker belongs "in the company of Faulkner" for her achievement in *The Color Purple* (183).

As Charles S. Proudfit highlights, ever since the novel's debut, both *The Color Purple* and Walker herself "continue to elicit a wide range of praise and censure" from critics, reviewers, and readers alike" (12). The fact that the novel has spurred such strong feelings in its readers suggests just how powerful the novel remains. It also suggests just how taboo the subject of domestic violence still is—even in the 21st century (since the book keeps ending up on the list of banned books). Moreover, though the intense debates surrounding *The Color Purple* point to the controversial nature of the book's (and film's) subject matter, they also offer testimony to the resonant effects *The Color Purple* has had on cultural and racial discourse in the United States.

The Structure of *The Color Purple*

The violent subject matter of the novel is made more immediate and intense for readers by the way Walker presents Celie's story. As a way to establish intimacy between the novel and its readers, Walker relies upon an epistolary structure, "laced with diaries, letters, and prayers as forms of female expression" (Floyd-Thomas and Gillman, 530). The epistolary, or letter-writing, form of *The Color Purple* resembles a diary, since Celie tells her story through private letters that she writes to God. Therefore, as Celie narrates her story with total candor and frankness, she presents a personal and startling account of the abuse she faces as a poor African American woman in rural Georgia in the early to middle parts of the 20th century. The structure of the book works to powerfully render Celie's experiences since, as a victim of domestic abuse, she is almost completely voiceless and disenfranchised in everyday society; through the act of writing the letters, however, Celie becomes able to speak out. Writing, then, for Celie is a form of protest, for, through these letters, she can privately break the silence that her family and society have tried to impose upon her.

The structure of the novel bears scrutiny for yet another reason: in some ways, Celie's confessional narrative is reminiscent of African American slave narratives from the 19th century. Like the autobiographical accounts provided by Frederick Douglass, Harriet Jacobs, and the many voices represented in the Slave Narrative Collection of the Federal Writers project, Celie provides a day-to-day account of her life and struggles in the face of oppression. She offers an eye-witness account of the oppressive nature of society at the same time she records the horrific domestic abuse she's subjected to because of her stepfather and husband. In this sense, she raises awareness about an issue that society has tried to, alternately, hide and minimize: the problem of domestic violence.

Though the structure of the novel works well on several levels, not the least of these being how Walker provides a first-hand perspective (through Celie's eyes) on the abuse she suffers at the same time as Walker links Celie's story up with the legacy of slavery in a tangible way, there are nonetheless challenges stemming from how Walker chooses to present Celie's story. Shanyn Fiske discusses the difficulty associated with the structure of *The Color Purple* in her short article "Piecing the Patchwork Self: A Reading of Walker's *The Color Purple*." Fiske argues that the novel's "inclusion of so many individual stories makes it difficult to tell whether these narratives are enclosed within Celie's account of her life of whether Celie's story is part of a larger whole. The formal destabilization of a dominant narrative emphasizes that an individual cannot be considered apart from the matrix of his or her relationships" (Fiske, 150–151). It is in this context—as an individual woman who is part of larger social order—that Walker asks us to consider Celie.

Early Abuse: Celie's Childhood and Adolescence

When Celie's mother, who has grown ill and no longer wants the burden of pregnancy, rejects her husband's advances, he begins to rape and beat Celie. This physical and sexual abuse that she suffers at the hands of her stepfather plays a large role in defining young Celie, not only because of the trauma it causes her, but also because he uses her shame and fear to manipulate her. Alphonso warns Celie, "It'd kill your mammy" if she were to find out what he was doing, thus threatening her into silence and submission (Walker, 11). Through this threat he equates Celie's speaking up about the abuse with bringing about her mother's death, thus putting the young and naive Celie in an impossible situation. Celie does remain silent, but her mother, whose health has been failing for some time, dies anyway, leaving Celie and her younger sister Nettie alone with the abusive Alphonso. Alphonso eventually remarries, but this new marriage does not stop him from abusing Celie. Celie grows increasingly concerned that Alphonso will turn his unwanted attention toward young Nettie.

As the two sisters mature, Nettie catches the eye of a widowed farmer who lives nearby (Celie initially refers to the man simply as "Mr. _____"). Alphonso, however, refuses to let the man marry Nettie and he, instead, bargains with him about a possible match with Celie. The result is that Celie is then forced to marry "Mr. _____" (Albert), who is looking for a wife to take care of his home and his four children. Making matters worse, this arranged marriage forces Celie to separate from her younger sister.

Celie's Abusive Marriage

Alphonso, fearing that Celie might reveal to Albert what he has done to her—and in an attempt to shield himself from any accusations that Celie might one day make against him—again silences Celie when, as the two men discuss her, he says that she "tell lies" (Walker, 18). This time, however, Alphonso renders Celie powerless by calling into question "her credibility" (Lewis, 238). Celie has no choice about marrying Albert, and once in the marriage, she remains voiceless.

Though she is no longer under Alphonso's thumb, violence remains a grim reality for Celie as Albert's wife. On their wedding day, Albert's twelve-year-old son Harpo greets Celie by injuring her head by hurling a rock straight at her. Albert does little to intervene. As Lewis notes, when Harpo "splits her head open with a rock," there is "negligible reproach from Albert" (Lewis, 239). Albert's reaction—or lack thereof—fits a pattern that reveals much about this society and underscores just how precarious a position Celie holds within a patriarchal context. Specifically, it bespeaks the powerful position men occupy relative to women. As Lewis explains, there is a clear "privileging of young males" that is "resonant with *The Color Purple* in that Celie, upon marriage to Albert, is prey to the actions of 12-year-old Harpo" (239). The injured Celie spends the rest of her wedding day cleaning Albert's messy house and chasing after his unruly children.

Albert has little or no provocation for his mistreatment of Celie; nonetheless, he frequently beats her. At one point, his son Harpo asks him why he abuses Celie. Albert responds, "Cause she my wife. Plus, she stubborn" (Walker, 22). For her part, Celie feels that his abuse of her is a way for punishing her for not being Shug, and she confides to Shug that she thinks Albert beats her for not being "you." Despite the fact that Celie is clearly suffering in her marriage to Albert, she passively accepts her husband's physical abuse of her. Though at numerous points in the novel other women tell Celie to fight back or speak up for herself, Celie, accustomed to abuse and still traumatized from her stepfather's horrid violation of her, stoically endures Albert's beatings.

It is only when Celie realizes that Albert has been deliberately hiding the letters that her sister Nettie has been sending her that Celie speaks up for herself. Though the two sisters have been separated for years, the two still share a remarkable bond. Celie has never stopped loving and worrying about Nettie, who she's grown to fear may be dead. When Celie confides these fears to Shug, Shug mentions that she often sees Albert removing mysterious letters from the mailbox and hiding them in his coat pockets.

> He been keeping your letters, say Shug.
> Naw, I say. Mr. _____ mean sometimes, but he not that mean.
> She say, Humpf, he that mean.
> But how come he do it? I ast. He know Nettie mean everything in the world to me [Walker, 115].

About a week later, Shug obtains the most recent of these letters. The letter has stamps from Africa on it, and it's from Nettie, who reveals that she is alive and well—and that she has been sending letters all along!

The discovery of these letters—and her discovery of Albert's treachery—is a revelation for Celie, and it marks a real change for her as a character. Indeed, this realization proves pivotal for many reasons. For starters, it prompts Celie toward action in a way that none of Albert's other behavior has before. Though Celie has for so long remained silent and compliant, Albert's deception is more than she can take. She sees his actions as spiteful, and she cannot tolerate his keeping her away from her sister for all these years. Celie begins to watch Albert closely, and she contemplates violence against him as a way to repay him for his cruelty:

> I watch him so close, I begin to feel a lightening in the head. Fore I know anything I'm standing hind his chair with his razor open....
> All day long I act just like Sofia. I stutter. I mutter to myself. I stumble bout the house crazy for Mr._____ blood. In my mind, he falling down dead every which a way. By the time night come, I can't speak. Every time I open my mouth nothing come out but a little burp [Walker, 115].

Celie is out for "blood" now, as the passage above makes clear. Though Albert's physical abuse of Celie may rank worse in some people's minds, for Celie, hiding the letters from her proves to be a far crueler thing to do.

His actions clearly represent a particular form of domestic abuse (recall that abuse is defined as any behavior that is designed to control and subjugate another human being). Thus, through the revelation that Albert's been keeping Nettie's letters away from Celie, Walker shines a light on yet another dimension of domestic violence: the emotional abuse and psychological abuse that so often takes place in the domestic sphere. Albert's withholding of the letters is a form of domestic abuse, and it is simply too much for Celie to bear.

Psychological abuse and emotional abuse have traditionally garnered less attention from policy makers and researchers who specialize in domestic abuse. One reason for the relative neglect of the problem of psychological abuse is that there are difficulties in arriving at a common definition of it that might be useful to both the mental health and legal professions. Another reason for the relative inattention to the problem of psychological abuse is that there has been an implicit assumption that physical abuse exacts a greater psychological toll on victims than does psychological abuse. Despite this assumption, research into the problem suggests otherwise. In fact, studies suggest that psychological abuse actually appears to have as great an impact as physical abuse on its victims. Daniel K. O'Leary discusses this phenomenon in his article "Psychological Abuse: A Variable Deserving Critical Attention in Domestic Violence," where he cites data which supports this theory. Indeed, according to the findings O'Leary describes in his article, retrospective reports, longitudinal research, and treatment dropout research all provide evidence that psychological abuse can exact a negative effect on relationships that is as great as that of physical abuse. As O'Leary further points out, a direct comparison between psychological and physical abuse by women in physically abusive relationships indicates that psychological abuse has a greater adverse effect on them than physical abuse. Celie clearly feels this way, as well, for her reaction to the discovery of the hidden letters infuriates her in a way that Albert's physical abuse of her never did.

The discovery of these letters does much more than enrage Celie, though. Indeed, when she and Shug uncover the pile of letters Albert has kept hidden in a locked trunk, she learns what her younger sister has been doing for all of the time the two have been apart. Celie learns that Nettie became friends with a married couple named Corrine and Samuel who were members of a Christian ministry planning to travel to Africa for missionary work. Nettie developed a love of learning, and after reading all of Samuel and Corrine's books about African history, she decided to accompany them to Africa to help them start a missionary school. Years of correspondence from Nettie describe her experiences living as a Christian missionary in West Africa. Celie also learns through these same letters that her two children, Adam and Olivia (who she feared were also dead), are actually alive and have been adopted by Nettie's benefactors. Nettie's long-lost letters strengthen Celie's sense of self by informing her of her personal history and of the fate of her children. Feeling empowered and emboldened when confronted with the news that Nettie and her two children have survived, and strengthened by Shug's friendship and support, Celie finally finds the courage to leave Albert and her abusive marriage.

Finding Her Voice

Despite the horrific abuse she endures and the many trials she faces, Celie comes to depend on other women, and this, too, proves to be a crucial part of her emerging identity. Sofia, Harpo's wife, plays a pivotal role in Celie's development. Unlike Celie, who for so long passively accepts the abuse that Albert doles out, Sofia is a fighter. Sofia resists whites and rejects their view of what her place should be. She also refuses to submit to her husband and, when he tries to control her, she fights back (at one point, she gives Harpo a black eye). Like Sofia, Shug plays a significant role in helping Celie develop her sense of self. Lewis argues that when she is with Shug and while she is among other women, Celie begins to come into her own, for, as her life becomes "more and more stable," her "ability to relate to women" also grows (Lewis, 239). Celie "finds her voice louder and more clearly with them first, and then she is able to eventually face the men in her life" (Lewis, 239–240). Women help Celie along her journey, but in the end, Celie finds her voice in spite of Albert.

Indeed, when she finally stops being silent, Celie uses her voice to speak out against him. In the aftermath of finding Nettie's letters, Shug and Celie decide together that Celie will go stay for a while with Shug in Memphis. When Shug tells Albert about this plan, he forbids it. Celie's feelings of hurt, betrayal, and rage (which she's for so long suppressed) finally come to the surface, as the following exchange between Celie and Albert makes clear:

71

I thought you was finally happy, he say. What wrong now?

You a lowdown dog is what's wrong, I say. It's time to leave you and enter into the Creation. And your dead body just the welcome mat I need.

Say what? he ast. Shock.

All round the table folkses mouths be dropping open.

You took my sister Nettie away from me, I say. And she the only person love me in the world [Walker, 181].

Not only is Albert shocked to see Celie finally standing up herself, but others in the family are, too. Celie relates how, in response to witnessing this scene, "Sofia so surprise to hear me speak up she ain't chewed for ten minutes" (Walker, 181). Scenes such as these demonstrate how, without a doubt, Celie changes throughout the novel. Her connections with women such as Shug, Sofia, and her sister Nettie prompt this change: "Celie develops in the novel, moving from a non-fighter for a fighter-for-love" (Worthington, 50).

After this, Celie and Shug move to Memphis. Celie develops her own sewing business, and because of her hard work, talent, and dedication, the business does quite well. Her customer base increases to the point that she is self-supporting and, eventually, an employer. Not only do this profession and her new status as a business owner help Celie financially, but through the creation of this business, she gains emotional strength. In many ways, Celie's "talent for sewing pants" comes to represent "her independence, her talent, her freedom to love" (Worthington, 50).

Because Celie is now free of Albert's abuse and is also able to support herself through her own efforts, she moves closer toward self-actualization. Celie, who for so long has been oppressed, abused, and diminished by society and the men in her life, transforms into a contented, successful, and independent woman. Tellingly, Celie is able to transform through the act of sewing, a skill which is traditionally viewed as a chore for women who are confined to the domestic sphere. For Celie, however, sewing is not a sign of her continued oppression; rather, she is able to turn it into an outlet to creatively express herself (as well as a means to support herself financially). Though so much has changed for Celie, something is still missing until she is reunited with her family. When Nettie, Olivia, and Adam return to Georgia from Africa, Celie finally gets the reunion she has for so long needed—and deserved. Though Celie goes through so much hardship, she delights nonetheless in seeing her sister and children again.

The Cyclical Nature of Violence and Gender Oppression

Despite the claims that Walker portrays black men in a rather negative light in *The Color Purple,* it is worth noting that the majority of those who commit violence in Walker's novel are not stereotypical, one-dimensional villains. Indeed, more often than not, the men who perpetuate violence are themselves victims, oftentimes of racism and discrimination. Moreover, many of the men who perpetrate domestic abuse were themselves raised with violence. For example, Celie's husband Albert, who commits terrible acts of violence, is himself a product of a violent home. His son, Harpo, is made to witness Albert's abuse of Celie—and Harpo himself sometimes falls victim to his father's physical abuse as he grows up—so his desire to control his wife, Sofia, stems in part from these early experiences.

Society at large plays a significant role in the oppression that Celie and the other female characters face in *The Color Purple,* as well. There are many societal factors that contribute to perpetuating violent relationships such as cultural mores, religious practices, economic and political conditions, and rigidly viewed gender roles (as well as the gendered division of labor), any or all of which may set the precedence for committing and perpetuating domestic violence. In the case of the society Walker depicts in *The Color Purple,* the strictures of the rural South work to oppress and confine women such as Celie and Sofia who are subject to patriarchy. Walker portrays a society which does much to diminish women like Celie and Sofia, "who are bound physically, legally, psychologically, and socially by male codes" (Lewis, 239). Walker depicts the violence that these women face as an outcome of these social codes.

Women, too, sometimes play a role in causing other women to be abused, as the situation of Celie and Sofia so poignantly illustrates. Harpo, who is initially attracted to Sofia because of her fierce will and spirit, and who woos her in large part because of her feisty nature and strong personality, begins to worry that his masculinity is threatened by her behavior. Although when they are first married, Harpo seems quite proud of Sofia's independence, Albert causes him to feel that Sofia is too strong-willed. In fact, Albert frequently admonishes his son for not being better able to control his wife. After much prodding, Harpo, feeling that his masculinity is in question, and succumbing to his father's wishes, tries to assert control over Sofia. His desire to subjugate her clearly stems, at least in part, from his father's prodding.

Not quite sure what to do, Harpo approaches Celie for advice about how to make Sofia obey him. Celie tells Harpo to beat Sofia. Though advising Harpo to abuse Sofia may appear out of character for Celie, it actually makes sense on a couple of levels. Not only do her remarks highlight her precarious position in society, but her counsel points to the cyclical nature of domestic abuse and gender oppression. By asking for Celie's advice, Harpo presents her with a rare opportunity to participate in the control and abuse of another woman. Celie, who for so long has been disempowered, takes this opportunity to exercise authority over another person (Sofia). Celie, however, quickly regrets giving Harpo this advice, and she actually confesses to Sofia what she's done. Sofia, who is initially upset with Celie, comes to understand that it was Celie's feelings of jealousy—combined with her own sense of powerlessness—that has prompted her to give Harpo the bad advice. For her part, Sofia doesn't let Harpo get away with abusing her. Unlike Celie, she knows how to fight back against abuse, and Harpo gets a black eye for his trouble. When Harpo later asks Celie for more advice, Celie tells Harpo that abusing Sofia is not the answer. Thus, this situation reveals the cyclical nature of patriarchy and male dominance, but it also shows how these forces can be resisted.

Indeed, by asserting their objections and independence, the women in *The Color Purple* are ultimately able to break the chains of patriarchy. Through Celie and Sofia's resistance to Albert and Harpo, the cycle of violence appears to be broken by the end of the novel, as well. For his part, Harpo seems to learn that there is a better way. When Albert falls ill, he nurses him back to health, and he shows more kindness to his children than what was shown to him as a child.

The Novel's Resolution

The Color Purple deals with the violence and oppression that shape the lives of women like Celie and, consequently, much of the novel presents a sad picture of life in the rural South. Nonetheless, Walker ultimately offers a rather hopeful message through the novel's conclusion. Celie and Shug reside in Memphis for some time, where Celie spends her days designing and sewing individually tailored pants at Folkspants, Unlimited, the business she has founded. Celie, finally free from oppression, also begins to take better care of herself, and she really comes into her own.

The fact that Celie is now a changed woman becomes evident to others when she returns to Georgia for Sofia's mother's funeral. At the service, many of her old friends comment about how pretty she looks. Celie learns that Harpo and Sofia have reconciled and are living together as a happily married couple. Celie meets up with Albert again and finds that he is a different man. He now works hard on his land and cleans his own house. She learns that Albert has reevaluated his life and attempted to correct his earlier wrongs. When the two speak, Albert finally listens to Celie, and the two come to enjoy spending time together. Albert expresses his wish to have an equal and mutually respectful marriage with Celie, but she declines. Nonetheless, the two decide to remain friends, and at the end of the novel, Walker presents a scene where the two of them "sit sewing and talking and smoking" their pipes together (Walker, 238).

Therefore, as Diane Gabrielsen Scholl emphasizes in her article "With Ears to Hear and Eyes to See: Alice Walker's Parable, *The Color Purple,*" Walker ends this novel hopefully, with "a scene of reconciliation, a reunion that begins when Celie makes her peace with a contrite" Albert, who is now "willing to talk about their past and attempts to understand and apologize for her excessive domination" (Scholl, 260). Not only have Albert and Celie reconciled, but the tone of reunion permeates the book's final pages. Indeed, as Jacqueline Jones points out in her article "Fact and Fiction in Alice Walker's *The Color Purple,*" the novel "ends with a series of reconciled dyads," including Celie and Albert, Harpo and Sofia, and others (654).

When Celie returns to town for the funeral, she also discovers that Alphonso has died, which means that her parents' land and home are now hers. She moves into her own home and lives life there on her own terms. Thus, by the end of the novel, Celie has transformed from a "depressed survivor-victim of parent loss, emotional and physical neglect, rape, incest, trauma, and spousal abuse" to a woman who has achieved "an emotional maturity and a firm sense of identity that is psychologically convincing" (Proudfit, 13–14). Indeed, the novel shows Celie finally finding her voice and able to live her life as she sees fit. Walker has successfully depicted "Celie's movement away from an existence as a victim" to the point where she has become "the author/subject of her own story" (Cutter, 163). Thus, the novel ends on a rather promising note for Celie; at the same time, the novel presents an overall positive message by suggesting that "hope, strength, and love can grow no matter what" (Worthington, 50).

CHAPTER 5

Violent Spaces: Gloria Naylor's
The Women of Brewster Place
and *Linden Hills*

Born in New York in 1952, Gloria Naylor is a novelist, essayist, screen-play writer, columnist, and educator. Much of her fiction deals with oppression, and she uses a lot of her writing to call attention to the violence and suffering that women endure. The focus of this chapter will be two of Naylor's novels, *The Women of Brewster Place* (1982) and *Linden Hills* (1985), both of which raise awareness about domestic abuse. In these novels, Naylor shows how domestic violence remains hidden because the private nature of the domestic sphere works to cover up the problem, at the same time as the supposedly "private" setting discourages involvement by law enforcement or other members of the community. These two novels, which clearly also operate as broader social indictments of women's treatment and the larger sociopolitical and economic conditions in contemporary America, demonstrate, as well, the relationship between women's literal—meaning physical and geographic—and figurative places in society. Thus, these novels stress the roles environment and geography play in shaping women's lives. Naylor also highlights through her literary representations of domestic abuse its regulatory function—that is, how domestic tyranny can function as a way to create order in the home.

Order in the Home

The order Naylor's violent men crave is defined by, and operates as part of, the larger power structure of 1980s America, a sociopolitical and economic system whose continuation is dependent not only on men remaining in charge, but also having their authority go unchecked and (largely) unchallenged. The majority of the abusive men featured in these Naylor novels act violently primarily to maintain the status quo, that is, to quell any type of outward resistance from, usually female, family members or others close to them who question their authority. This aspect of, and explanation for, domestic violence has been addressed in detail by professionals in the medical, psychological, and legal communities, including Diane L. Zosky, for example. She discusses this explanatory mode in her article "The Application of Object Relations Theory to Domestic Violence," where she points out that sometimes men "resort to domestic violence as a mechanism to maintain power, control, and privilege in a patriarchal society" (Zosky, 57). Similarly, in their book *Partner Violence: A Comprehensive Review of 20 Years of Research,* Jana L. Jasinski and Linda M. Williams address the roles played by male dominance, control, family power, and societal norms when they point to the dynamics and risk factors involved with domestic abuse. They highlight that "results from previous research suggest that wife beating is more common in households where power is concentrated in the hands of the husband or male partner" (Jasinski and Williams, 5). They also note that in male-controlled households, "physical violence may be used to legitimate the dominant position of the male" (Jasinski and Williams, 5). The characters who perpetrate domestic violence in these novels clearly fit the above descriptions.

Setting and Its Importance

The Women of Brewster Place and *Linden Hills* pair well together because—in addition to the fact that both were written and set in the 1980s—both of these novels illuminate the regulating function of domestic abuse. Importantly the settings of these two novels play significant roles in the dilemmas and abuse faced by the female characters. Far from existing solely as backdrops for the action that occurs, the settings of *The Women of Brewster Place* and *Linden Hills* allow Naylor a means to explore how characters' environments shape them and contribute to their struggles. In *The Women of Brewster Place,* which is set in a poor neighborhood where many characters struggle just to pay the bills and put food on the table, Naylor identifies the link between women's economic disenfranchisement and their subordinate role by portraying violence as a way to keep underclass women in their place. In *Linden Hills,* set in an affluent neighborhood, she underscores how domestic violence functions as a way to police women who transgress the acceptable boundaries in the home.

Even though many of the female characters in *Linden Hills* are largely isolated from the economic hardships that plague their more economically disenfranchised sisters in *The Women of Brewster Place,* both groups of women are largely defined by where they live, and both face similarly oppressive situations in the home. There is also a considerable degree of intertextuality in these two novels, in that there are characters, albeit usually minor ones, who figure into both of these novels, and Naylor specifically references the two neighborhoods in both, as well, which suggests that these two novels collectively address her more general interests.

Naylor's concerns in these two novels—which sometimes overlap— seem to be at least fourfold: exposing problems related to violence in the home, highlighting how the power structure of contemporary America oppresses women, critiquing marriage and other family dynamics, and, finally, making a broader social indictment about 1980s America. Naylor accomplishes this last task by revealing the poverty and despair intrinsic to certain geographic areas—areas whose inhabitants are economically dis-enfranchised (as Naylor's fiction makes clear) because of issues related to race, gender, sexuality/sexual orientation, and social class. The importance of class becomes especially evident when Naylor presents the generational cycle of poverty. Such is the case in *The Women of Brewster Place.*

The neighborhood of Brewster Place proves to be, as Jill L. Matus points out in her essay "Dream Deferral and the Closure in *The Women of Brewster Place,*" the proverbial "'end of the line' for most of its inhabitants" (50). These remarks underscore the severity of the poverty and other social problems the women in this novel face, and they also work to starkly con-trast the literal place they inhabit with the environment which shapes the women in the Linden Hills neighborhood. While *The Women of Brewster Place* shows the detrimental effects of poverty, racism, and sexism, as well as how these social practices have a negative impact on the novel's charac-ters, in *Linden Hills,* Naylor highlights how those who have attained a degree of power and privilege often use it to oppress others, all the while they themselves suffer from an excessive fixation on the outward trappings of wealth and success, often at the cost of their values or worse—indeed, some characters are so tainted by Linden Hills that they lose their lives. As Charles E. Wilson, Jr., discusses in his book *Gloria Naylor: A Critical Com-panion,* in *Linden Hills,* Naylor "explores questions about the black middle class and critiques the misguided value system of that community" (64).

What all of these observations help to suggest is that earning money and a degree of privilege actually often work to skew individuals' values and belief systems. Indeed, in their effort to "make it" (that is succeed), the inhabitants of Linden Hills have had to give up other freedoms, so in a way, this affluent neighborhood proves to be just as confining as Brewster Place, whose residents have landed there largely because they do not have anywhere else to go. The sense that Naylor depicts the community as confining and stultifying—despite its inhabitants' outward emblems of success—is only heightened by the fact that she structures the neighborhood to suggest the different levels of hell described in Dante's *Inferno,* with different streets and addresses in *Linden Hills* corresponding to levels from Dante's classic work. This sustained allusion, as Christine G. Berg argues, allows Naylor "the opportunity to condemn American materialism as a root of her characters' sins" (3). Thus, by showcasing the problems intrinsic to certain areas, Naylor is able to make a broader critique of American society as well as to reveal how social problems can affect rich and poor alike.

Looking at *Linden Hills* and *The Women of Brewster Place* side by side also encourages readers to consider how violence in the home manifests itself across lines of social class. *The Women of Brewster Place* is set in an urban working-class neighborhood that is populated mostly by African Americans who struggle desperately just to get by. Naylor takes pains to show how the characters in this novel are largely defined by their poverty, oppressive and stultifying living conditions, and lack of choices. In contrast, *Linden Hills* is set in an affluent suburb populated by educated African American professionals. Naylor shows through these two novels that domestic abuse affects both rich and poor. By depicting domestic abuse as something that crosses class lines, she counters the prevalent and often misleading stereotype that the problem is largely confined to working-class homes. She also acknowledges how widespread the problem is. Naylor suggests, too, that domestic violence—far from existing as a separate issue— is intimately connected to and part and parcel of larger social problems endemic to contemporary American society, including the exploitation and disenfranchisement of the poor, the oppression of women, and the devaluing of anything that doesn't yield a product. Indeed, both *The Women of Brewster Place* and *Linden Hills* depict domestic abuse as merely one symptom of many of a deeply flawed society.

The Women of Brewster Place

Naylor's debut novel, *The Women of Brewster Place,* was published in 1982 and won the 1983 National Book Award. In 1989, it was adapted as a film of the same name. *The Women of Brewster Place* explores the lives of a group of men and women in an urban setting. Throughout the seven interrelated stories that make up the novel, Naylor depicts these characters' troubled and complicated relationships, as well as the violent backdrop of their interrelated lives. As she represents these characters and their dilemmas, Naylor also makes a scathing indictment of 1980s American society.

As Wilson notes, "*The Women of Brewster Place* shows in poignant detail the detrimental effects of men's emotional and physical violence on women, and in more subtle detail the ill effects of racism on black lives" (58). These social problems surface time and time again as Naylor traces the tragic lives of her characters, depicting them as trapped—both literally and figuratively—in a poverty-stricken urban neighborhood. Judith Branzburg underscores this point in her review of the novel. She argues that the neighborhood "has become a dead end, literally and figuratively" (Branzburg, 117). These critics' remarks help to characterize the novel's setting and correctly identify how it is a social critique—a point which becomes apparent even before it begins because of Naylor's choice of epigraph (which sets the stage early for the novel's violent tone and tragic themes, one of which is the failure of the American dream).

These remarks, however, useful as they are, do not emphasize the large role domestic violence plays in the lives of these women, nor do they treat domestic abuse as a theme of the novel. In my reading, this is a book about the abuse women suffer—and the violence that Naylor's women face is usually in the home—as well as the collective efforts of women to rail against the stultifying and oppressive conditions that have come to define them. The closing scene of the novel emphasizes this theme since it finally shows the neighborhood's residents banding together to fight their oppressive living conditions.

The book ends with women of the community working together to tear down the wall that created an alleyway, a literal and figurative dead-end, outside their homes; thus, the novel's conclusion shows these women coming together to protest their, again, both literal and metaphorical, entrapment. Tragically, it takes two unnecessary deaths—Ben, the maintenance man, and a child both die—and the brutal gang rape of a woman to spur the community to action. That the women of the neighborhood are the ones who ultimately band together is telling, not only because it plays into the novel's title, but also because it highlights how the structure of patriarchy has conspired to oppress women as a group and how these women have finally realized their subordinate position and are fighting against it. That a rape proves to be the final catalyst to tear down the wall underscores Naylor's broader themes, as well. As Laura Tanner argues in her article "Reading Rape: *Sanctuary* and *The Women of Brewster Place*," rape proves to be a dividing line between men and women. She asserts, "The very possibility of rape serves as a cultural dividing line that enforces a hierarchy of autonomy in which the male, free to think, imagine, and act without fear of sexual violation, is always in a position of power" (Tanner, 579). Indeed, this fear of sexual violence underscores the difference between men's and women's lived experiences, a difference Naylor seeks to expose through this novel.

The actual violence perpetrated on female characters, along with the threat of violence, goes a long way to shape women characters' experiences in this novel, as well. Betrayal, abandonment, and violence were the catalysts that forced Mattie Michael from her parents' home when she was a young woman, and betrayal by her own son lands her in Brewster Place in her elder years. In these ways and others, Mattie Michael is a character whose economic and social situation is intricately tied to her personal life. Mattie Michael is the novel's matriarch. Naylor begins the novel with her story, and she continues to occupy a central role throughout. Indeed, Mattie plays a key role throughout the entirety of the novel, as the following comments about her suggest: "If there is a central character in a novel that so avoids definition and homogeneity, she is Mattie. Mattie's is the first story, and from it we understand that she knows what it is to love and to suffer loss, paternal abuse, betrayal, and dispossession" (Matus, 52).

The account we are given of the character Mattie's life conflates sexuality, domestic violence, abandonment, and betrayal. This proves a lethal combination for her, whose story operates to communicate her individual dilemmas and also sheds light on the dilemmas other characters face. Mattie was originally from the South; she was raised by her mother, Fannie, and strict father, Sammy Michael, a man who for many years dotes on Mattie, but who ultimately turns on her.

The chain of events that leads to the rift between Mattie and her father are as follows: Butch Fuller, the local Lothario, seduces Mattie when she's a young woman. He comes by her house while her family is out, asks her for a drink of water, and begins to talk with her. Mattie knows that her father would vehemently disapprove of even this level of contact between the two of them, so she is wary of Butch initially. Though she enjoys his company, she remains reserved at first.

> They laughed again—Butch heartily and Mattie reluctantly—because she realized that she was being drawn into a conversation with a man her father had repeatedly warned her against. That Butch Fuller is a no-'count ditch hound, and no decent woman would be seen talkin' to him [Naylor 9].

Mattie hears her father's voice in her head as she visits with Butch, so she is slow to follow him, but when Butch invites her down to the cane fields and promises to carry back some of the "nice fat canes" for her, she can no longer resist (Naylor, 10). Mattie worries that "her father would kill her if he heard she had been seen walking with Butch Fuller," so they take an alternate route to the fields, thinking that they will not be spotted by anyone along the way (Naylor, 10). Though Mattie's fear of her father is presented as both figurative, to a degree, and as a cliché, her words also prove prophetic (since Sam Michael indeed, only weeks later, very nearly beats her to death), and they thereby foreshadow the violent attack Mattie will soon endure at the hands of her father.

Sam Michael has not only warned Mattie against associating with Butch Fuller, who has a reputation in town as a seducer of other men's wives and daughters, but he has forbidden her from spending time with any men at all, except for Fred Watson, a fellow congregant at their church, whom her father seems to like and respect. Watson, we learn, is "the only man in church that her father thought good enough for her" (Naylor, 14). Mattie's father is thus characterized in the novel as strict, protective, controlling, and possessive, a combination which suggests that he loves Mattie, but also wants to both police and micromanage her life. Mattie is already twenty-one, but she is quite naïve, especially when it comes to men, due largely to her strict upbringing and lack of experience with dating—indeed, the only man she'd ever dated was Fred Watson. The exchange between Mattie and Butch when she talks about Fred Watson is telling because it underscores her naïveté at the same time as it reveals her true feeling about Fred:

> For your information, Mr. Fuller, I already keep company on Sunday afternoons.
> With who?
> Fred Watson.
> Gal, that ain't keeping company. That's sitting up at a wake [Naylor, 13].

When Mattie hears Butch's retort, she cannot help but to give a "stifled smile" as she thinks of "those boring evenings with the deadpan Fred Watson" (Naylor, 13).

Unlike boring and unattractive Fred Watson, Mattie finds that Butch Fuller is both easy to talk to and look at. At one point we are told that she "admired the strong brown contours in his neck and arms," in spite of herself (Naylor, 10). After sweet-talking Mattie, Butch succeeds in seducing her in the field; she is impregnated as a result of the encounter. Mattie tells her mother who the father of her unborn child is, but doesn't tell her father. Her mother has promised not to betray her confidence in this matter. In fact, when asked, she says she would rather not be the one to tell him. Mattie asks her, "You didn't tell him it was Butch, did you?" and her mother replies, "Gal, you think I want to see my man in jail for killin' the likes of Butch Fuller? And besides, it ain't for me to tell" (Naylor, 20). Like Mattie's fear that her father would kill her for associating with Fuller, in this case her mother is being facetious, but her remark nonetheless underscores the violent undertones of their family dynamics and foreshadows the violent family encounter to come.

When her father first learns that Mattie is pregnant, he is hurt and disappointed, but does not immediately overreact because he assumes that Fred Watson, a young man he still generally approves of, is the child's father and that the two will marry. Mattie is at first "stunned that he would think it was Fred's baby," but then realizes he "was the only man he had allowed her to see, and his mind had been so conditioned over the years to her unquestioning obedience that there was just no space for doubt" (Naylor, 21–22). Mattie's thoughts here are telling because they highlight what a strict disciplinarian her father is. Though he has been kind to her at times, his good treatment of her was contingent on her obedience. When he felt able to maintain control of Mattie without violence, he was content to treat her well, but, as we and Mattie soon learn, Sam Michael is a man who will resort to violence if he sees it as the necessary means to retain—or in this case reassert—control over his daughter.

Sam, feeling certain that Fred is the father, feels completely baffled when he learns that he is not. He disapproves of Mattie's behavior, which he sees as transgressive, and he quickly tries to regain control of her and the situation by insisting that she tell him who impregnated her: "'Whose is it?' he demands" (Naylor, 22). When Mattie does not immediately respond to his question, the encounter quickly turns violent: "'I say, whose is it?' And he came toward her, grabbed her by the back of the hair, and yanked her face upward to confront the blanket of rage in his eyes" (Naylor, 23). The fact that Naylor describes his angry state as becoming visible to Mattie by the "blanket of rage in his eyes" suggests that Sam Michael—upset and shocked by Mattie's behavior—has lost control of himself because he has lost control of his daughter. His extreme reaction is an attempt to regain control.

Though "instinctively her body cried out to obey" her father because he is so badly injuring her, Mattie steadfastly refuses, which sets him off even further (Naylor, 22). Indeed, Mattie continues to remain silent about who fathered her unborn child, despite being hit and grabbed violently. As Mattie refuses to answer his question, Sam continues to assault her: "'I ain't saying, Papa.' And she braced herself for the impact of the large callused hand that was coming toward her face. He still held her by the hair so she took the force of the two blows with her neck muscles, and her eyes went dim as the blood dripped down her chin from her split lip. The grip on her hair tightened, and she was forced even closer to his face as she answered the silent question in his narrowing eyes" (Naylor, 22–23). Margaret Whitt comments on this scene in her book *Understanding Gloria Naylor.* Specifically, she highlights the dynamics that contribute to the escalating level of violence we observe: "When Mattie refuses to identify the baby's father, Samuel's reaction to her words is out of proportion. First, Naylor's language creates a whirlwind ... the erupting whirlwind suddenly becomes literal, as her father begins to slap her face, yank her hair, and beat her body with a broom" (Whitt, 20).

Tellingly, Whitt chooses to categorize Sam Michael's behavior as being directly responsive to Mattie's refusal to name the man who impregnated her. Sam is obviously angry at the man in question, but since his identity and whereabouts are unknown, Sam feels he has no other option than to transfer his rage to his daughter.

Importantly, Sam is also responding to the fact that Mattie is continuing to disobey him by her steadfast refusal. Indeed, as the scene continues and despite the increasingly severe harm inflicted on her, Mattie still refuses to answer his question, so her father, despite her mother's objections proceeds to beat her with a broom.

> Her silence stole the last sanctuary for his rage. He wanted to kill the man who had sneaked into his home and distorted the faith and trust he had in his child. But she had chosen this man's side against him, and in his fury, she tried to stamp out what had hurt him the most and was now brazenly taunting him—her disobedience [Naylor, 23].

As this passage further highlights, what sets Sam off to such a degree, and what proves to be the primary motivation for the severe violence he inflicts on his daughter, is "her disobedience." To Sam, this assault is an attempt to restore order in his home by forcing his daughter into obedience by beating her. Sam's behavior is a prime example of a man acting violently in order to regain control in his home, something Sam feels entitled to. When she still won't give him the information he wants, not only does he continue to beat her, but the violence we see even further escalates.

> Mattie's body contracted in a painful spasm each time the stick smashed down on her legs and back, and she curled into a tight knot, trying to protect her stomach. He would repeat his question with each blow from the stick, and her continued silence caused the blows to come faster and harder. He was sweating and breathing so hard he couldn't talk anymore, so he just pounded the whimpering girl on the floor [Naylor, 23].

His attack is so severe that Fannie (Mattie's mother), who had previously only pleaded with him to stop, finally physically intervenes. Sam Michael, whose violence was heretofore directed only at Mattie, assaults his wife, as well, when she attempts to defend Mattie from his brutal attack. Her initial attempt to stop the assault fails; Sam flings her "across the floor" when she tries to "wrestle the stick from him" (Naylor, 23). He continues to beat Mattie, now using "a jagged section" of the broom "in his fist" (Naylor, 23). That Sam Michael is now using a sharp, broken part of the broom in his attacks emphasizes his feelings of rage. To wit, he is willing, as we witness, to use *anything* at his disposal against her. Moreover, his choice of weapon suggests the violence of the encounter has even further escalated since the chances of inflicting grave harm to Mattie increase with his use of a sharp instrument in his attack of her. As Branzburg observes, "he beats her almost to death" in this scene (117).

Indeed, Sam has lashed out at his daughter to the point that her life, not to mention the life of her unborn child, is clearly in danger. Recognizing this, Fannie steps in, once again, and it is only when she shoots at their fireplace with a shotgun that he stops: "the blast stunned him for a moment, and he looked toward his wife" (Naylor, 24). Fannie, still armed, threatens his life: "'So help me Jesus, Sam!' she screamed. 'Hit my child again, and I'll meet your soul in Hell'" (Naylor, 24). The fact that Fannie, who has previously been depicted as docile and passive, feels it necessary to intervene and, moreover, the fact that she has to arm herself to stop Sam's assault on Mattie further suggest both how enraged Sam is and the severe danger Mattie is in. Naylor depicts Fannie's search for, and discharge of, the weapon as nothing more or less than a mother's desperate attempt to save her child, which further emphasizes how dire an encounter she (and we) witness.

Ultimately, the violent encounter between Mattie and her father proves to be a pivotal event in her life, for she is not only nearly killed by him, but she leaves home as a result of the attack, never to see either of her parents again. Thus, she is thrust out into the world alone, broke, and pregnant. Her circumstances come across as even worse when we remember that she doesn't have a husband, family support, an education, or marketable job skills. This violence in many ways defines her life by delineating her path moving forward. For Mattie, the consequences of violence are very real. In this way, Mattie's story sets the stage for the other interconnected stories to come; as a rule, the women who live in Brewster Place are facing hard times—and Naylor depicts their relationships with men as contributing to, if not causing, their struggles. Etta Mae Johnson, another Brewster Place resident, echoes this sentiment when she says to Mattie that there are no good men: "Let's face it Mattie, the good men are either dead or waiting to be born" (Naylor, 61). For Mattie, encounters with men tend to involve at least one of the following: sexuality, domestic violence, and betrayal. Mattie, in fact, is betrayed by her father, her son's father, and her own son, as well. Thus, for Mattie, her interactions with men prove to be the catalysts that lead her to end her days at Brewster Place.

Violence is at least in part responsible for Mattie's ending up at Brewster Place, an environment itself portrayed as violent. For many residents of this neighborhood, Naylor depicts violence as not only commonplace, but as a defining characteristic of their existence. The abuse these women suffer usually results from the male desire to maintain or reassert control. One example of this can be seen during the exchange between Eugene and "Ciel," the nickname of Lucielia Louise Turner, another neighborhood resident, who we soon learn faces domestic troubles. When Eugene comes home, the tension between him and Ciel becomes immediately apparent: "Ciel jumped when the front door slammed shut. She waited tensely for the metallic bang of his keys on the coffee table and the blast of the stereo. Lately that was how Eugene announced his presence home" (Naylor, 93). Moments later, Ciel notices that Eugene is in a foul mood and looking to argue with her.

> He wants to pick a fight, she thought, confused and hurt. He knows Serena's taking a nap, and now I'm supposed to say, Eugene, the baby's asleep, please cut the music down. Then he's going to say, you mean a man can't even relax in his own home without being picked on? I'm not picking on you, but

you're going to wake up the baby. Which is always supposed to lead to more: You don't give a damn about me. Everybody's more important than me— that kid, your friends, everybody. I'm chickenshit around here, huh? All this went through Ciel's head as she watched him leave the stereo and drop defiantly back down on the couch [Naylor, 93].

The thoughts running through Ciel's mind indicate that Eugene's behavior conforms to a pattern in their relationship. What is more, her thoughts also suggest that she knows he is deliberately provoking her, looking for problems, and expecting her to react in a certain way. When she doesn't outwardly respond to Eugene's blaring of the stereo, he follows her into the kitchen, tells her he lost his job, and complains about the fact that they have another baby on the way that they cannot afford. They disagree about what to do about Ciel's pregnancy.

The confrontation between Eugene and Ciel soon turns physical: "'What the hell we gonna feed it when it gets here, huh—air? With two kids and you on my back, I ain't never gonna have nothin.' He came and grabbed her by the shoulder and was shouting in her face. 'Nothin', do you hear me, nothin'!'" (Naylor, 95). Despite their financial circumstances, Ciel wants to keep the baby. She makes this clear by offering to get a job to help out financially; "'I'll get a job. I don't mind,' she says" (Naylor, 94). When he objects, she promises that after they have this baby, that she won't have any more: "Well, look, after the baby comes, they can tie my tubes—I don't care" (Naylor, 95). Neither of these options sounds feasible to Eugene, though, who prefers that Ciel terminate the pregnancy, which is what she ends up doing. The way that Eugene treats Ciel becomes clear through this lengthy passage. He wants control over her and will use any means at his disposal to get it.

Eugene's actions fit a pattern of abusive behavior that Michael Johnson, a sociologist who studies domestic violence, identifies: "the standard definition of domestic violence in the battered women's movement has been what I call 'intimate terrorism,' the kind of violence in which men control 'their women' using a variety of coercive control tactics, including physical and sexual violence" (Ooms, 2). Johnson further recognizes "domestic violence as a pattern of violent coercive control in which the coercive partner makes use of violence in combination with a variety of other tactics such as psychological or economic abuse to take virtually complete control" over his partner (Ooms, 2). In the case of Eugene and Ciel, domestic abuse is clearly about control: Eugene wants to control Ciel's behavior in matters small and large and has no qualms about using violence, the threat of a physical assault, or any other means to achieve it.

Cora Lee, another Brewster Place resident, recounts violent relationships with men, as well, which only further suggests the prevalence of domestic abuse. We learn that Cora Lee, who has "babies year after year by God knows who," reflects back on why none of her affairs with men lasted very long. At one point she recounts why the relationship between her and one of the men failed, a man (we never learn his name) who fathered two of her children, Sammy and Maybelline:

> She had really liked him. His gold-capped teeth and glass eye had fascinated her, and she had almost learned to cope with his peculiar ways. A pot of burnt rice would mean a fractured jaw, or a wet bathroom floor a loose tooth, but that had been their fault for keeping her so tied up she couldn't keep the house straight. But she still carried the scar under her left eye because of a baby's crying, and you couldn't stop a baby from crying [Naylor, 113].

In this account, Cora Lee underscores the violent nature of their affair, highlighting how he would beat her severely if she did not conform to his expectations. Moreover, Cora Lee highlights how his desire to control her (to make her keep the house in order) leads to this abuse.

The physical and emotional abuse perpetrated by Eugene and by Cora Lee's former lover stem from their male desire to control "their" women (Ciel and Cora Lee), but their willingness to resort to violence is a result of their own disenfranchisement by society at large. Eugene's remarks specifically suggest this, especially when we recall that he cites joblessness and lack of money/income as the primary reasons for not wanting another child. His complaint that he will never get "ahead" underscores his anxieties about the material realities of his life and that his economic disenfranchisement contributes to his behavior. Hampton, Oliver, and Magarian speak to this phenomenon in their article "Domestic Violence in the African American Community: An Analysis of Social and Structural Factors." They suggest that violence inflicted on female partners can stem from their own disenfranchisement: "The economic underdevelopment of African American men has historically been a source of anger and frustration" (Hampton et al., 537).

These authors situate their findings within a broader and more comprehensive study of partner violence in the African American community and discuss how the psychological community has coined a term to describe this pattern. According to their report, in 1964, a psychologist by the name of Nathan Hare introduced the concept of "frustrated masculinity syndrome" to describe how some African American men responded "to racial prejudice and various institutional barriers that blocked them from having equal access to the designated legitimate means to achieve manhood through conventional, societal avenue" (Hampton et al., 537). This explanatory model does shed light on the dilemmas faced by many of Naylor's male characters, for, in fact, many of the men depicted in *The Women of Brewster Place* do tend to suffer under an exploitative system, and so to a degree their behavior may be attributed to larger social factors, including their own lack of opportunities. Added to that are the pressure they feel as males to be breadwinners and the stereotypical image they want to conform to of the male being the de facto head of the household, both of which contribute to the pattern of abuse, as well. At the same time, though, the men depicted in *The Women of Brewster Place* have grown accustomed to male privilege and entitlement, a combination which encourages them to feel like they have a right to control and abuse the women in their families. There is little room to doubt, as the examples of Mattie Michael, Ciel Turner, and Cora Lee all demonstrate, that domestic violence is very much a part of life for many of these women. Moreover, the abuse they suffer at the hands of those close to them, whether the violence comes from a father or a partner, contributes to the tragedies of these women's lives; the violence these women suffer and witness to a large degree defines their existence.

Linden Hills

Though the characters *in Linden Hills* (a novel which Naylor published in 1985) are, as a rule, much better off financially than those in *The Women of Brewster Place,* they lead for the most part very unsatisfying lives, in part because they have misplaced values—residents are so consumed by materialism and so intent on keeping up with, if not surpassing, their neighbors that their pursuit of this dream eclipses any other possible concerns. As Catherine Ward, who characterizes the residents of Linden Hills in her article "Gloria Naylor's *Linden Hills:* A Modern 'Inferno,'" points out, in "their single-minded pursuit of upward mobility, the inhabitants of Linden Hills, a black, middle-class suburb, have turned away from their past and from their deepest sense of who they are" (Ward, 67).

Place, indeed, figures prominently in Naylor's fiction (as I suggested at the start of this chapter). In *Linden Hills,* this is true, as well. In fact, Naylor introduces us to the *neighborhood* of Linden Hills before we even meet the people who populate its streets, a feature of the novel which only further stresses the significance of the neighborhood that Naylor depicts.

> Linden Hills. The name had spread beyond Wayne County, and applicants were coming from all over the country and even the Caribbean. Linden Hills—a place where people worked hard, fought hard, and saved hard for the privilege to rest in the soft shadows of those heat-shaped trees. In Linden Hills they could forget that the world said you spelled black with a capital nothing. Well, they were something and there was everything around them to show it. The world hadn't given them anything but the chance to fail—and they hadn't failed, because they were in Linden Hills [Naylor, 15–16].

As this passage highlights, the neighborhood of Linden Hills is a place that defines its inhabitants, rather than the other way around; the people who live there believe themselves to be successful because they think that living there proves it—according to the logic of this passage, "they hadn't failed, because they were in Linden Hills" (Naylor, 16).

Yet, for all the apparent success Linden Hills' residents have achieved and despite the outward trappings of their affluence, the lives of these folks prove to be as hollow and unfulfilling as what Naylor presented in *The Women of Brewster Place*. Maxine Montgomery comments on the tragic nature of the neighborhood residents' lives in her article "Good Housekeeping: Domestic Ritual in Gloria Naylor's Fiction." She points out that "in *Linden Hills* the home place is an arena under patriarchal domination divorced from the political struggle of contemporary black America" (Montgomery, 62). As Montgomery's remarks imply, the neighborhood is full of people who do not seem to understand or care about the struggles those with less resources face. Though removed from many of the economic struggles that plague other Americans, Linden Hills' residents face their own troubles by way of domestic disputes, many of which are related to the male desire to control those in their household. This desire for control proves the undoing of several families.

Unhappy home life is the norm for these characters. Most of the marriages depicted are dysfunctional. John Noell Moore discusses Naylor's representation of marriage in *Linden Hills* in his article "Myth, Fairy Tale, Epic, and Romance: Narrative as Re-Vision in *Linden Hills*," where he explains,

> Most of the marriages in *Linden Hills* are miserable failures: four Luther Nedeeds and four brides; Chester and Lycentia Parker; and Laurel and Howard Dumont. When gay attorney Winston Alcott marries Cassandra,

he denies himselfhappiness with his real love, David. Naylor's Cassandra is a perfect symbol for the doomed marriages in the novel [1411].

As Moore puts it, in this novel, "marriage promises paradise but delivers hell" (1412). Moore's observations not only emphasize how, through this novel, Naylor critiques marriage as a social practice by highlighting how these presumably ideal matches result in couples who are miserable with one another and oftentimes lead tragic lives, but they also point to Naylor's sustained allusion to Dante's *Inferno*, which only further suggests the tragic tone of the novel.

One marriage that ends tragically is Laurel Dumont's. Once successful, Laurel Dumont is pushed to the brink when her marriage fails and she learns that, without a husband, she is nothing in Linden Hills. Luther Nedeed, who owns all the land in the area (his ancestors gave the original settlers one-thousand-year-long leases to the land) makes her aware that she has no right to stay in her home after her divorce. Ward discusses Laurel's situation in detail.

> After graduating Phi Beta Kappa from Berkeley, she works her way into a top executive position at IBM and marries a man predicted to become the next State's Attorney, but she remains emotionally detached from her husband and even from her deepest sense of herself. Laurel is an Amazon who mutilates her spirit in order to be both successful and free. She is what Smyth will become if he keeps on "moving down" in Linden Hills. When her husband of ten years decides to divorce her, she faces not just the emptiness of her life, but the emptiness of herself. Finally, a confrontation with Luther Nedeed makes Laurel realize that there is no inner core to her person, only a frightening void. When she kills herself by diving off the high dive into an empty pool, her faceless body symbolizes her spiritual state [71].

As these observations suggest, Laurel has traded in her autonomy for the privilege of living in this neighborhood. She has also forfeited her independence in order to be married, even though that marriage ultimately proves unfulfilling. This neighborhood has so thoroughly shaped and trapped Laurel that she cannot imagine a life outside of it, and she thus decides to kill herself. In his article "Suicide or Messianic Self-Sacrifice? Exhuming Willa's Body in Gloria Naylor's *Linden Hills*" Christopher N. Okonkwo discusses how Laurel cannot come to terms with her marriage's ending: "Laurel seems unable or unwilling to locate alternative paths of self-validation besides materiality, maleness, and marriage" (119). Thus, a once independent and successful woman is so broken down through this narrative that she sees no other option than suicide.

Though, at times, the subject of women's oppression is treated seriously in this novel, it is also mentioned offhandedly by characters, which suggests how pervasive the problems Naylor is critiquing really are—and how naturalized and normalized oppressive conditions such as those depicted in *Linden Hills* are. At one point, Lester and Willie, whom readers follow through most of the novel as they come into contact with many of the neighborhood's residents, are spending the evening with their friends, Norman and Ruth. Norman makes an offhand remark about abusing women: "'Man, you don't know how to handle a woman.' Norman cut his eyes to Ruth. 'You gotta put your foot on their necks and let 'em know who's boss'" (Naylor, 37). Though said as a joke, this sentiment works to underscore that the novel centers on themes of violence and oppression. Moreover, it works to foreshadow the extreme example of physical and emotional abuse that we will see in the Nedeed household. The fact that Luther Nedeed's household is full of violence and that his power is the result of a legacy of generational abuse against women speaks to the nature of the whole community. As owner of all of the property in Linden Hills— and owner of the real estate company and funeral home, as well—Luther Nedeed is the epitome of success by Linden Hills' standards. Other residents compete to try to attain what he has, and a house at the bottom of the hill (near where he lives), on "Tupelo Drive," is the ultimate sign of success. It is thus both fitting and ironic that Nedeed's own house is in such disorder. As Charles Wilson observes, "the dysfunction of the present-day Nedeed household represents the generic tensions of the larger Linden Hills community" (Wilson, 65).

Luther, readers learn, has locked his wife Willa in the basement because he believes she has been unfaithful to him; he further suspects that he is not the true (meaning biological) father of her son, Sinclair (Luther suspects that the child is not his because he is light-skinned and all of the other Nedeed men, though they have all married light-skinned wives, have had dark complexions). As Ward notes, the boy is, indeed, "Nedeed's but carries the light-skinned genes of his maternal ancestors" (78). Luther's jealousy and crazy accusations have prompted him to punish his wife, Willa, for these imagined transgressions: "Willa Prescott Nedeed, the wife of Linden Hills' most prominent citizen Luther Nedeed, has been locked in the basement of the Nedeed home, along with her five-year-old son Sinclair, for several weeks because her husband believes that someone else has fathered the boy" (Wilson, 64–65). Determined not to let this woman ruin him, Luther starves Willa and the child (the boy dies) in an attempt to teach his wife a lesson. His goal, as we will learn, is to keep Willa down in the basement long enough that when she emerges, she will rejoin him, resume her wifely duties, and, having learned her lesson, obey Luther going forward. Luther does not want to kill Willa—he needs her—but he does want to control every aspect of her life. This control is necessary because Luther's lifestyle depends on Willa caring for him. He is not only dependent on the actual work she performs for him in the home, but his image as a male is bound up with his roles as husband, father, and breadwinner. As the following passage illustrates, Luther has grown to be quite dependent on the domestic duties that Willa performs:

> He took another sip of his drink and grimaced. He always managed to add too much brandy. Now her absence even lay at the base of his burning throat. Six years of decent brandy and soda weren't going to wash down the drain because of one problem. His father was right: breaking in a wife was like breaking in a good pair of slippers [Naylor, 67].

This excerpt also sums up how Luther views his wife (and wives in general)—he values Willa because she waits on him and, moreover, he thinks wives need to be "broken in," suggesting violence and control—among other things.

This mindset is a product of bourgeois ideology. As Angela Davis explains in *Women, Race, and Class,* "the housewife, according to bourgeois ideology, is, quite simply her husband's lifelong servant" (225). Luther considers Willa his lifelong servant, which is similar to how his father and the other Nedeed men who came before him saw their wives. Luther also (as I suggested previously) also depends on the image of himself as the Nedeed family patriarch, a position contingent not only on him being married to Willa but on their marriage conforming to a pattern whereby he is in control of her and their relationship. When she threatens the status quo of the relationship and when she—as Luther perceives it at least—transgresses the boundaries of acceptable behavior for a wife, Luther seeks to punish her with the hope that she will conform once again to his expectations. In his effort to regain control of Willa, Luther abuses her and imprisons her.

The suffering bound up in—and the violent nature of—Willa's imprisonment becomes evident in many of the novel's passages. One instance of this is when she hears Luther turn on the water, and begins to reflect on what she has endured while locked in the home's cellar:

> Once that sound had meant salvation that was prayed for and bargained for.... And it came as an answer from that untouchable region, sending her

in a flight across the basement hurriedly to catch what she needed for bathing and drinking. And then to wet the dry cereal after the milk was gone. But then even the cereal had gone [Naylor, 70–71].

The details of Willa's imprisonment and the desperation evident as she recalls her "flight" to catch as much water as possible both emphasize the depravity of what Luther forces her to go through. Pausing to consider her options, Willa realizes the course of action she will take if she ever escapes; she "sat there calmly and irrevocably immersed in the simple fact that had become part of her being. Luther was a dead man if she ever left that basement alive" (Naylor, 71).

Luther decides he will keep her locked in the basement a few weeks— just long enough, he figures, to teach her a lesson. He reflects, "Well, in a few weeks she would have learned her lesson. And then in the spring, she'd conceive again and he'd have the son he should have had in the first place" (Naylor, 67). Luther's thoughts emphasize the reason for his violence—he has gravely abused Willa (and his actions have killed their son) in order to regain control over her. He acknowledges his desire to control her as well as how he more broadly views women when he thinks over what went wrong in his marriage.

> He couldn't understand what had gone wrong. He had never been cruel or abusive to her. He must have given her at least six lines of credit in his name, never questioning what she bought or why. And he asked so little of her in return. Just come into his home and respect him and the routines of his household. Work along with him to continue the tradition of several generations. Simply honor what his family had done, just as he honored it. And she couldn't bring herself to do even that [Naylor, 68].

This excerpt works to underscore Luther's desperate need for control; at the same time, it also helps to point out how Luther has normalized and naturalized his unrealistic and unjust expectations of Willa. He says that all he wants is "respect" and for her to honor the "routines of his household," sentiments which stress that he obviously does not view Willa as a partner, but rather as a servant whom he can control. This passage suggests, as well, that Luther, like some of the other male abusers discussed earlier in this chapter, perpetrates what is referred to as "intimate terrorism," the type of abuse in which men control "*their*" women" (my italics) using a variety of coercive tactics, including physical and sexual violence.

One of the many tactics used by Luther is his withholding of food and water. His reasons for mistreating her in this fashion become even clearer as he reflects on what has transpired: "By now she understood that he controlled her food and water and light. Whatever she had been allowed—upstairs or down—was hers not by right, but as a gift" (Naylor, 68–69). Further stressing that his motive for the horrible abuse he perpetrates is control, Luther blames Willa for her situation and comments on how her refusal to comply with his wishes contributed to her imprisonment: "She wouldn't have been down there in the first place if she hadn't tried to make a fool of him" (Naylor, 69).

While locked in the basement, Willa goes through old family albums and recipe books; through carefully studying these materials, she learns how she is the last in a long line of Nedeed women who have been, in various ways, abused and oppressed by their husbands. She comes to the conclusion that she is not to blame, regardless of what Luther believes. She decides, "If there was any sickness, it was in this house, in the air. It was left over from the breaths of those women who came before her. The Luwana Packervilles, Evelyn Cretons, and God knows who else" (Naylor, 204). What Willa is referring to here is the systematized abuse perpetrated on all of the Nedeed wives by the husbands, men intent on "breaking in" wives and forcing them to comply with their desires.

In wading through the pieced-together family history that she is able to construct via the pictures, notes, and recipes she has found, Willa learns of the legacy of abuse that (her) Luther is carrying on. As Jewelle Gomez points out, "Leafing through journals and photograph albums during her imprisonment, Willa sees a pattern of overbearance and abuse that has left the Nedeed women less than whole" (Gomez, 8).

Luther's mother, grandmother, and great-grandmother, Willa realizes, have suffered at the hands of ruthless Nedeed men, as well. As Ward asserts, "Theirs is a tale of progressive depersonalization, as each husband became in turn more cruel and evil than his father" (Ward, 78). They have served merely to bring the next generation of Nedeed into being: "The Nedeed reign of terror" has been sustained through "a systematic dehumanization of women as papa-copying machines" (Okonkwo, 122–123). By seeming to transgress this role by committing adultery and thereby humiliating Luther— of course, these transgressions are based on Luther's unfounded, but alleged charge of adultery against Willa—she has incurred Luther's wrath.

Willa almost starves to death in the basement and, in fact, seems to recognize her perilous situation: "She knew she was dying" (Naylor, 266). She also palpably detects her body growing weaker: "she could feel it happening: the passage of air through lung tissues that had disintegrated a little with each breath" (Naylor, 266). It takes feeling like death is imminent before Willa decides, once and for all, to act. Only moments before this transpires, Luther decides that Willa has been locked away long enough.

> He had forgiven her. It was his fault anyway; he had chosen that woman and was willing to accept the responsibility of that choice. It was an error in judgment, one that his father would never have made, but unfortunately he had. But it wasn't irretrievable; it's just that the child had died. Luther frowned and sipped slowly. He had truly never meant for it all to get so out of hand [Naylor, 287].

Willa, unaware that Luther has made his mind up to release her, grows determined to leave the basement and climbs the staircase, all the while thinking the only thing stopping her "was simply a bolted door" (Naylor, 297). Willie (he and Lester are doing some work in the Nedeed home while this transpires) had, only seconds before, inadvertently unlatched the bolt, so when Willa reaches for the door, "Miraculously, the bolt slid back" (Naylor, 298). When she enters the main floor of the house, she looks disheveled and nearly starved to death; in her arms, she carries her dead five-year-old son. Now freed, Willa begins to clean the house; it's only after she cleans the kitchen that she confronts Luther: "'Luther'—her voice was cracked and husky ... 'your son is dead'" (Naylor, 299). Luther, unsure what Willa is doing, grabs her and the child; in the commotion that ensues, a veil that was trailing behind Willa catches fire from contact with an ember; their last words uttered are, "My God, we're on fire" (Naylor, 300). Fire quickly spreads, killing Luther and Willa; the flames not only engulf them, but also the body of their (already dead) son and the entire home.

As Willie, Lester, and other neighbors watch, they refuse to intervene and, as the novel closes, we are told, "They let it burn." Thus, the novel ends with the destruction of the Nedeed home. As Okonkwo highlights, "the apocalyptic battle takes place in a private space, without any witnesses," thereby ending a family tragedy in a domestic space (127).

The novel's ending transforms the Nedeed's private tragedies into a public spectacle, thereby literally and figuratively tearing down the boundary between private and public spheres that have helped to cover up the terrible abuse that has so long plagued the Nedeed home. The nature of the destruction of the Nedeed home and family is significant for other reasons, as well. It sustains the allusion to Dante's *Inferno* until the end of the novel (the concluding image is of the Nedeed house engulfed in flames— an "inferno" of sorts). The destruction takes down not only these individuals, but also the Nedeed home and legacy with them.

Thus, in *Linden Hills,* Naylor shows how affluent individuals are plagued by some of the same problems that surface in poorer communities. In *The Women of Brewster Place,* she shows how violence can result from being entrapped. In both novels, she draws our attention to one explanatory model for domestic abuse: its regulatory function. Ultimately, Naylor, through her representations of domestic violence in these novels, gives voice to abused women and further suggests that domestic violence crosses lines of social class and results from, at least in many cases, the male desire to control women—a product of 1980s American society, which Naylor takes pains to critique through these works.

CHAPTER 6

Family Violence and Popular Fiction: Terry McMillan's *Mama* and *A Day Late and a Dollar Short*

The chapters appearing thus far in this book examine representations of domestic abuse (and violence against women in general) in novels that are generally considered to be part of the canon of African American literature. Though these canonical novels do much to call attention to these problems and how they affect women, popular fiction also plays a crucial role in raising awareness about the issue of violence in the home. This chapter examines two of bestselling author Terry McMillan's novels, *Mama* (1987) and *A Day Late and a Dollar Short* (2002), and explores her treatment of the themes of domestic abuse and family violence. The first novel discussed, *Mama*, focuses on Mildred Peacock, a mother of five who struggles with poverty, domestic abuse, and alcoholism as she tries desperately to raise her children. Set in the 1960s and 1970s in Michigan, California, and New York, this novel tells the story of a flawed but sympathetic woman who moves from man to man, job to job, and place to place, all the while trying to make a life for herself and her family. McMillan's more recent novel, *A Day Late and a Dollar Short,* is set in the 1990s, primarily in Las Vegas, Nevada. Throughout this novel, McMillan offers a moving portrayal of the large and dysfunctional Price family. Told from multiple points of view, *A Day Late and a Dollar Short* revisits many of the same themes that she introduced in *Mama,* but here McMillan provides a more contemporary spin on the troubling issues families so frequently face.

Terry McMillan and Popular Fiction

Terry McMillan was born in Michigan in 1951. She worked at a library as a teenager and, as many scholars who discuss her life have suggested, this experience sparked her interest in books. Although McMillan studied journalism at University of California, Berkeley, she has made a career and a name for herself as a writer of popular fiction. McMillan's many novels include *Mama* (1987), *Disappearing Acts* (1989), *How Stella Got Her Groove Back* (1996), *A Day Late and a Dollar Short* (2002), and *Getting to Happy* (2010). It was McMillan's third—and best known—novel, *Waiting to Exhale* (1992), which remained on the *New York Times* Bestseller list for many months and made McMillan a household name. McMillan's novels are characterized by relatable female protagonists whose struggles with contemporary issues resonate with her readers. Because of the immense commercial success of some of her novels, like *Waiting to Exhale, Disappearing Acts,* and *How Stella Got Her Groove Back* (all of which were made into films), McMillan has been criticized for (supposedly) pandering to the marketplace. Even critics who have not been quite so harsh in their criticism of McMillan remain resolute in categorizing her as a popular writer—and all too often dismissing her novels on those grounds.

The practice of disparaging a writer's creative work for being too "popular" is, of course, nothing new. Without a doubt, popular fiction has long been criticized or, more often, ignored by literary critics who prefer to devote their energies to more "serious literature." Writing in 2010, Matthew Schneider-Mayerson addresses this practice in his essay "Popular Fiction Studies: The Advantages of a New Field." Schneider-Mayerson also discusses the label "popular fiction" and teases out the implications of what it means to label a literary work as popular fiction.

> "Popular fiction" has been defined in a number of ways (in Western, English-language criticism) over the last half-century. Although the specific terminology has often reflected the author's approach to this topic, the subject's actual domain is rarely questioned. Popular fiction is defined by what it is not: "literature." Most critics openly or implicitly adhere to the following claims: Whereas "literature" is indifferent to (if not contemptuous of) the marketplace, original, and complex, popular fiction is simple, sensuous, exaggerated, exciting, and formulaic [21–22].

Not only are the novels themselves subject to this form of criticism, but the writers of popular fiction are frequently dismissed as "genre hacks," who "produce a new paperback each year, to be 'consumed' in airports and quickly discarded" (Schneider-Mayerson, 22).

Similar criticism has been levied against Terry McMillan (and her bestselling novels), a point Janet Mason Ellerby makes in "Deposing the Man of the House: Terry McMillan Rewrites the Family." In this essay, she highlights how "McMillan has been disconcertingly diminished by those who should know better" (Ellerby, 116). Indeed, as Ellerby notes, prize-winning African American women writers, as well as others, have "diminished McMillan's novels as pulp fiction" (Ellerby, 116). Robin Virginia Smiles makes a similar point in "Romance, Race, and Resistance in Best-Selling African American Narrative," where she examines three of McMillan's novels. As part of her examination, Smiles asserts, "Few scholars have addressed McMillan's novels in a serious and sustained manner" (109). Smiles further argues that, due to their commercial success, McMillan's novels have not received the critical attention they deserve. In fact, as she points out, the more "popular" McMillan's fiction has become, "the less likely critics have been to engage in a 'scholarly' discussion about her works" (Smiles, 109).

Smiles also contends that the way McMillan's novels have been labeled, as well as the way her fiction privileges the themes of love and romance that appeal primarily to a mass-market audience, has deemed her fiction irrelevant in some critics' eyes. Smiles points out that novels written by McMillan and other African American novelists (such as Connie Briscoe, E. Lynn Harris, Omar Tyree, Eric Jerome Dickey, and others) became difficult to categorize, so new labels—"'sistah fiction,' or 'sista girl' and 'brotherman' novels"—came about (Smiles, 113). These new labels, according to Smiles, were "colloquialisms that characterized the genre's ostensible appeal to an 'everyday' black reading audience and its central focus: portraying the intimate relationships and friendships between and among black males and females" (113). These labels, however, served to further diminish McMillan's novels by treating them as if the concerns she takes up through her characters and the dilemmas they face are not worthy of "real," or serious, academic inquiry.

Yet, despite this type of criticism, McMillan's fiction is deserving of critical attention. Her novels raise awareness about a whole host of social problems that were important in the late 20th century and that remain highly relevant today. Indeed, through her fiction, McMillan confronts such timely issues as drug and alcohol abuse, domestic violence, sexual violence against women, child abuse, oppression, and the many ills associated with poverty and economic injustice. Not only does McMillan's fiction call attention to these serious issues, which matter in the real world, but her creative works also function as social protest. As Smiles observes, however, the "signs of social protest and resistance appear in McMillan's fiction in more contemporary forms," such as her characters' insistence "on pursuing educational and professional opportunities outside their home communities, or their refusal to adhere to proscribed gender roles within heterosexual unions" (123).

McMillan's fiction has been unfairly criticized on the basis that it's popular and appeals to a mainstream audience. Although McMillan's target audience and writing style may differ from other African American female novelists,' her work remains relevant and deserving of attention nonetheless. As Ellerby puts it, "perhaps McMillan does not write with the same polished facility as Walker, Morrison, and Naylor, nor does she have the historical range of some of her contemporaries, but it is only critical blindness that prevents readers from seeing McMillan's work as squarely within the African American canon" (116). Smiles makes a similar argument for McMillan's place in the canon, citing both the cultural importance of the popular and the literary value of McMillan's oeuvre. As a rule, accessibility is one of the hallmarks of popular fiction. Popular fiction, by definition, appeals to a broader audience and tends to present relatable characters and scenarios to its readers. McMillan's novels deserve attention for many reasons, not the least of these being their realistic portrayals of characters with contemporary problems and the vital role they play in showcasing the changing dynamics of the family in the 20th and 21st centuries.

Indeed, McMillan's "novels are a significant contribution to understanding the evolving African American family," a point Ellerby makes (116). Using her novels to showcase the African American family and the typical problems that they confront is one way that McMillan uses her fiction to explore the day-to-day struggles of real people. This a feature of her writing, as well as part of her motivation for writing the types of novels that she does. As she states plainly in a 2013 NPR interview, she's "interested in watching real people go through real problems in a real way" (McMillan).

Though some critics may view novels that are commercially successful and have mass appeal as being subordinate to more "literary" works of fiction, the very qualities that open popular fiction up to harsh criticism— the accessibility of the books and the connections readers feel with so many of popular fiction's characters—provides these books with the opportunity to shine a light on controversial and problematic issues, such as family violence and violence against women. Indeed, since popular fiction has the potential to reach more readers, commercially successful books, like bestselling author Terry McMillan's novels, raise awareness about domestic abuse in ways that canonical literature or literary fiction cannot.

Mama

Terry McMillan's debut novel, *Mama*, was first published in 1987. Many of the events that make up the novel were inspired by McMillan's own upbringing, and she loosely based the novel's main character, Mildred, on her own mother (in fact, McMillan dedicated this novel to her mother). Critics have discussed this aspect of the novel, noting that *Mama* is "largely autobiographical" because it tells the story of McMillan's own "mother's difficulties" (Champion and Austin, 248). Michael D. Sharp, who writes about McMillan in his book, *Popular Contemporary Writers,* comments on McMillan's use of autobiography in her fiction, as well. He points out that her "inspirations are overwhelmingly autobiographical" (Sharp, 1062). Even McMillan herself has acknowledged this dimension of her fiction and has gone on record as saying that her mother was an inspiration for the novel. McMillan speaks with pride about incorporating details of her personal life—and the lives of her family members—in her fiction, by explaining that her writing is about "my story, and telling it, and feeling it. And that's how I write. And that's why I write" (Porter, 42). This dimension of McMillan's fiction makes her novels relevant to readers, a point Paulette Richards emphasizes in her book *Terry McMillan: A Critical Companion;* she notes that McMillan's "ability to draw on her own experiences and evoke her own emotional truth in her novels is one important element of her tremendous popular appeal" (1).

Although its publication was not met with the same hoopla as *Waiting to Exhale* or some of her other, more recent novels was, *Mama* sold out its first hardcover printing of 5,000 copies, largely due to McMillan's own efforts to market the book (using the word processor at the law firm where she worked as a night typist, she sent out thousands of letters to bookstores, college organizations, and news media—with a strong emphasis on black groups—urging them to stock and promote her book and invite her to read from it). It has since been reprinted many times. The novel's sustained popularity connects directly with how relatable its characters are. As Richards points out, "McMillan created in her first novel" a story that many "readers can identify closely with" (53). The novel's protagonist, Mildred Peacock, is a flawed but sympathetic woman who defies traditional stereotypes about what it means to be a black woman in the 1960s and 1970s, yet she remains relatable and real as she confronts domestic abuse, poverty, economic injustice, and sexual exploitation, all the while trying to raise her five children and make a life for herself and her family. Through largely episodic depictions and told from the point of view of an omniscient narrator, the focus of the novel remains on the protagonist, Mildred Peacock: "the novel chronicles her life and maturation from her late twenties into middle age" (Sharp, 1062). At the same time, the novel also provides a glimpse into the lives of "African American inner-city families" (Sharp, 1062).

McMillan portrays Mildred Peacock as a young, energetic mother of five children—Freda, Money, Bootsey, Doll, and Angel—who lives in the small town of Point Haven, Michigan (a town McMillan based on Port Huron, Michigan, where she was born). When Mildred decides to leave her husband, Crook, due to abuse and infidelity, her life of continuous struggle begins. She is forced into taking low-wage jobs to support her family. Making matters worse, many of the companies in Point Haven are laying off, so between jobs she must depend on welfare to raise her four young daughters and one young son. To cope with the grim realities of her life, Mildred abuses alcohol and "nerve pills."

Though McMillan addresses a range of social issues through her depiction of Mildred and her family, domestic violence is a major theme of *Mama*, and it propels much of the action in the early parts of the novel. Domestic violence is introduced very early in the novel. Beginning with its opening scene, the novel pits Mildred "against her abusive husband" as she scrambles to defend herself from his rage (Richards, 54). Readers are thus thrust into the middle of a very dramatic—and potentially lethal—domestic conflict in which Crook, "Mildred's childhood sweetheart, husband, and the father of her five children," is beating Mildred as part of a jealous, drunken rampage (Smiles, 144). The novel's first few paragraphs present readers with a twenty-seven-year-old Mildred Peacock hiding an "ax beneath the mattress of the cot in the dining room," checking the kitchen's three butcher knives "to make sure they were razor sharp," and strategizing additional ways to defend herself from Crook, who had, just hours before, beaten Mildred's face to the point that her "bottom lip was swollen" and had also run over her foot with his '59 Mercury (McMillan, 1). Crook had attacked Mildred as a result of the crazy jealousy he felt when he spied her "carrying on a friendly two-minute conversation with Percy Russell," a man whom Crook "had always despised" because of a lingering rumor that Percy was the true (biological) father of their oldest daughter, Freda (McMillan, 2). Since this is the initial scene McMillan presents us with, readers' first picture of Mildred is amidst a violent, domestic encounter. Indeed, because McMillan begins in medias res, readers are confronted with dramatic, and, in this case, violent, action, which introduces the theme of domestic abuse early on in the narrative.

As disturbing as those opening paragraphs of *Mama* are, what transpires in the pages that follow proves even more troubling, for that passage (quoted below) reveals Mildred's five young children being forced to witness as Crook beats their mother with a belt:

> Crook kicked the door shut and the kids cracked theirs. Then they heard their mama screaming and their daddy hollering and the whap of the belt as he struck her.
> "Didn't I tell you you were getting too grown?" *Whap.* "Don't you know your place yet, girl?" *Whap.*
> "Yes, yes, Crook." *Whap.*
> "Don't you know nothing about respect?" *Whap.* "Girl, you gon' learn. I'm a man, not no toy." *Whap.* "You understand me?" *Whap.* "Make me look like no fool." *Whap.*
> He threw the belt on the floor and collapsed next to Mildred on the bed. The terror in her voice faded to whimpers and sniffles. To the kids she sounded like Prince, their German shepherd, when he had gotten hit by a car last year on Twenty-fourth Street [McMillan, 10–11].

Being forced to witness this scene terrorizes all five of the children. They cry and huddle together in fear—and for mutual protection.

Freda, the oldest, "hushed the girls," but finds they are inconsolable (McMillan, 12). Not wanting to provoke Crook's anger, Freda warns them that "we'll be next" if they don't quiet down, and she tries "to comfort the two youngest, Angel and Doll, by wrapping them inside her skinny arms, but it was no use. They couldn't stop crying." (McMillan, 12). Although Freda, being the oldest, "felt it was her place to act like an adult," she soon "started to cry, too" (McMillan, 12). In response to witnessing this scene of domestic abuse, Money, the only boy, wets himself (in fact, McMillan reveals, "the fighting always made him lose control of his bladder") and he prays "hard" and swears "that when he got married he would never beat his wife" (12). Not only are Mildred's children clearly terrified—as their reactions demonstrate—by the violent encounter they witness, but there is little doubt that seeing Crook beating their mother haunts them for long after the attack is over.

Domestic violence affects every member of the family, including the children—and this holds true with the family McMillan depicts in *Mama*. As a rule, family violence creates a home environment where children live in constant fear. In fact, studies suggest that children who witness family violence are affected in ways similar to children who are themselves physically abused. Although children who live in violent homes react to their environment in different ways (reactions can vary depending on the child's gender and age, for example), the children who are exposed to family violence are more likely to develop social, emotional, psychological and/or behavioral problems than those who are not. Recent research indicates that children who witness domestic violence show more anxiety, low self-esteem, depression, anger and temperament problems than children who do not witness violence in the home. The trauma they experience can show up in emotional, behavioral, social, and physical disturbances that affect their development and can continue into adulthood.

Indeed, witnessing domestic violence can lead children to develop a range of emotional and behavioral problems. In recent years, research has been done to locate the specific effects witnessing domestic abuse has on children. As Melissa M. Stiles, M.D., notes in her 2002 article "Witnessing Domestic Violence: The Effect on Children,"

> Children who witness violence in the home and children who are abused may display many similar psychological effects. These children are at greater risk for internalized behaviors such as anxiety and depression, and for externalized behaviors such as fighting, bullying, lying, or cheating. They also are more disobedient at home and at school, and are more likely to have social competence problems, such as poor school performance and difficulty in relationships with others. Child witnesses display inappropriate attitudes about violence as a means of resolving conflict and indicate a greater willingness to use violence themselves.

Moreover, the line between witnessing abuse and being directly victimized by it is blurred, if not altogether obscured, in McMillan's novel, *Mama*—and in general.

Children who witness domestic abuse are also likely to be themselves abused, and whether or not the children are themselves physically assaulted, the mere threat of being beaten takes an emotional toll on the children who reside in violent homes. This very real threat is suggested in *Mama* when the children, recognizing that they are in danger from Crook, "hide under the covers" because they are so scared (McMillan, 6–7). Crook batters Mildred, but, by his abuse of her, he also victimizes the five children by terrorizing them and forcing them to witness him beating their mother. Children who witness violence in the home tend to suffer the effects of it for years to come—and such is the case with Mildred's five children, all of whom are frightened as Crook savagely beats their mother and who continue to reel from the trauma of witnessing domestic violence for years to come.

The theme of domestic violence is central in *Mama,* and this is only reinforced by the novel's opening scenes and the way that McMillan sets the stage for the rest of novel. By launching readers headfirst into the volatile scene between Mildred and Crook and then, immediately afterward, showing the children's reactions to witnessing such violence in the home, McMillan portrays domestic abuse as a catalyst for much of what will come later for the Peacock family. Indeed, taken as a whole, the beginning parts of *Mama* are powerful for a number of reasons, not least of which is that they set the stage for what is to come. Though Mildred struggles to raise her children and do her best for them, the effects of witnessing domestic abuse—and well as the economic realities of their existence (the family's chronic poverty as well as Mildred's frequent unemployment and reliance on government benefits)—take a real toll on them.

Freda, determined not to follow in her mother's footsteps, grows up dreaming of leaving Point Haven (and she eventually lands in Los Angeles). Money (the only son) gets into frequent trouble as a teenager, and as an adult he is constantly in and out of jail. The other three daughters, Bootsey, Doll, and Angel, all want to become adults before their time, and Doll and Angel try to find love and acceptance through men. The fact that all of Mildred's children have emotional issues as teenagers and adults, and that some of them also have legal troubles and substance abuse problems later on, suggests the long-lasting effects of growing up in a violent home.

These same early scenes of the novel prove important for another reason, as well, for they introduce some of the book's other tensions: fidelity, marital discord, and substance abuse (all of which reemerge again and again in the novel). Because Crook's jealousy provokes his rage in the novel's opening scene, readers are confronted with the issue of marital fidelity, which surfaces time and again in *Mama.* The problem of substance abuse is highlighted in this scene because Crook and Mildred's violent encounter is (even further) fueled by their alcohol abuse. Yet, not only are we confronted with the harsh realities of Mildred and Crook's violent relationship through the drunken violent encounter that begins the novel, but we also catch a glimpse of Mildred's resilience and drive to protect herself. As Michael Awkward (who was a contemporary reviewer of the novel) points out, Mildred's scrambling for weapons in this scene is her attempt at a "self-protective scheme," which serves as an "accurate reflection of the survivalist mentality that compels her subsequent adventures and misadventures" (Awkward, 649). This aspect of her personality will, indeed, surface later—and will (ultimately) serve her as she struggles to take care of her children.

The early scenes of *Mama* prove important for yet another reason. By the way McMillan depicts Crook and through her portrayal of the cycle of violence, she highlights the role sociological factors play in domestic abuse. Though Crook does not come across as the most sympathetic of characters, McMillan does take pains to show how he, too, remains trapped because of his position in society. Indeed, his inability to make a decent living in America and his sense of powerlessness because of the role allotted to him (because of his race, social class, education level, and gender) clearly affects him and his treatment of Mildred. As Smiles emphasizes, "Unable to keep a steady job in a town plagued by the demise of American manufacturing jobs, Crook spends most of his time down at the local bar. He takes his anger and frustration out on the 27-year-old Mildred by beating her and then forcing her to have sex with him" (Smiles, 144). As several recent sociological studies have addressed, poverty, joblessness, substance abuse, and a number of other factors clearly contribute to the cycle of domestic abuse.

For example, in *Domestic Violence at the Margins: Readings on Race, Class, Gender, and Culture,* Natalie J. Sokoloff and Christina Pratt examine "structural factors in relation to domestic violence" (5). They note that, among the sociological factors that are significant, "poverty, especially extreme poverty within the African American community, has been correlated with higher rates of severe and lethal domestic violence" (Sokoloff and Pratt, 5). In another examination of domestic abuse in the African American community, *Family Violence and Men of Color: Healing the Wounded Male Spirit,* Ricardo Carrillo and Jerry Tello argue that "substance abuse, and specifically the use of alcohol, has been identified as one of the most powerful predictors of domestic violence" (71).

Along with these sociological factors, Crook's psychological makeup pushes him to abuse Mildred as he does. Already feeling vulnerable because of how society has systematically devalued him, Crook feels further threatened by Mildred when she flirts with Percy. Crook perceives this as a challenge to his (already fragile) sense of self, as well as a deliberate attack on his masculinity. As Ellerton suggests, this scene results in Mildred "being beaten because she has challenged her husband's masculine subject position" (Ellerton, 109). To be clear, McMillan does not excuse Crook's behavior, but she does provide a rationale for it, which is part of how her novel functions as a social protest. Moreover, details such as these indicate that *Mama* is a work of realism by the way it depicts life in the 1960s and 1970s—and the promises and disappointments that era meant for all black people.

Mildred, sick of being on the receiving end of Crook's abuse, finally decides to kick him out of the house. Though Mildred is resourceful and sly, life without Crook proves difficult for her because of her and her children's chronic poverty. She'll do anything to pay the bills, but she loses job after job, and goes from one man to another, until alcohol and nerve pills are her only comfort. In this sense, McMillan presents us with a flawed woman who nonetheless loves her five children and strives to do what she thinks is best for them. In his description of her character, Awkward clarifies that "Mildred Peacock is no transcendent or unquestionably triumphant exemplar of 'the black woman's experience,' but an alcoholic, nerve-pill popping, frequently self-centered character whose strength is manifested in her ability to survive (sometimes barely) the difficulties" she faces (Awkward, 650).

It's important to note that the Peacock family's problems do not evaporate after Crook's out of the picture. By depicting this family as having such desperate financial struggles after the abuser (in this case, Crook) is no longer in the picture, McMillan highlights a reality for many victims of domestic abuse, at the same time as she calls attention to one reason abused women so frequently do not leave their abusers: many simply cannot afford to. Though Crook never made much money, he was the family's breadwinner; so, when Mildred kicks him out of the house, she loses the financial support he provided to her and her children. Consequently, Mildred and her five kids find themselves subject to the harsh economic realities of life in a depressed Michigan town. Mildred bounces around from job to job, and there is never any semblance of financial security for her or her children. Life as a single mother proves very difficult for Mildred in other ways, as well, and she never feels fulfilled. Life is also hard for her five children. Growing up in a one-parent home means that Mildred's children are often home alone without any adult supervision. This leads them to get into trouble, and in the case of Freda, being home alone also leads to her being sexually assaulted by a family friend named Deadman, who shows up at the family's residence one night when Freda (now a young teen) is there by herself.

When Deadman arrives, it's clear that he has been drinking. He offers Freda "five dollars" for "one little kiss" (McMillan, 94). When she rebuffs his advances, Deadman grows angry and throws "Freda onto the couch," where he proceeds to pull "down her slacks past her trembling knees" (McMillan, 95). Overcome with fear, Freda passes out, and when she awakens, she finds him "on top of her, fumbling with himself and pressing his body hard against hers" (McMillan, 95). Freda doesn't tell anyone about the assault at the time; instead, feeling "embarrassed and humiliated," she tries to clean herself and the house up to hide what's happened to her (McMillan, 96). In many ways, Freda's reaction to Deadman's violent sexual assault is reminiscent of how Mildred would react in the aftermath of Crook's abuse of her, for Mildred would always try to clean up the house and act like things were back to normal after she and Crook would fight. Though Mildred is not to blame for Deadman's behavior, Freda's response to his sexual assault fits the pattern that she witnessed so many times when she was a younger child. This encounter thus reflects the sad reality that violence has become a way of life for this family.

Indeed, in addition to the many personal and financial problems that Mildred faces over the years, Mildred herself also continues to encounter domestic violence in her later relationships. After a string of failed relationships and after taking pretty much any job she can get just to put food on the table, Mildred marries a longtime acquaintance named Rufus. Initially, this marriage seems to promise a better life for the family because of the relative financial stability that Rufus can provide, but soon this relationship, too, turns sour. At first, "Rufus tried to be a good stepdaddy" and "bought them as much junk as he could afford. Now they had all the things they dreamed would fill up the refrigerator," like "too many hotdogs and potato chips, too much popcorn, and plenty of soda pop and ice cream" (McMillan, 100). He is able to pay the bills, but, "like Crook, Rufus drank too much" (McMillan, 100). Soon, spurred on by his own "pitifulness, his own worthlessness and powerlessness," Rufus began to "spit it out" at Mildred (McMillan, 101). Heavy drinking would send Rufus into "a purple rage," and he would take it out on her (McMillan, 101).

In her marriage to Rufus, Mildred again finds herself on the receiving end of violence, and her children, once again, find themselves forced to witness violent encounters in the home. At one point, when Mildred, sick of his abuse and general mistreatment of her, threatens to leave Rufus, he comes at her with a knife and grabs her arm as her daughters watch on in horror. Freda attempts to intervene on Mildred's behalf, screaming "Let go of my mama, you son of a bitch!" and tells her sisters, who also witness this scene, to "run and call the police" (McMillan, 103). This incident results in injuries for both Mildred and Rufus. Mildred realizes, "Rufus had cut her. Her blouse was bloody," and she retaliates by jabbing "Rufus in his side" with a broken beer bottle (McMillan, 104). This heated domestic dispute between Mildred and Rufus halts when the police arrive, but they seem "bored with the incident" and soon leave the scene (McMillan, 105). The fact that the responding officers react in this way hints at just how commonplace domestic abuse is for families like Mildred's. Their lack of response also suggests a general apathy by law enforcement with respect to addressing domestic violence and their unwillingness to try to help victims of family violence. In this sense, McMillan provides another layer of realism (by highlighting the prevalence of the problem of domestic violence) as well as additional social commentary, through the way she shows the police officers' inappropriate handling of the violence that had just occurred.

Mildred ends the relationship with Rufus, but her problems are far from over. She continues to struggle financially at the same time as she works unsuccessfully to find romantic love and emotional fulfillment. Unable at times to cope, Mildred relies all the more heavily on alcohol and drugs (the "nerve pills" she has become addicted to) to get by. In this respect and in others, McMillan provides a complicated picture of Mildred. As Ellerton summarizes it, McMillan portrays Mildred as a character who "driven by impossible bills, she turns tricks, hosts poker parties, remarries, divorces, and moves from house to house, from state to state" in an "effort to maintain some form of family stability" (Ellerton, 110). Indeed, despite her many problems, Mildred tries desperately to raise her five children, who are growing up to have problems of their own.

Though the novel does not have a happy ending in many respects, it does offer a glimpse of hope through Mildred's tenacity and perseverance in the face of seemingly insurmountable obstacles. McMillan's novel also closes with the possibility of a better future for Mildred's children, who are striving to overcome their many problems by finally confronting them. In the case of Mildred, her ultimate ability to not only survive but keep her family going makes her likeable despite her many flaws. In all, through *Mama,* McMillan provides a poignant depiction of the difficulties faced by this family at the same time as she raises awareness about the problems they face such as poverty, domestic abuse, and the cyclical nature of both.

A Day Late and a Dollar Short

A Day Late and a Dollar Short (2002) is Terry McMillan's fifth novel. The novel features a multigenerational family dealing with a range of contemporary problems. A novel set primarily in Las Vegas, Nevada, in 1994, *A Day Late and a Dollar Short* contrasts in many ways with her 1987 novel, *Mama,* where McMillan confronts domestic abuse and its effects through her depiction of Mildred Peacock and her family, as they try to make lives for themselves in America during the 1960s and 1970s. While domestic abuse was one of the major themes of *Mama,* in *A Day Late and a Dollar Short,* domestic violence is just one of the many problems that the large and dysfunctional Price family must confront. Like in *Mama,* family takes center stage in *A Day Late and a Dollar Short,* but, as Jill Hallett emphasizes in her essay "New Voices in the Canon," the focus of this novel is "on strained relationships and how they are resolved" (Hallett, 419). Through the use of multiple narrative voices and offering a 21st century perspective, McMillan explores the Price family's many dilemmas. Viola Price, the family matriarch, is the dominant voice in this novel, with a plot revolving around her strained marriage with Cecil.

Together, they have four grown children located in various places throughout the country. Their tumultuous marriage has lasted nearly forty years, but it's now on the brink of ending, which Viola alludes to in her early description of her husband and family:

> I don't even want to think about Cecil right now, because it might just bring on another attack. He's a bad habit I've had for thirty-eight years, which would make him my husband. Between him and these kids, I'm worn out. It's a miracle I can breathe at all. I had 'em so fast they felt more like a litter, except each one turned out to be a different animal. Paris is a female lion who don't roar loud enough. Lewis is a horse who don't pull his own weight. Charlotte is definitely a bull, and Janelle would have to be a sheep—a lamb is closer to it—'cause she always being led out to some pasture and don't know how she got there [McMillan, 1–2].

The burden of bringing her family together weighs heavily on Viola, who is also facing financial troubles and chronic health problems. She dies near the end of the novel from a final asthma attack, but Viola's death ultimately does bring the family together through her efforts. Together, the family seems to move past many of their problems as they comfort each other by reading letters she wrote to them before passing away. Through these letters, she teaches them that nothing is more important than family.

Though this family's struggles and eventual coming together make up the focus of this novel, just as she does in *Mama,* McMillan succeeds in raising awareness about domestic abuse through *A Day Late and a Dollar Short.* In the case of this novel, however, her message seems to be how family violence is just one of a number of problems facing families today, for she explores the problem of family violence at the same time as she addresses a range of other problems that characterize life for so many in the late 20th and early 21st centuries. Even though McMillan addresses a variety of concerns throughout *A Day Late and a Dollar Short,* her treatment of domestic abuse in this novel bears scrutiny, for she calls attention to the problem by addressing the various mechanisms that allow violence in the home to occur.

Of the many dilemmas the Price family members face, there are three situations in this novel that feature family violence. The first concerns Lewis, Viola's grown son who, as a child, was sexually abused by his male cousins, who were teenagers at the time. Lewis's sexual abuse from his cousins merits attention because his violation departs from the stereotypical representation of male on female violence, and it shows the vulnerability of male children to abuse. Another instance of abuse involves Todd (Lewis' son's white stepfather) and Jamil, Lewis' son by his ex-wife, Donnetta. Todd throws things at and punches the teenaged Jamil for being disrespectful and smoking marijuana, which provokes Lewis. Like his father before him, Jamil faces abuse at the hands of an older male (although in Jamil's case, it is physical abuse, not sexual abuse), so this shows another situation with male-on-male family violence. Todd's mistreatment of Jamil is an example of a child facing violence at the hands of an abusive stepfather, a pattern which presents in more insidious fashion through another character in the novel, George Porter. A high ranking LAPD officer, Porter is married to Janelle (Cecil and Viola's daughter), and he is caught sexually abusing her 12-year-old daughter, Shanice (who is his stepdaughter). Janelle is, at first, loathe to believe that her husband George, who holds a position of power and relative prestige, could be sexually abusing young Shanice, but she later learns that George Porter has a history of abusing girls—his other victims include another one of his stepdaughters and his own daughter.

Lewis, described by his mother as "a horse who don't pull his own weight," is generally considered to be the black sheep of the family (McMillan, 1). Lewis has constant money problems and he struggles to find stable employment. Having to face these problems, and confronted with the reality that he's not been very successful compared to his sisters, all of whom are middle class, makes Lewis "feel small" (McMillan, 50). His frequent legal troubles further confirm his family's low opinion of him, as do his failed personal relationships. His marriage to Donnetta, the mother of his son, has fallen apart, and his relationship with his son, Jamil, remains strained, as well. Reflecting on his bond with Jamil, Lewis admits at one point, sometimes "I just pretend like I don't have a kid" (McMillan, 49). Lewis convinces himself that since he's not "in a better position to do for him," it's better for him to just forget about his son (McMillan, 49). He blames his drinking on his bad relationship with his son, and he clearly blames Donnetta for his financial hardship, as the passage below makes clear:

> If it wasn't for Donnetta, I'd be in much better shape financially. She's the reason I have to work under the table half the time, because right after we split up she insisted on taking me to court, knowing I wasn't making nothing but two dollars over minimum wage. She didn't care. She wanted *that*. And she *got* it [McMillan, 49–50].

Lewis finds it easier to blame his ex-wife than to take financial responsibility for son. Moreover, he also finds it convenient to blame Donnetta that he doesn't have more money. In this manner, McMillan thus presents readers with a rather disparaging picture of Lewis. Indeed, from the time he's introduced in the novel, she portrays him in a rather negative light. When Lewis first arrives on the scene at the hospital (he's there to visit his mother, Viola, who has been hospitalized because of her severe asthma) he makes a bad impression on readers because he shows up drunk, broke, and asking his family for money.

Many of Lewis' personal problems, however, stem from the trauma he experienced from being sexually abused as a child. In the following passage from *A Day Late and a Dollar Short*, Lewis describes his abuse at the hands of his cousins and he points to the long-lasting effects that this abuse has had on him:

> As much as I'd like to, I've tried hard to forget the fact that my sixteen- and seventeen-year-old cousins—Boogar and Squirrel—pushed me inside the trapdoor of our fallout shelter when I was ten years old and made me suck their penises. I couldn't believe they was making me do it and I didn't

understand why. We were boys. Plus, we were cousins. I ain't never felt so humiliated and confused in my life as I did that day. When I threw up afterwards, they just laughed and told me if I ever told anybody about this they would kill me. To this day, I ain't never told a soul [McMillan, 50–51].

Lewis admits in this passage that he would like to forget this assault ever occurred. This reaction is all too common for survivors of incest and sexual abuse. Karen L. Kinnear, who addresses victims' typical responses to abuse in *Childhood Sexual Abuse: A Reference Handbook,* discusses various "coping methods such as withdrawal and attempts to forget the experience" (315). Lewis has clearly done both—he's attempted to forget what happened to him and he's withdrawn, since he cannot make sense of what transpired in the fallout shelter. Even as an adult, Lewis struggles to reconcile how family can do "unspeakable, despicable" things to one another (McMillan, 50).

The fact that his abuse constituted incest understandably disturbs Lewis (when he reflects on what's happened, he considers, "we were cousins"), as does the fact that he and his attackers were all male ("We were boys," he also thinks). Significantly, and as many researchers have suggested, boys are sometimes affected differently by sexual abuse than girls are. In his book *Victims No Longer: Men Recovering from Incest and Other Sexual Abuse,* Mike Lew describes some of these key differences.

Since men "are not supposed to be victims," abuse (and particularly sexual abuse) becomes a process of demasculinization (or emasculation). If men aren't to be victims (the equation reads), then victims aren't men. The victimized male wonders and worries about what the abuse has turned him into. Believing that he is no longer an adequate man, he may see himself as a child, a woman, gay, or less than human: an irreparable damaged freak [41].

This scenario describes precisely what Lewis must contend with, and he finds that he cannot reconcile his masculinity with his victimhood and the powerlessness it represents for him.

At the same time, the sexual abuse his cousins subjected him to has shattered Lewis' sense of trust in people and especially in family members. As Lewis sums it up, he realizes that "relatives can do more harm to you than a total stranger" (McMillan, 50). For Lewis, the aftermath of the abuse he endures is significant, yet he is so full of shame and self-recrimination for what's happened that, even as he grows up, he never tells anyone about the abuse. When his abusers die (both die young because of the life of crime they've taken up), Lewis refuses to attend their funerals. Sadly, even after their deaths, Lewis remains unable to move past the trauma he endured.

For many years, he assumes that the rest of his family is unaware of what occurred between him and his cousins, but at the very end of the novel, he learns that his mother and siblings did eventually come to suspect that Lewis had been abused.

Jamil, Lewis' thirteen-year-old son by his ex-wife Donnetta, finds himself embroiled in dysfunctional family dynamics, both because he's the product of Lewis and Donnetta's messy divorce and since his stepfather, Todd, mistreats him. Jamil has been living with his mom and Todd when Todd grows tired of the boy's behavior. Todd disapproves that Jamil's been experimenting with marijuana and that his grades have been slipping. At one point, Todd punches the teenaged boy in the eye for being disrespectful. When Lewis learns of this incident, he and Jamil talk about what happened.

> "So Todd hit you and your mama just watched?"
> "She asked him to stop when she saw that he'd hurt me."
> "He ever hit you before?"
> "He threw something at me once."
> "Really?"
> "Yeah, but he missed."
> "What'd he throw?"
> "A bat."
> "A bat, huh?" [McMillan, 238–239].

Although in the case of Todd and Jamil there may not yet be a clear pattern of abuse, as the exchange above makes clear, punching the boy is far from an isolated incident. As Jamil's explanation demonstrates, Todd has resorted to physical violence as well as the threat of violence to force the teen into submission.

When Lewis learns of Todd's bad behavior, he becomes angry. Though Lewis has been far from a perfect father, he has never once raised his hand against his son. It is understandable that he'd want to confront the man who has punched and threatened his son (and his motive to retaliate against Todd no doubt stems in part from his protective paternal instincts), but McMillan also creates the sense that Lewis' reaction links up in a very real way with his own memories of abuse and feelings of powerlessness. It is perhaps his own experiences of being abused that provoke Lewis to not only confront Todd, but to violently attack him with his hands as well as with "the wooden handle of a mop" (McMillan, 286). This incident sends Todd to the hospital and lands Lewis in jail.

In *A Day Late and a Dollar Short,* the problems and physical confrontations that take place between Todd and Jamil do more than simply create another layer of drama for the novel. Indeed, by depicting the tense and violent relationship between stepfather and stepson, McMillan calls attention to a specific type of family violence: the abusive stepfather. As David J. Buller notes in his book *Adapting Minds: Evolutionary Psychology and the Persistent Quest for Human Nature,* several recent studies suggest that children who live in the home with a stepfather are at an elevated risk for violence. These same studies further demonstrate that this risk "is due primarily to abuse by the stepfather" (Buller, 400).

In the novel, another character faces abuse at the hands of a stepfather. Young Shanice, Janelle's 12-year-old daughter, gets sexually molested by George Porter, her mother's husband and a well-respected LAPD officer. Shanice shows many of the telltale signs of abuse, but her mother at first refuses to believe that anything's happened. Though Shanice confides to her mom, "George is mean and sometimes hits her," Janelle tells Viola that she's sure that it's all an elaborate lie: "Mama, George has never hit Shanice. She's been lying about a lot of things lately. She's just being dramatic" (McMillan, 21–22). Not only does Shanice make clear claims that she's been abused, but her behavior suggests that abuse has taken place, as well. She acts skittish around George and admits to being afraid of him, going as far as to beg her mother not to leave her alone with him. Shanice suffers from trichotillomania (an impulse disorder characterized by pulling out bits of one's own hair), a disorder which usually is triggered by a life trauma, such as sexual abuse. Though Janelle and Viola notice that Shanice has been pulling out her hair, Janelle insists that this self-destructive behavior has nothing to do with George.

Even when Viola (who believes what her granddaughter has told her) pleads with Janelle to listen to Shanice's account, Janelle continues to make excuses for George and discounts her own daughter's story, despite the fact that the young girl has many of the telltale signs of abuse. Indeed, Janelle remains in denial that the abuse is occurring until she catches George, pants down, in the act of molesting young Shanice. Finally confronted with the truth, Janelle asks herself, "Why didn't I see the signs?" and is forced to admit to herself that it was because she "wanted to believe him" because, without George, she feared that she'd "lose everything" (McMillan, 76). Janelle eventually learns that George's sexual abuse of Shanice began when her daughter was quite young (it started when she was just six or seven years old, from what Shanice can remember) and that it has been going on for many years.

In the case of George Porter, McMillan not only presents readers with a man who used his relationship (that of stepfather to Shanice) to exploit the young girl and abuse her for many years, but she also shows how a man with a position of power and the community's respect can be guilty of this terrible sort of violation. As a high-ranking policeman, Porter occupied a position of relative prestige and privilege, and he used his station to hide his perverted crimes. The irony of this high-ranking policeman's being guilty of criminal behavior is not lost on Janelle. When she kicks George out of the house, she screams, "Get out of here before I call the police. Oh. I forgot. You are the fucking police" (McMillan, 75).

Society holds those in law enforcement to a higher standard, and this is especially true with decorated officers who have moved through the ranks of the police department, such as George Porter has. Yet, for a time at least, George Porter was able to misuse this trust and rely upon his wife's (and society's) good opinion of him to get away with terrible crimes. When Janelle finally stops denying what's happened, and when she finally stops making excuses for George, who promises her that he'll change and get help, she starts to uncover a long history of abuse. She eventually learns that he had abused other girls including another one of his stepdaughters (with another woman) as well as his own daughter. Thus, through the case of George Porter, McMillan shines a light on a specific type of family violence at the same time as she shows how those in power sometimes use their power to subjugate others.

Though domestic violence is just one of many themes that McMillan addresses in *A Day Late and a Dollar Short,* this novel serves as a way for her to raise awareness about the problem. Through the book's characters and the dilemmas they face, McMillan shows different types of family violence as well as the mechanisms that allow these forms of abuse to occur. Because the novel was written in 2002, it provides a more recent perspective on abuse than did *Mama.*

Mama and *A Day Late and a Dollar Short*: Common Themes

For all their differences, there are some common themes that bind McMillan's *Mama* with her more recent novel *A Day Late and a Dollar Short.* Both provide compelling portraits of black families. Both present readers with characters who are flawed but sympathetic. Both of these novels also prove to be readable and relatable, qualities which make them connect to McMillan's readers—and which allow her messages of social protest to reach a wide audience. When examining these books side by side, it easy to locate "very poor and upwardly mobile, ambitious Black women" alike, which is true, too, when looking at the body of McMillan's fiction (Ellerby, 109). This feature of her novels works as part of McMillan's project of raising awareness, for she depicts rich, middle class, and poor alike facing many of the same issues—including the problem of family violence, which she does much to confront through her portrayals of the Price and Peacock families.

McMillan has gone on record as saying, "I don't write about victims. They just bore me to death. I prefer to write about somebody who can pick themselves back up and get on with their lives. Because all of us are victims to some extent" (Sawhill, et al. 76). This statement most certainly holds true for the characters she creates in *Mama* (1987) and *A Day Late and a Dollar Short* (2002), for though they suffer from the effects of violence, have personal problems, and face obstacles in their path, they show a remarkable resilience, which gives her novels a hopeful note. This same sense of hope pervades in McMillan's depiction of domestic abuse because, though she creates characters who undergo all sorts of trauma, she shows their repeated and constant efforts to rise above their problems.

CHAPTER 7

Family and the Legacy of Violence:
Toni Morrison's *Love*

Like so many of the novels already discussed in this book, Toni Morrison's *Love* reveals the violent undercurrents so common in the domestic sphere. As she does in *The Bluest Eye* (1970), in her 2003 novel, *Love,* Morrison highlights the hidden and secretive nature of much of the violence that occurs within the home, but since *Love* was written over thirty years after *The Bluest Eye* was first published, she is able to offer a 21st century perspective on the problem of domestic abuse. In *Love,* however, Morrison is also able to offer a retrospective glance at many of the problems that characterized the 20th century because the events of the novel span so many decades. By tracing the exploits of the character, Bill Cosey, whose legacy of violence continues well after his death, Morrison also shows both the cycle of violence and its long-lasting repercussions.

There is an awful lot of violence in this novel (which is ironically entitled *Love*). Indeed, a veritable laundry list of misdeeds makes up the narrative, many of which fall into the category of domestic abuse. These include, as Laura Miller, one of the book's contemporary reviewers, succinctly rattles them off,

> murder, arson, the maiming of a little girl, fetishism, pedophilia, rape, gang rape, statutory rape, prostitution, blackmail, sadomasochism, defenestration, the corruption of various minors, masturbation and an angry mob containing a kid who throws a bucket of "animal waste" all over the owner of a nice hotel [Miller].

These events—far from being incidental to narrative—work to paint a society and family structure that is rife with problems.

If Morrison, in *The Bluest Eye,* indicts 1940s American culture and illustrates how those who are themselves marginalized and excluded from society at large leave a legacy of pain to their children through physical, sexual, and emotional abuse, in her much more recent novel, *Love,* published over thirty years later, she provides a retrospective view of the 20th century through the abuse suffered by two of the novel's main characters, Christine and Heed, childhood friends turned bitter enemies. In *Love,* as she does quite pointedly in *The Bluest Eye* (as well as, to varying degrees, in several of her other novels), Toni Morrison portrays the domestic sphere as violent, and she underscores how viewing the domestic sphere as a "private" space alternately covers up and legitimizes the abuse that takes place there.

In *Love,* Morrison points to social problems that she sees as consistently plaguing America. At the same time, she reveals how those who have attained a degree of power use their privileged position to oppress others. Throughout this novel, Morrison reveals that, rather than existing and operating separately, the larger social problems that plague 20th-century American society—including sexism, racism, and poverty—are tied directly to the objectification, commodification, and violation of women by those intimately acquainted with them. In *Love,* Morrison highlights how the family as a "social unit continues to have a preponderant role in molding the destiny of individuals" (Sathyaraj and Neelakantan, 10). This role takes on a sinister dimension when we consider all that transpires in the novel and how many of characters' dilemmas originate within the domestic sphere.

The Premise of *Love*

Love centers on the character of William "Bill" Cosey. Though he was murdered twenty-five years before the events that make up the present of the story take place, he is nonetheless the focus of the novel. Cosey is also still a very real presence to the women who shared his life. Indeed, even years after his death, they cannot stop obsessing over him, a point made even clearer by the way Morrison divides up this novel. All of the chapters in *Love,* "Portrait," "Friend," "Stranger," "Benefactor," "Lover," "Husband," "Guardian," "Father," and "Phantom," refer to him and illustrate Cosey's many different roles.

Beyond using the titles of these chapters to highlight just how much a presence Cosey truly remains in the novel, Morrison relies on them, as well, to present him as multifaceted. Cosey is hardworking and financially successful. Indeed, in many ways he embodies the qualities that 20th-century American society values in a man—and, in the minds of many, he is considered the "county's role model" (Morrison, 37). Though many people think well of Cosey, we learn, however, that he is guilty of a range of misdeeds, ranging from corruption to child molestation to participating in a financial exchange that is tantamount to human trafficking. Despite these flaws, Cosey has "made it" on his own in America, and for those reasons, he is wealthy and respected. By creating a character such as Cosey—an individual who embodies so much that American society respects in a man, but at the same time commits atrocious deeds without repercussion—Morrison questions the supposed values of 20th-century American society.

Love as a Social Indictment

Tessa Roynon points to Morrison's critique of American values in her discussion of the novel. She argues,

> Cosey is an obvious embodiment of the American dream, and given the fact that he creates a "fabulous, successful resort" described as a "paradise" and as a "fairytale that lived on even after the hotel was dependent for its life on the people it once excluded," it is not hard to read the man as an allegorical representation of America itself [Roynon, 33].

The fact that a major part of Morrison's critique about America involves how invested our society is in attaining material and financial well-being is further reinforced by the central conflict between Christine and Heed in the present of the novel. When Bill Cosey dies, he leaves his estate to his "sweet Cosey child," and he thus reignites a bitter fight between two women who were at one time friends—Christine, his granddaughter, and Heed, his second wife, whom he married when she was only eleven—over which of the two women he meant to include in his will (Morrison, 79).

This bizarre triangle is further complicated—and Morrison's point about the degree to which our society places value on money is further underscored—by the manner in which their feud is depicted and the way the two women were treated by Cosey in the past: "The one who had been sold by a man battled the one who'd been bought by one" (Morrison, 86). The fact that these two women perpetuate the cycle of violence even after Bill Cosey's death points to several things. First, it shows the insidious nature of domestic abuse and operates as a way to criticize the family structure, which Morrison wants to point out as flawed. Second, the fact that these women are fighting over an inheritance only serves to reinforce the role capitalism plays in the problems that manifest in the home. By this point in the novel, both Heed and Christine have fully adopted the same belief system that has worked to oppress them (namely, patriarchal capitalism).

A number of social scientists and feminists have discussed the relationship between the system of patriarchy and the abuses suffered by individual women. For example, in their book-length study *Understanding and Preventing Violence: Social Influences,* social scientists Albert J. Reiss and Jeffrey A. Roth examine the role that a "violent-tolerant culture" plays in permitting—and sometimes encouraging—violence against women, particularly violence committed by those close to them (207). Reiss and Roth acknowledge, as well, how "power motives and adherence to patriarchal ideology converge in research on patriarchy and marital violence" (209). Similarly, in their article "Patriarchy, Family Structure and the Exploitation of Women's Labor," economists Judith A. Heath and David H. Ciscel note that "the family's power relationships mirror society's stratification system" and suggest that this contributes to women's abuse and exploitation in the domestic sphere (793). Further suggesting how important it is to consider the role played by patriarchy when studying the American family, Heath and Ciscel contend, as well, that "economics needs to integrate the assumption of patriarchy into the analysis of the family" (783–784).

In their book *Feminists Negotiate the State: The Politics of Domestic Violence,* Cynthia R. Daniels and Rachelle Brooks cite a position held by second-wave feminists about the relationship between society (or the state) and individual men, in terms of perpetuating women's abuse and oppression. Their analysis breaks down how the two (the state and individual men) intermingle and, ultimately, conspire to subjugate and politically disenfranchise women.

> The state and individual men work together in their use of sexual violence to terrify women into submission. The state's failure to provide basic bodily protection forces women to make arrangements with individual men to gain protection from other men. Because the state itself is an organization of men, the result is analogous to a male protection racket. The lack of physical protection also suggests that women are not members of political society [Daniels and Brooks, 103].

As their argument makes clear, not only "do men control the state," but they use it as an "instrument of domination over women. Domestic violence thus emerges as a ploy by the state to subordinate women" (Daniels and

Brooks, 103). It is precisely this dynamic that is present—and which Morrison makes visible—in *Love*. Cosey, with his power, privilege, and influence, is able to subordinate the women in his life. In the case of Heed, he is able to continue to sexually abuse her (abuse that, in my mind, amounts to multiple counts of child rape—remember, Heed is only eleven years old when the two marry), yet his behavior remains sanctioned by society.

Rather than rejecting these hegemonic notions, Heed and Christine (even though they do not fare well by this system) begin to identify their positions within a patriarchal domestic order and in relation to a man (in their case, Bill Cosey). As Jean Wyatt points out in her essay "*Love*'s Time and the Reader: Ethical Effects of *Nachtraglichkeit* in Toni Morrison's *Love*," even after Cosey dies, Heed and Christine remain preoccupied with the signifiers of capitalist patriarchy, using the terms that the "Law of the Father endows with meaning: inheritance, property, legitimacy" (198). For instance, Heed insists redundantly that she is Bill Cosey's "lawful wedded wife," and Christine attempts to use the legal system to establish (again redundantly) that she is "the last, the only, blood relative" of Bill Cosey, so she must thus be the "sweet Cosey child" his will designates as the rightful (and lawful) heir (Wyatt, 198–199).

Consequently, the legacy of Cosey's violence and oppression of these women continues long after he is gone. This shows the long-lasting repercussions of domestic abuse and reveals it to be a problem without a simple solution. Even when the perpetrator—in this case, Bill Cosey—has died, the trauma from the abuse he perpetrated still lives on for his victims. The fact that Cosey is able to reach from beyond the grave (so to speak) and continue to affect these women's lives also emphasizes the *structure* of patriarchy at work—and it shows how its effects are long-standing.

Adding to the sense that Morrison wants to critique America's value system, and also what contributes to the sense that she places the blame on society for domestic abuse, is the way she takes care to show that Cosey's bad, and sometimes abusive, behavior is allowed and, at least to a degree, hidden under the guise of his supposed respectability, as well as because of the fact that much of it takes place in his home. Cosey's supposed respectability rests, in part, on the fact that he, with his wealth and relative position of power in the community, has managed to ingratiate many of his neighbors by the financial help that he has, in one way or another, given them. In fact, it's fair to say that a number of the townsfolk owe their financial well-being to Bill Cosey, for, as Doreatha Drummond Mbalia reminds us, he has made a habit of "lending money and providing jobs" for so many of them (215). This, yet again, suggests the roles that money and the system of patriarchal capitalism play in allowing Cosey to get away with criminal behavior.

Through a series of flashbacks, we learn of Cosey's various misdeeds and about the dysfunctional nature of his family. We also learn how he first becomes sexually interested in his twelve-year-old granddaughter's eleven-year-old playmate. The two girls are playing outside of Cosey's upscale waterfront resort when Heed decides to run inside to fetch some jacks to play with.

> Heed runs into the service entrance and up the back stairs, excited by the picnic to come and the flavor of bubble gum. Music is coming from the hotel bar—something so sweet and urgent Heed shakes her hips to the beat as she moves down the hallway. She bumps into her friend's grandfather. He looks at her.
>
> Embarrassed—did he see her wiggle her hips?—and in awe. He is the handsome giant who owns the hotel and who nobody sasses [Morrison, 190].

From this moment on, he is sexually attracted to her. Indeed, Cosey, described in the novel as "the Big Man who, with no one to stop him, could get away with it and anything else he wanted," knows no bounds (Morrison, 133).

Cosey takes advantage of being alone with the young girl by touching Heed in a sexual, and highly inappropriate, manner.

> He touches her chin, and then—casually, still smiling—her nipple, or rather the place under her swimsuit where a nipple will be if the circled dot on her chest ever changes. Heed stands there for what seems an hour but is less than the time it takes to blow a perfect bubble. He watched the pink ease from her mouth, then moves away still smiling [Morrison, 191].

Cosey's fondling of her body registers with Heed as inappropriate; the self-consciousness and shame she clearly exhibits in the moments following the encounter reveal as much. For a moment, she stands there stunned and speechless while the "spot on her chest she didn't know she had is burning, tingling" (Morrison, 191). Moments later, she realizes that "she is panting" (Morrison, 191). The sexual abuse that Heed experiences in this moment traumatizes her—and, as the narrative makes clear, the trauma of this molestation stays with Heed throughout her whole life.

The encounter is significant, as well, for Cosey, though in a much different way. He retreats to his granddaughter's bedroom right after touching Heed and proceeds to masturbate while standing in front of the room's window. Christine, who didn't see her grandfather touch Heed, and, hence, does not put the two things together at the time, sees him touch himself: "her grandfather is standing there, in her bedroom window, his trousers open, his wrist moving with the same speed L. used igaday to beat egg whites" (Morrison, 192). Witnessing this makes her vomit. This encounter links Christine and Heed through the violation they share and experience in different ways. As Jean Wyatt points out, both Christine and Heed experience the trauma of Bill Cosey's "sexual intervention as a 'thing'—unsignifiable and unassimilable—that resides within their own bodies" (212). For both Heed and Christine, this trauma causes them to feel overwhelming feelings "of shame—still—because it is an 'inside dirtiness,' which they are afraid will leak out and expose them to the world. Since the 'dirtiness' is within, each of them blames herself" (Wyatt, 212). For these women, the self-recrimination they feel and the traumas they experience prove to be long-lasting.

For Bill Cosey, nothing is off limits. Once his sexual interest in Heed is provoked, he finds a way to legally have her for himself by marrying her. Indeed, he more or less buys her from her parents. The fact that marrying the young girl he desires sexually is a way to sanction his pedophilic and abusive desires suggests that Morrison is attacking the institution of marriage. She paints it as an arrangement that not only hides, but also allows, excuses, and justifies, the abuse and oppression of women—and, in this case, children. Morrison also highlights the economic component of marriage, and as Anissa Janine Wardi puts it in her article "A Laying on of Hands: Toni Morrison and the Materiality of *Love*," how "heterosexual relationships, which, as Cosey's poker game unmasks, are easily bargained—bought, won, and lost—by men" (208). After Cosey and Heed marry, Christine feels betrayed. Christine later tells Junior, who works for the elderly Christine and Heed, her version of what transpired: "One day we were playing house under a quilt; next day she slept in his bed. One day we played jacks; the next she was fucking my grandfather" (Morrison, 131–132).

Though Christine seems to realize that her grandfather basically bought the eleven-year-old Heed from her parents, she nonetheless places some of the blame on Heed, and she taunts her former friend because of that. Before Heed married Cosey, the two girls had made up a secret language called "igaday," similar to "pig latin," which they used to communicate in private. As part of a gesture that suggests that Cosey's perverse sexual desires have infected even this shared, special language, Christine turns what was once their secret weapon against others against her friend when she hurls this insult to her: "Ou-yidagay a ave-slidagay! E-hidagay ought-bidagay ou-yidagay ith-widagay a ear's yigagay ent-ridagay an-d igaday a andy-c ar-bigaday!" ("You a slave. He bought you with a year's rent and a candy bar") (Morrison, 188). The significance of these insults is not lost on Heed, who says, "That hurt, Christine. Calling me a slave" (Morrison, 188). The fact that Morrison has Christine invoke notions of a slave economy through this jab is not accidental. Instead, it works well to further reinforce the marginalized position young Heed occupies. As a young, African American female from a poor family, she is extremely vulnerable and Cosey takes advantage of this. Christine is not alone in blaming Heed. Vida, a onetime employee of Cosey's, acts as if "Heed had chased and seduced a fifty-two-year-old man, older than her father. That she had chosen to marry him rather than been told to" (Morrison, 147).

Indeed, society is quick to label Heed as "bad" and just as quick to overlook Bill Cosey's behavior: "In their minds, she was born a liar, a gold digger unable to wait for her twelfth birthday for pay dirt. They forgave Cosey. Everything. Even to the point of blaming a child for a grown man's interest in her" (Morrison, 147). Heed and Cosey soon settle into their marriage, but the rift between the girls only grows worse when they are all living under one roof as a family. Christine and May (Christine's mother and Cosey's daughter-in-law) are relentless in their mocking of Heed and insult her every chance they get.

Things eventually grow so bad that Cosey sends Christine away from his house, choosing the company of his wife over his granddaughter, much to Christine's chagrin. When Christine returns home for a short visit, the acrimony she shares with Heed is palpable. The rift between the two girls worsens when, during this visit, a dinnertime quarrel between Christine and Heed leads to Cosey spanking Heed in full view of the others and then leaving her home alone for the evening. Heed retaliates by setting Christine's room on fire. When Christine, her mother May, and Cosey return home, they notice "smoke billowing from her bedroom window" (Morrison, 134). Christine and May are horrified by Heed's behavior, but Cosey finds some humor in it: "'She's going to kill us,' May hissed. 'The bed was empty,' he said, still chuckling" (Morrison, 134).

Heed vs. Christine: The Legacy Cosey Leaves Behind

In the novel, Morrison delineates in careful detail why the two girls have turned on each other to such a degree. As L. (short for "Love"), the novel's narrator, explains,

Heed and Christine were the kind of children who can't take back love, or park it. When that's the case, separation cuts to the bone. And if the breakup is plundered, too, squeezed for a glimpse of blood, shed for the child's own good, then it can ruin a mind, And if, on top of that, they are made to hate each other, it can kill a life way before it tries to live. I blame May for the hate she put in them, but I have to fault Mr. Cosey for the theft [Morrison, 199–200].

Though the cycle of abuse that plagues both Heed and Christine begins with Bill Cosey, who, as the novel suggests, likely inherited it from his dysfunctional relationship with his own father, it is a legacy that survives him. Morrison reveals through a flashback that Christine and Heed literally "fought over his coffin" at the funeral—a fight that could have potentially had fatal consequences since Christine is armed at the time with a "switch-blade" (Morrison, 34).

In the present of the story, the two women live together, alternately fearing, plotting against, and tormenting one another, as Wardi's characterization of the two, now elderly, women highlights: "Heed the Night, the child bride of Bill Cosey, and Christine Cosey, his granddaughter" are now "bitter enemies occupying the family home on Monarch Street" (Wardi, 205). Again, the fact that their resentment for one another outlives Cosey makes sense on a number of different levels, and it points to some of the novel's broader messages, as well. Part of the pain they feel, to be sure, must have its roots in the deep betrayal both women feel.

Christine, of course, blames Heed for marrying her grandfather, and this disrupts both their friendship and the family. Heed, on the other hand, feels that her friend Christine let her down by turning on her for something that was not her fault to begin with. Yet another dimension of the two women's bitterness derives from the claim each wants to lay to Cosey. As Wyatt emphasizes, this rivalry links up directly with their alignment with patriarchy, which ironically, is the system to blame in the first place for many of their former and present dilemmas. As Wyatt explains it, it is within the patriarchal order that Christine and Heed come to see each other "only as rivals—first for the man's favor, then for the man's estate" (199). Indeed, even after Cosey's death, the dysfunctional pattern he began lives on in the two elderly women, through their schemes and abusive behavior. As one of the book's reviewers sums it up, "Christine, forced to work as a servant in her childhood home, carries a switchblade and has retained a lawyer to win her inheritance back. Each devotes herself to thwarting and tormenting the other. It's like 'What Ever Happened to Baby Jane?' with two Bette Davises" (Miller).

Indeed, Christine—in the spirit of *What Ever Happened to Baby Jane?*—uses mealtime as a chance to torment Heed. At one point, she serves Heed a shrimp dinner, which she steadfastly refuses to eat, not because she fears the food to be poisoned but because, as Christine knows all too well, Heed dislikes eating shrimp. The passage in question follows:

> Christine entered carrying a tray. No knock preceded her and no word accompanied her. She placed the tray on the desk where Heed and Junior faced each other and left it without meeting a single eye.
> Heed lifted the casserole dish lid, then replaced it. "Anything to annoy me," she said.
> "Looks delicious," said Junior.
> "Then you eat it," said Heed.
> Junior forked a shrimp into her mouth and moaned, "Mmmm, God, she sure know how to cook."
> "What she knows is that I don't eat shellfish" [Morrison, 27–28].

Though the abusive relationships between Heed and Christine, and within the larger Cosey family take center stage in the novel, it is worth pointing out that Morrison depicts other dysfunctional families in *Love,* as well.

(Additional) Dimensions of Family Dysfunction in *Love*

One such example is Heed's family. Her parents, who the townspeople claim have an "unapologetic shiftlessness" about them, participate in her abuse by their complicity in the arrangement made with Bill Cosey (Morrison, 193). Unable to financially provide for their daughter themselves— before her marriage, Heed "slept on the floor and bathed on Saturday in a washtub full of water left murky by her sisters"—her parents quite literally sell her to Cosey (Morrison, 75). They figured, "why not let their youngest marry a fifty-two-year-old man for who knew how much money" (138). Heed is not ignorant about why her parents allow her to marry the much older Cosey. In fact, she even seems to know the particulars of the exchange that took place. At one point, she says "I heard it was two hundred dollars he gave my daddy, and a pocketbook for Mama" (Morrison, 193). The fact that money was the motivation Heed's parents needed only works to further underscore that their marriage—and by extension I believe Morrison is saying marriage in general—is about buying and selling. This agreed-upon arrangement points to "an economic model for marriage: slavery. The father who was said to have smiled on Cosey's courtship and marriage as 'a true romance' turns out to have been smiling because he had just pocketed $200 in exchange for his eleven-year-old daughter Heed" (Wyatt, 210). Rather than entering into marriage as a partnership, by marrying young Heed, Cosey bought the pleasures of a "slave-owner" and can consequently claim "absolute power over another human being, the license to subject her to his sexual whims" (Wyatt). Because of her position in relation to Cosey, for Heed, getting married meant that she was reduced, just "like the slave narrator Harriet Jacobs, to 'the condition of a chattel,'" and must live entirely subject to the will of another (Cosey), without agency or a will of her own (Wyatt, 210).

The dynamic that exists between Cosey and Heed—and the way their marriage is bartered—works to further underscore the connection between the domestic sphere and the marketplace, which is, of course, part of the larger socioeconomic fabric of American society. This thus reinforces the sense that Morrison wants to convey how larger social problems that plague 20th-century American society—including sexism, racism, and poverty— are tied directly to the objectification, commodification, and violation of women by those intimately acquainted with them. They also link up quite specifically with a statement Christine makes late in the novel. Again invoking the slavery metaphor, she says to Heed, "It's like we started out being sold, got free of it, then sold ourselves to the highest bidder" (Morrison, 185).

Heed does not know quite what Christine is getting at, but her answer is nonetheless quite telling: "Who you mean 'we?' Black people? Women? You mean me and you?" (Morrison, 185). The fact that Heed cannot put a finger on who exactly Christine is referring to suggests the prevalence of selling "ourselves to the highest bidder" (Morrison, 185). By depicting marriage as primarily an economic and sociopolitical arrangement, rather than one based on love or affinity, Morrison makes a critique of the nuclear family and the institution of marriage by suggesting that all married women live in a power structure which is "governed by the idea of woman-as-property," a point Wyatt emphasizes (211).

We learn that yet another character, Junior (also known as "June"), the young woman who comes to work for Christine and Heed, is the product of an abusive family, as well. Junior has landed there after being on the streets and in juvenile detention. In her back story, we learn that it was family violence which led to her unfortunate circumstances, since she ran away from her home to escape her abusive uncles. Though, as a rule, Junior lived in fear of her uncles, a specific violent encounter with them leaves her feeling that she has no choice other than to run away. This encounter involves their retaliation against her for removing a snake from the settlement (settlement is how they refer to the backwoods area where they live).

The sequence of events that leads to this confrontation are as follows: It was difficult for Junior to make friends at school.

> The girls in her class avoided her and the few who tried to sprinkle the seeds of friendship were quickly forced to choose between the untidy Rural with one dress and the crafty vengeance little girls know how to exact. Junior lost every time [Morrison, 56].

Junior, however, finally does make a friend, Peter Paul Fortas, a young boy who "after having lived through eleven years of being called Pee Pee" grows "insolent and unyielding to popular opinion" and decides to befriend her (Morrison, 56). Unlike the little girls who abandon Junior, this boy stands up to his classmates and remains her friend despite the classmates' insults. Peter is a proud boy and the "son of the bottling-plant manager, who could hire and fire their parents—and told them so" (Morrison, 56). Peter gives Junior much-needed presents, "a ballpoint pen, a pair of socks, a yellow barrette for her finger-combed hair," so for Christmas June gives him "a baby cottonmouth curled in a bottle"—and he was thrilled (Morrison, 56–57). The gift of the snake, however, is what "did them in" (Morrison, 57). Junior's uncles, "idle teenagers" whose "brains had been insulted by the bleakness of their lives, alternated between brutality and coma," become enraged when Junior gives her friend the snake. In fact, "the act was deeply offensive to them. Something belonging to the Settlement was being transferred to the site of a failure so dismal it had not registered on them as failure at all" (57). As revenge, the morning after Christmas, they wake up with their minds on "fun-seeking" (57). This leads to them chase Junior with their truck, a ride which ends when "the front fender knocked her sideways, the rear tire crushed her toes" (Morrison, 58). Her uncles lie about what happened and tell the family, instead, that they had "found her sprawled on the roadside" (Morrison, 59).

This incident is the catalyst that causes Junior to drop out of school and run away from home at the age of eleven. Though, as this passage and others make clear, there is much tragedy in *Love,* the novel does offer a small, hopeful note toward its conclusion, through the partial reconciliation between the friends-turned-bitter-enemies, Christine and Heed. Not only do the two women seem to call a truce before they die, but they also seem to have a better understanding of each other. Christine, who initially blames Heed, later realizes that the marriage wasn't Heed's fault and tells her that she was "too young to decide" (Morrison, 186).

The Structure of *Love*

In *Love* Morrison emphasizes how characters' families as well as society at large are to blame for many of the predicaments we see in the novel. Morrison relies on both the content and structure of *Love* to underscore that fact. Though *Love,* especially in comparison to some of her other literary works, seems in many ways like a realist novel, it nonetheless has a decidedly fragmented and postmodern feel to it, which helps emphasize the sociopolitical messages within. One such message involves how Cosey abuses his power and privilege to the detriment of Heed and Christine alike—leaving both women "bereft and emotionally infirm for life" (Gillespie, 118). The structure and chronology of the novel—both of which are fragmented—only reinforces the long-lasting repercussions of Cosey's actions. Thus, as Wyatt argues, the text is deliberately disruptive in order to show the disruptive nature of Cosey's actions. She explains how the sequence of events that disrupt their temporal order are themselves a violation of chronology:

> Heed's marriage at eleven to her twelve-year-old playmate Christine's grandfather, the successful black entrepreneur Bill Cosey—and, hidden behind that marriage, the earlier intrusion of adult sexuality into the childhood world through Cosey's molestation of Heed. From the moment Heed is catapulted untimely into the world of adult sexuality and marriage [Wyatt, 192–193].

As a result, Heed and Christine lose the ability to order their lives in relation to time's passage. The fragmented narration of the novel affects how readers perceive these characters, in part because it defers the moment when readers learn the circumstances that led to Heed and Cosey's marriage. The effect of this is that it is "belatedly, then, the reader understands that the adult sexual world broke into the childhood world of Christine and Heed before the inappropriate marriage" (Wyatt, 212). Readers are also slow to learn that the "sexual violation of a child came first, marriage after," a revelation that shows the marriage took place so that Cosey could "conceal a brute abuse of power: or, in Lacanian terms, the Law of the Father conceals and thus gives license to the father figure's uninhibited, unbounded exercise of sexual impulse" (Wyatt, 212).

The choices Morrison made in terms of how she structured this novel help to underscore the deeper messages of *Love,* including her portrayal of marriage and family life in 20th-century America as sinister—a point only further emphasized by Morrison's own pronouncement that the "little nuclear family is a paradigm that just doesn't work. It doesn't work for white people or for black people" (Morrison, 260). In the case of *Love,* Morrison thus relies on both its form and content to represent how the domestic sphere is a place where violence is sanctioned and that, rather than existing and operating separately, the larger social problems that plague 20th-century American society—including sexism, racism, and poverty— are tied directly to the objectification, commodification, and violation of women by those close to them. Ultimately, *Love* proves to be a novel about domestic abuse, and, through this narrative and the dilemmas that the novel's characters face, Morrison brings to light how society and the private nature of the family work together to hide, excuse, and justify perpetrators who commit terrible acts of domestic abuse.

CHAPTER 8

Domestic Violence through a Science Fiction Lens: Octavia Butler's *Seed to Harvest*

The preceding chapters of this book have centered on novels that are realistic and that, consequently, attempt to present a (more or less) realistic view of domestic abuse—as well as its myriad causes and consequences. Discussing these literary works has provided a window through which to consider family violence in the 20th and 21st centuries, as well as a means to address how our society has struggled to come to terms with the issue. Much can be gleaned by analyzing the treatment of family violence in these more traditional literary works since realistic fiction offers a window through which we can view contemporary social problems and anxieties. Yet, though these realistic novels can offer much in terms of revealing the patterns intrinsic to so many abusive family relationships, considering these same issues through the lens of science fiction literature opens up new possibilities not typically afforded to more traditional literary genres.

Science fiction is a significant component of popular culture, and popular culture is an important source of information about life and how the world works—this is true of every source of popular culture, where relevant information about our world is revealed, oftentimes in a continuous stream. This final chapter will focus on the treatment of domestic abuse in science fiction literature by offering literary analyses of the science fiction novels that make up the *Patternist* series by Octavia Butler (1947–2006), a Hugo and Nebula award-winning science fiction author. In *Seed to Harvest* (2007), also known as her *Patternist* series, Butler confronts timely and provocative questions about family, gender, race, and domestic violence at the same time as she explores the themes of identity and transformation. By including a chapter on Butler's *Patternist* series in this book-long exam-

135

ination of domestic violence in African American women's fiction, we can consider how the genre of science fiction not only functions as social commentary and raises awareness about domestic abuse, but we can also explore how the genre creatively addresses many of the (difficult) problems associated with family violence.

The Structure of *Seed to Harvest*

Seed to Harvest is a science fiction series that includes the following novels: *Wild Seed, Mind of My Mind, Clay's Ark,* and *Patternmaster.* The first two books of the series, *Wild Seed* and *Mind of My Mind,* focus on the complicated romantic relationship between two supernatural beings, Doro, an African man who survives by transferring his consciousness from one body to another, and a shape-shifter named Anyanwu (who later goes by the name Emma). Throughout *Wild Seed* and *Mind of My Mind,* Butler presents a startling image of domestic violence and exposes the pattern of coercive control that so frequently characterizes abusive relationships. The latter two books of this series, *Clay's Ark* and *Patternmaster,* portray the fascinating and frightening consequences of the union between Doro and Anyanwu/Emma (both of whom are now deceased). In *Clay's Ark* and *Patternmaster,* Butler also tackles ethical dilemmas related to human rights issues through her characters and the struggles they face—and all of this takes place amidst a backdrop of a violent new world created by Doro and Anyanwu's (not-quite human) descendants.

Themes of the Series

Because the series is so expansive (four separate novels comprise *Seed to Harvest*), there are a number of overall messages and themes that emerge, but a hallmark of the series is how Butler brings to light the dynamics of power versus subordination and captivity versus freedom. Through her sustained engagement with these issues, Butler is able in these novels to comment on the history of the transatlantic slave trade, plantation slavery in the United States, and latter day racism and discrimination—all the while she simultaneously raises awareness about domestic abuse and family violence. By depicting the interpersonal struggles between characters such as Doro and Anyanwu (and, later, among their many descendants), Butler reveals the pattern of coercion and control that is so common in abusive intimate relationships.

The *Seed to Harvest* series begins, chronologically, at least, with *Wild Seed*, a novel that is set centuries ago. The book opens with Doro first encountering Anyanwu in 1690 in West Africa. Even before the two come face-to-face, Butler suggests there is a strong link between them which pulls them toward each other. Upon meeting, Doro and Anyanwu are instantly fascinated with one another and, in many ways, the two seem made for each other. Nonetheless, Butler portrays their budding romantic relationship in a very troubling manner. Doro, though enamored by Anyanwu, seems equally invested in using her and her special abilities to accelerate a breeding program that he's dreamed up and already begun—so far with limited results. Anyanwu is not only clearly attracted to Doro, but she's also greatly interested in what he promises he can deliver her—and, by the second book of the series, *Mind of My Mind,* it is clear that she has grown to love him and that she doesn't want to live without him. There are, however, disturbing elements within (and violent undercurrents to) their relationship that run throughout the first two books of the series. For instance, Doro repeatedly threatens to kill Anyanwu and her offspring, he mercilessly commits barbaric and frightening acts with little provocation, and he forces Anyanwu to sleep with another man. Doro's sadistic treatment of Anyanwu is a recurring conflict in *Wild Seed*, one with consequences that resonate throughout the entire series, yet it remains an underexplored dimension of the series.

The complicated relationship between Doro and Anyanwu (who later goes by the name Emma) bookends the first two books of the series, and their relationship provides the overarching plot of these two books. Their relationship takes center stage in *Wild Seed,* a novel that introduces the two characters and shows the early years of their relationship as well as their voyage from Africa to the New World. In *Mind of My Mind,* Butler depicts their lives in a more contemporary America and shows Doro's efforts to develop his breeding program. Doro and Anyanwu both die before the events within the latter books of the series take place, but the new world order created by them exists long after they are gone. Moreover, both Doro and Anyanwu remain important throughout the series because it is their descendants—descendants who were born as a result of Doro's breeding program—who remain the focus of *Patternmaster.* In *Clay's Ark* and *Patternmaster,* Butler imagines a new kind of world populated by new kinds of families. Through those novels, Butler reflects upon the violent ties that so often bind individuals to one another at the same time as she raises challenging questions about human rights in a post-human world.

Because this series is science fiction, Butler can creatively explore possibilities that simply couldn't be realistically played out—largely because they would seem too far-fetched—in more traditional, that is, more realistic, literary genres. Indeed, the genre of science fiction has long been heralded as a forum wherein authors can confront controversial social issues. Many different scholars and critics have weighed in on the value of science fiction as a tool of social criticism. For instance, Elaine J. O'Quinn and Heather Atwell write about this dimension of science fiction in their essay "Familiar Aliens: Science Fiction as Social Commentary." There, they contend that, while "classic texts remain powerful tools of discussion and historical relevance," science fiction provides a window through which we can challenge and question the world around us (O'Quinn and Atwell). Science fiction scholars John Moore and Karen Sayer seem to concur on this point. As they emphasize in their Introduction to the book *Science Fiction, Critical Frontiers,* "science fiction—at its best—represents an invaluable tool for analyzing the current malaise and envisioning alternatives to it" (Moore and Sayer, xi). The genre of science fiction indeed offers a quality not found in realistic literature for, only through science fiction literature, can authors push "back the boundaries of the known and the possible" (Moore and Sayer, xi).

Those interested in history can learn much from science fiction, as well, for we can use science fiction literature and film to better understand and criticize reality. Science fiction presents us with not only opportunities to "escape" reality, but also to criticize those realities. The (oftentimes fantastic) scenarios that science fiction authors present us with are, essentially, different takes on the past and present; by viewing the past and, in fact, even the present from a different perspective, we may be able to imagine alternate circumstances as possibilities for the world they are currently living, or have lived in.

Some critics have gone as far as to suggest that the lens of science fiction literature is a particularly useful way to view marriage and the family. For example, Val Clear and the other editors of *Marriage and Family through Science Fiction* draw attention to the important role played by science fiction literature in imagining the future of the family. They note, for instance, that in science fiction, the "speculation can leap great bounds in anticipating the future of the family" (Clear et al., 6). Science fiction encourages careful examination of family structures, structures which are so intimately associated with other aspects of society that it is often difficult to parse up all the many connections between the two. Yet, this task remains a crucial one because there is constant tension between the family and society, a point highlighted by Clear who notes that, "inevitably, the individual, the family, and society are in dynamic tension, constantly interacting and effecting change in each other. So complex is the interaction that it is difficult to assign cause-effect relationships" (4). Science fiction literature, then allows readers a lens through which to consider these complex relations, but it also encourages a skeptical eye in terms of rushing toward major social changes. In other words, science fiction literature also "makes it obvious that not all possible changes are desirable" (Clear et al., xiv).

Octavia Butler and Genre

Octavia Butler was born in 1947 in Pasadena, California. After earning an associate's degree from Pasadena City College in 1968, Butler enrolled at California State University, Los Angeles. She eventually left CalState and took writing classes through an extension program affiliated with UCLA. Through her enrollment in a series of writing workshops, Butler met fellow writers Harlan Ellison and Samuel L. Delaney, both of whom would become her mentors (Butler and others credit Delaney and Ellison for influencing much of her science fiction writing). At the time of her death in 2006, Butler had published several science fiction series: The *Parable* series, the *Patternist* series, and *Lillith's Brood* (also known as her *Xenogenesis* trilogy); she'd also written stand-alone novels such as *Kindred* and *Fledgling*, as well as many short stories, some of which were published in her collection *Bloodchild and Other Stories*.

Octavia Butler is now widely recognized as a science fiction writer, and as one of the few black science fiction writers publishing in English, "her work needs to be understood within the context of the traditions of the genre," a point Patricia Melzer makes in her book *Alien Constructions: Science Fiction and Feminist Thought* (43). *Seed to Harvest,* which is the focus of this chapter, is a work of science fiction and thus offers readers a unique lens through which to consider dysfunctional family dynamics. The books that make up the series present in vivid detail the cycle of violence, control, and exploitation that characterizes abusive families. Discussing Octavia Butler's fiction and its genre, however, means going beyond simply using the term science fiction to describe the many literary works Butler wrote over her prolific and decades-long career. Though Butler is best known for being a science fiction writer, her relationship with the genre bears some scrutiny.

Like Melzer, Gregory Jerome Hampton discusses Butler's work in the context of science fiction literature. In his book *Changing Bodies in the Fiction of Octavia Butler: Slaves, Aliens, and Vampires*, Hampton examines Butler's oeuvre and comes to the conclusion that there is a "distinct line between Butler's work and the traditional SF written by white males" (xx). Butler's fiction diverges from some traditional science fiction in both its scope—she remains actively invested in interrogating race, class, gender, sexuality, and difference, among other issues—and in its target audience. The stereotypical science fiction reader is, of course, a "predominantly heterosexual adolescent white male," and Butler's plots and protagonists, many of whom are "black, female, and bisexual," run the risk of alienating this type of reader (Hampton, xx). Butler herself seems keenly aware of how her treatment of race and sexuality differ from more traditional science fiction writers. Speaking about her interest in race, Butler at one point told the interviewer Rosalie G. Harrison that the "universe is either green or all white" in the typical science fiction novel (31). Unlike these more conventional science fiction writers, Butler presents a complex view of race in her *Patternist* series (as well as in so many of her other novels).

Truly, Butler is one of just a number of African American science fiction writers (others include Samuel Delaney, Steven Barnes, Charles Saunders, Virginia Hamilton, and Nalo Hopkinson) for whom matters of race and ethnicity figure prominently into their works. As Gregory Jerome Hampton emphasizes, "race matters a great deal in" Butler's fiction (Hampton, xiii). Butler, through her creative works, forces readers to directly confront race, ethnicity, and otherness. She does this, as Hampton suggests, by locating "highly visible (race, sex, of species) and non-visual (gender and sexuality) identities at the center of her text" and then makes readers "grapple with otherness as more than metaphor or allusion" (xx). This remains true in her *Seed to Harvest* series, where Butler presents readers with a constellation of concerns that gained recognition in the late 20th century; these include not only issues related to race, but also concerns such as domestic violence, gender issues, human rights issues, and the history of slavery.

In addition to moving beyond the usual concerns of science fiction, Butler also departs from tradition by blending elements of other literary genres into so many of her novels. As Patricia Melzer notes, there is "a strong interweaving of elements from different genres" in Butler's work, even though her fiction "is mostly categorized as science fiction" (39). For example, both *Wild Seed* (which is part of her *Patternist* series) and her 1976 novel, *Kindred*, "contain structures found in both the historical novel and the slave narrative, and stylistic elements of fantasy are present in *Wild Seed, Patternmaster,* and *Mind of My Mind*" (Melzer, 39). As Melzer points out, there are elements of the historical fiction, fantasy, and slave narrative genres in much of Butler's fiction. Her literary works, however, also show the influence of two other literary trends that became popular with black writers in the late 20th century: Afrofuturism and the neo-slave narrative genre.

Indeed, to understand Butler's messages, her fiction must be considered in the context of both Afrofuturism and the neo-slave narrative genre. Afrofuturism is an emergent literary and cultural aesthetics that combines elements of science fiction, historical fiction, Afrocentricity, fantasy, and magical realism with non–Western cosmologies in order both to critique present-day dilemmas and to reexamine and interrogate historical events of the past. Afrofuturism addresses themes and concerns of the African Diaspora through a technoculture (a term which refers to the interactions between, and politics of, technology and culture) and science fiction lens. Afrofuturism encompasses a range of mediums and artists who have a shared interest in envisioning black futures that stem from Afrodiasporic experiences.

A genre related to science fiction, the lens of Afrofuturism sheds light on concerns that interest Butler and emerge in her fiction, yet the publication of many of Butler's earlier novels also coincides with the emergence and the popularity of yet another literary genre: the neo-slave narrative. Many of Butler's literary works address slavery. *Seed to Harvest* is one example, but other novels she's written also provide extensive examinations of slavery, including *Kindred*. Not only do these literary works contain overlapping themes, but both *Seed to Harvest* and *Kindred* share similarities in terms of the generic conventions that Butler employs in each since each borrows elements from the neo-slave narrative genre. Written by contemporary authors, neo-slave narratives are modern fictional works set in the slavery era that are primarily concerned with depicting the experience or the effects of enslavement in the New World. In the case of *Kindred*, Butler (using the mechanism of time travel) has her protagonist Dana travel back and forth between 1970s California and antebellum Maryland to probe her own history, as well as to confront the realities of life under plantation slavery. In *Seed to Harvest,* Butler offers a broad view of life under the conditions of slavery by tracing Anyanwu's centuries-long existence, starting from her point of origin in West Africa, moving across the Atlantic Ocean and, thus, re-creating the transatlantic slave voyage, settling down temporarily in New England, moving on to Louisiana, and finally settling in California. Thus, through Anyanwu, Butler presents the story of an extraordinary African woman whose travel replicates and re-creates the journey that so many others of African descent made centuries ago.

There are political implications associated with writing a neo-slave narrative, and Ashraf Rushdy discusses many of these in his book *Neo-Slave Narratives: Studies in the Social Logic of a Literary Form,* where he also probes the popularity of the genre. He claims that the literary form of the neo-slave narrative is unique because it employs contemporary techniques to experience history and thus offers incisive commentaries both on the nature of the past and on the present. He argues that while the neo-slave narrative is concerned with the past, its implications reside in the present as well as with the future. Rushdy considers questions such as these:

> What is the meaning of the particular aesthetic choices made by authors who were mediating between a nineteenth-century Ur-textual form and a late twentieth-century period of textual and formal play in American writing? Finally, we must ask, what is the political significance of this body of American fiction? What are we to make of this novel development in American culture at the end of the twentieth century? [87].

Rushdy's concerns remain relevant when analyzing Butler's fiction, especially her books that confront the legacy of slavery (such as *Kindred* and the novels that make up her *Patternist* series). Rushdy's questions about the neo-slave narrative genre highlight the aesthetic choices Butler makes in *Seed to Harvest,* and they, in particular, draw attention to her depiction of Anyanwu, since through this character Butler presents an extraordinary African woman whose myriad life experiences carry her from West Africa, across the Atlantic Ocean, and to the New World.

With respect her protagonist Anyanwu, Butler's concerns in *Seed to Harvest,* in fact, coincide with themes common to both neo-slave narratives and dystopian narratives. As Maria Varsam emphasizes in her essay "Concrete Dystopia: Slavery and Its Others," there are many themes developed in neo-slave narratives and in dystopian narratives, but "a common thread unites them: a conspicuous preoccupation with obtaining freedom" (204). Varsam argues that this is especially true with female-authored texts (like Butler's) since this preoccupation so frequently "centers on issues of reproductive freedom, sexuality, and the control over one's body" (204). Tellingly, these are all issues that Anyanwu confronts. Since Anyanwu is (virtually) enslaved by her lover-turned-captor/master Doro (who tells her where to live and with whom to breed, among other things), she wrestles with freedom in the same sense that so many enslaved women did, yet Butler's depiction of Anyanwu's captivity remains more complicated than in a traditional captivity narrative, in part because of Anyanwu's special abilities (her abilities to shape-shift and to heal herself and others) and in part because Doro also fulfills the role of her romantic partner.

Though opinions vary about how best to classify Butler's fiction, what becomes clear is that there are traits to her writing that recur again and again, such as her continued focus on kinship relations, her repeated exploration of the themes of power versus subordination and captivity versus freedom, and her continued focus on issues of race. These elements make Butler's fiction very timely. Butler wrote the books that make up *Seed to Harvest,* as well as many of her novels (*Kindred,* for example), in direct response to a confluence of events that were occurring in the late 20th century including various human rights movements (such as the Civil Rights movement and the Women's Rights movement), the emergence of late capitalism, and a host of global conflicts and catastrophes. Significantly, the initial publication of the books that make up *Seed to Harvest* also coincided with a heightened awareness of the issue of domestic abuse. These myriad concerns are all reflected throughout *Seed to Harvest.*

It is no accident, nor is it mere coincidence, that Butler addresses both slavery and domestic violence in her *Seed to Harvest* series, for there is a clear relationship between the two. A handful of contemporary scholars, Kai Erickson and Ron Eyerman being two such examples, have suggested a link between slavery and domestic abuse that derives from the legacy of slavery's abuses such as the sexual commodification and victimization of women of African descent. These scholars argue that there is a pattern which originated during slavery times that gets reproduced in abusive relationships between black men and women in the middle of the 20th century. Discussing this phenomenon, Erikson contends that slavery represented a collective (or communal) trauma for African Americans. It is a communal trauma, he claims, because the result was not just a community composed of individual trauma sufferers, but a community whose very nature was transformed as a consequence of the traumatic event (slavery). In such instances, "traumatic experiences work their way so thoroughly into the grain of the affected community that they come to supply its prevailing mood and temper, dominate its imagery and its sense of self" and, consequently, dictate the way its members "relate to one another" (Erikson, 190).

In his book *Cultural Trauma: Slavery and the Formation of African American Identity,* Eyerman builds upon this notion of communal trauma. There, he examines the ways that slavery continues to structure the experiences of African Americans in the 20th century. Eyerman extends the definition of collective trauma even further by describing how it can get passed down from one generation to the next. He understands the trauma of slavery to be incorporated into the collective memory of the African American community to the degree that individuals traumatized by its effects need not have experienced the traumatic events themselves in order to suffer. In lieu of direct experience, Eyerman suggests that subsequent representations of the traumatic past (slavery's myriad abuses) preserve it as a part of the collective memory. A closer examination of the novels that comprise *Seed to Harvest* will highlight the relationship between slavery and domestic abuse, as well as reveal the series' other timely concerns.

Wild Seed and *Mind of My Mind*

The first two books of Octavia Butler's *Patternist* series, *Wild Seed* and *Mind of My Mind,* focus on the troubling romantic relationship between two supernatural beings, Doro and Anyanwu. Published in 1980, *Wild Seed* is the fourth book Butler wrote in her *Patternist* series, but it is the earliest book in the chronology of the *Patternist* world. In *Simians, Cyborgs, and Women: The Reinvention of Nature,* Donna Haraway describes *Wild Seed* as the story of an "African Sorceress [Anyanwu] pitting her powers of transformation against the genetic manipulations of her rival" (179). To an extent, that is what the novel is about—indeed, many characters in the novel believe Anyanwu to be a witch, and she reveals that she has been tested for "witchcraft" several times over the course of her life—but the novel, however, also recounts the early years and evolving nature of Anyanwu's centuries-long romantic relationship with a fellow supernatural being (Butler, 7). Anyanwu's rival and love interest are, indeed, one and the same: Doro.

Wild Seed is in many ways the key to the rest of the *Patternist* series because the novel shows how everything began between Doro and Anyanwu, and without the two of them, the series of events needed to create "the Pattern" could never have taken place. As Gregory Jerome Hampton and Wanda M. Brooks point out in their article "Octavia Butler and Virginia Hamilton: Black Women Writers and Science Fiction," the "book of genesis for the *Patternmaster* series is *Wild Seed*" (72). They explain how, "much like the biblical Book of Genesis, *Wild Seed* is the beginning of a creation story and the introduction of a patriarch and matriarch, Doro and Anyanwu" (Hampton and Brooks, 72). Both Doro and Anyanwu are powerful beings who possess supernatural abilities, and together they become the progenitors of a new race of beings.

Doro is an immortal character who is able to remain alive by jumping from one body to another. His ability to transfer his consciousness from one body to the next gives him the potential to live forever, but his constant need for new bodies compels him to kill. Over time, Doro becomes desensitized to the death of human beings, yet he longs for companionship. Spurred by this longing, Doro eventually dreams up an elaborate breeding program. His hope is to create beings with powers similar to his own. He sees this dream becoming a real possibility when he encounters Anyanwu, a shape-shifter living in West Africa. She has the ability to transform herself into other human beings as well as to turn into different animals. She also is a powerful healer who has a good understanding of how the human body works, so she, like Doro, has the potential to live forever.

Butler portrays Anyanwu as very different from other women living in tribal Africa, as Butler's account of her from early in the novel suggests. Rather than conforming to the traditional gender roles of her time, Anyanwu is described in the novel as a "priestess who spoke with the voice of god and was feared and obeyed" (Butler, 9). As Kameelah L. Martin points out in her book *Conjuring Moments in African American Literature: Women, Spirit Work, and Other Such Hoodoo*, the (human) men Anyanwu encounters are no match for her because she "consciously uses her spiritual knowledge and shape-shifting abilities to humble men who demand too much of her body" (87). Yet, when Anyanwu encounters Doro, she finds him to be much more powerful than any human man—and stronger than even she could imagine. Doro sees Anyanwu's potential and decides that he needs to bring her to one of his colonies in the New World with the hope that, through his elaborate breeding plan, she will be able to pass on her many abilities and/or combine her gifts with other powers. Anyanwu is resistant to Doro, and throughout the novel the two are at odds trying to reconcile that they will both be alive forever as long as Doro does not take her body. Thus, their relationship and their rivalry remain the focus of *Wild Seed*.

Wild Seed is divided into three books (or sections): "Covenant: 1690," which contains the first six chapters of the novel; "Lot's Children: 1741," which includes chapters seven through ten; and "Canaan: 1840," which includes chapters eleven through fourteen, as well as the novel's Epilogue. The structuring and organization of the novel prove significant in part because of the biblical allusions and parallels that are set up in each. Some critics have picked up on these allusions and addressed their importance. For example, in his essay "Octavia Butler Writes the Bible," John R. Pfeiffer discusses Butler's choice of section titles, as well as her use of biblical analogues in the novel's three books. He argues that the novel's first book, "Covenant," substitutes "the Doro/Anyanwu relationship for the God/ Abraham relationship of Genesis" (Pfeiffer, 144). Pfeiffer suggests the second book, "Lot's Children," brings to mind the story of Lot's daughters at the same time as it highlights the incest theme of the section, and he further argues that while the Louisiana plantation setting in "Canaan" (the third book of the novel) is not a "promised land," it nonetheless "encourages the hope of one" (144). Hampton, who also discusses Butler's use of biblical allusions, goes as far as to suggest that her employment of religion and religious themes "makes her fiction both accessible and plausible as a source of social commentary" (85). The biblical allusions suggested by the sections' titles are one reason it's important to scrutinize Butler's choice of how to structure the novel, but *Wild Seed*'s organizational structure also merits discussion because of how each book within the novel shows a different aspect of the evolving relationship between Doro and Anyanwu—and since each section clearly correlates with a different geographical setting (settings that are all important to African American history).

Doro first encounters Anyanwu in 1690 in West Africa in "Covenant," the first book of *Wild Seed,* as he is searching for "what was left of his seed villages" (Butler, 5). Anyanwu becomes alerted to Doro even before they meet since she can sense someone watching her as she attends to her garden, but since she's accustomed to being around mortals, who pose no real threat to her, she mistakenly believes that whoever is watching her is harmless, and she continues to work. Doro, however, is far from harmless, and he immediately takes an interest in Anyanwu, an extraordinary woman whom he correctly guesses to be "about three hundred years old" (Butler, 11). He reveals the truth about his own existence to Anyanwu by confessing that he has achieved something akin to immortality through his power to "kill a man and wear his body like a cloth" (Butler, 13). After disclosing his true nature to Anyanwu, Doro insists that she similarly make known her own special abilities. When Anyanwu hesitates, Doro "gently and effectively" threatens the lives of her sons (Butler, 13). Prompted by this threat, she tells him about her ability to transform not only into other humans, but also into "animal shapes" when necessary (Butler, 16). She also demonstrates her extreme physical strength and reveals how she is able to heal herself, birth extraordinarily healthy children, and even father children when she has taken a male form. When Doro learns what she can do, he becomes convinced that he wants Anyanwu with him. Through coercion—he repeatedly threatens her life as well as the lives of her many children—and through the promise of giving her children like herself who will never have to die, Doro succeeds in enticing her "away from this place" (Butler, 18). Though Anyanwu is hesitant to go with Doro, she eventually leaves everything behind with the assurance that her family will be left alone and safe, and they travel together to the coast of West Africa.

Once there, they board a ship sailing for the New World. During their voyage across the Atlantic, they each learn more about the others' abilities. After seeing first-hand what she can do, Doro worries that he has underestimated Anyanwu, who he fears could successfully escape him by taking animal form. He also believes she may have "too much power" and, despite his fascination with her, "his first inclination" is to kill her (Butler, 83). Though he fears her power, Doro feels it would be a shame and a waste to dispose of Anyanwu, so he decides, instead, to "teach her, instruct her quickly and begin using her at once" as a breeder to bring to fruition his elaborate scheme for creating a master race (Butler, 85). He freely admits that he plans to make Anyanwu "fear him and bend herself to his will," as well as to "use her children, present and future," to forward his designs (85). At this point, Anyanwu is afraid of Doro, but she does not fully comprehend what his intentions toward her are. Despite her fears, Anyanwu remains attracted to Doro and comes to see him as her husband, as the following passage makes clear:

> She considered Doro her husband now. No ceremony had taken place, but none was necessary. She was not a young girl passing from the hands of her father to those of her first husband. It was enough that she and Doro had chosen each other [Butler, 87].

The attraction between the two of them is clearly mutual. Butler at one point reveals how much Doro "liked to touch" Anyanwu, and she describes, as well, how, Anyanwu also "enjoyed his touches," even "when she thought they were more imprisoning than caressing" (89).

Their relationship is further complicated as their power struggles continue. When Anyanwu begins to learn the true nature of Doro's plan, she offers a degree of resistance to him by, among other ways, refusing at first to cooperate with his plans to use her as a breeder: "Within her body, she killed his seed" because she wanted to "avoid being used" (Butler, 121–122). As Martin glosses it, this passage reveals how Anyanwu "aborts the child she and Doro, her captor, conceive," once she learns about his plans (87). By revealing details such as these, Butler presents a rather complicated view of Doro and Anyanwu's budding relationship. The two clearly have romantic and sexual feelings for each other, but Doro's plan to manipulate Anyanwu for his own designs is ever present and an essential part of the reason he is with her. Moreover, the fact that Doro will stop at nothing to control Anyanwu remains abundantly clear by his treatment of her, as well as by the insights into his mind that Butler provides. These scenes also show, however, the seeds of Anyanwu's resistance, which prove important later in the novel.

In the first section of *Wild Seed,* the focus remains on Doro and Anyanwu's initial meeting and the early part of their relationship. To an extent, this time they spend together in Africa and on the ship can be characterized as a "honeymoon period," because Butler presents Doro as wooing Anyanwu, whom he's clearly attracted to (both because of her beauty and because of her potential to him as a breeder). This period, however, also gives Doro an opportunity to establish control over her by feeling out her abilities and her weaknesses. Thus, in this respect, this part of the novel shows the pattern of coercion and control that comes to define the relationship between Doro and Anyanwu (as well as so many abusive relationships). Indeed, by the end of "Covenant," Doro seems to be very much in control. By the time the ship they were sailing on has landed in America, Doro has convinced the reluctant Anyanwu to sleep with his son, Isaac, who has his own brand of abilities. Doro wants the two of them to breed, and he has forced Anyanwu to cooperate, even though she at first thought it wrong for her to be with Isaac. Isaac, considered by Doro to be his favorite child because of the strength of his ability, is a very powerful telekinetic. He demonstrates his power in the novel by flying, directing his father's ship through a storm with his mind, and easily killing characters throughout the novel. Isaac grows to be quite fond of Anyanwu and wishes to be with her (a desire that aligns itself with his father's plan to breed the two in hopes of creating a powerful line of special children).

The next section of *Wild Seed,* entitled "Lot's Children: 1741," takes place in New England, primarily in the community of Wheatley, where Doro has created a settlement for his people. Anyanwu has abilities of her own, but her existence during this time is tantamount to the life of a slave, for the powerful and manipulative Doro has taken such control over her that her own desires have been almost completely overshadowed by his. Though Anyanwu's special gifts (that is, her abilities to shape-shift and heal herself and others) function as part of her power, they paradoxically are also what define her reproductive slave status under the "ownership" of Doro. In other words, her abilities mark her eligibility for enslavement. During their time in Wheatley, Doro makes many decisions for Anyanwu, telling her how to spend her time, what kind of work to do, and with whom to breed. In this respect, Doro is very much like a slave master. He forces Anyanwu to bend herself to his plans, regardless of her feelings, a practice reminiscent of life under the conditions of plantation slavery. As Maria Varsam points out in her essay, "Concrete Dystopia: Slavery and Its Others," the roles that women were assigned in slavery "adhere to strict sexual functions that benefited the masters without regard for the women's own desires" (213). This is precisely the predicament that Anyanwu finds herself in.

Doro also resembles a slave master by his selective breeding program. He only breeds individuals who are exceptional. When people are no longer of use to him, he kills them because his main focus is to breed a race of people who have supernatural abilities. Indeed, Anyanwu realizes that Doro may dispose of her, too, once he has used her for his purposes. By using others in this manner, Doro takes the humanity away from "his" people (the people he breeds), which was another significant component of slavery.

Because *Wild Seed* is about slavery among other concerns, it is an example of a black science fiction novel that simultaneously reflects on African Americans' past at the same time as the novel remains concerned with the present. Butler (though clearly also invested in commenting on life in the 20th century) includes many parallels to slavery as part of her political message. Her inclusion of practices common to slavery and her creation of Anyanwu constitute deliberate attempts on her part to call attention to the institution of slavery and, in particular, the specific dilemmas female slaves faced. In preparing to write her own works of fiction, Butler read and relied upon many well-known accounts of the history of the slave trade and the Middle Passage. She also reportedly read such works as Iris Andreskis' *Old Wives Tales: Life Stories from Ibibioland* (1970),

George Basden's *Niger Ibos: A Description of the Primitive Life* (1966), and Sylvia Leith-Ross' *African Women: A Study of the Ibo of Nigeria* (1965) in order to make her characterization of Anyanwu more authentic. The combined effect is that, through Anyanwu, Butler makes visible much of the suffering intrinsic to life under the conditions of bondage. At the same time, through the character of Anyanwu and her volatile relationship with her lover-captor Doro, Butler reveals the pattern of coercion and control so common to abusive romantic relationships.

When Anyanwu finally decides to flee from Doro, she brings to mind both an escaping slave and a battered woman who's had enough abuse at the hands of her partner. Realizing that life with Doro means life under his tyrannous rule, Anyanwu devises a plan to leave and, indeed, this section of the novel ends with Anyanwu escaping Wheatley and Doro's clutches. Finally fed up with being used, Anyanwu uses her shape-shifting abilities to transform into a dolphin, and she swims away. As she leaves him, she thinks, "If Doro had not found her an adequate mate, he would find her an adequate adversary. He would not enslave her again. And she would never be his prey" (Butler, 181).

The third book of *Wild Seed,* entitled "Canaan: 1840," is set in Louisiana. Anyanwu, who has escaped Doro for the time being, establishes a small agricultural community near New Orleans and lives in relative harmony with her surroundings there. Through her ability to shape-shift— and her recent practice of disguising herself as a white plantation owner—she has evaded Doro for some time, but Doro eventually finds her. He manages to insinuate himself back into her life, taking control over her community and using Anyanwu's people for his own designs. Doro has not changed at all, for he kills at will and even goes as far as to kill a woman named Susan—one of Anyanwu's favorites (Doro knows how much Anyanwu "liked" Susan)—simply because she was the "kind of kill he needed" (Butler, 241). Thus, Doro (who is as ruthless as ever) quickly falls back into his old pattern of attempting to control Anyanwu and use her as he wishes, all the while disregarding her feelings or what's important to her.

Doro's character plays an important role here (and elsewhere in the novel) because of his ability to attain almost total control over all of the other characters. His gift (and curse) of being able to take on the body of anyone he desires gives him great power, but it also gives others a real reason to fear him. Another reason that Doro has so much control is because he is manipulative. Though Anyanwu is physically strong enough to resist

Doro, there are times where she does not retaliate against his physical abuse. In the case of Anyanwu, Doro's ability to regain control of her is bound up with his knowledge of her weaknesses as well his own ruthlessness (since he'll do whatever it takes to hold onto his power). As Hampton summarizes it, "through his usual threats on the lives of Anyanwu's children Doro managed to take over her settlement" in Louisiana (Hampton, 39). Doro's callousness grows to be too much for Anyanwu, and she falls into despair in the face of his cruel actions, which she sees as having little or no justification: "You kill your best servants, people who obey you even when it means suffering for them" (Butler, 250). She worries that killing gives Doro "too much pleasure," and she tells him that she can no longer ignore what he's been doing (Butler, 250).

Though Anyanwu realizes her power is ultimately no match for Doro's, she reveals to him that she has found a way to escape him for good: by bringing about her own death. Her knowledge of her body has grown so sophisticated that she has learned that she can will herself to die. Her understanding of Doro has also grown, and though she realizes that she cannot defeat him, she warns him that he, despite all his power, will one day meet his match. "You are not infallible," she tells him, and someday someone "will find a way to rid the world of you" (Butler, 251). Though Doro is "furious" with Anyanwu, the prospect of her dying is too much for him to bear. He realizes that he loves and needs her so much that "he could not leave or kill" her, and when he fears that she will kill herself, he begs her not to leave him (Butler, 251). Thus ends "Canaan."

Butler explains in the Epilogue to *Wild Seed* the terms of their now-changed relationship.

> He did not command her any longer. She was no longer one of his breeders, nor even one of his people in the old proprietary way. He could ask her cooperation, her help, but he could no longer coerce her into giving it. There would be no more threats against her children [Butler, 252].

Yet, in spite of these concessions, and though Doro could "no longer have all that he had once considered his right," Anyanwu has not fully prevailed over him (Butler, 252). She "could not have all she wanted" either, a point Butler emphasizes (252). Nonetheless, the terms of their relationship have been redefined, which Christopher N. Okonkwo highlights in his book *A Spirit of Dialogue: Incarnations of Ogbanje, the Born-to-Die, in African American Literature*: "*Wild Seed* ends on that note of gendered triumph and delicate truce" (81).

By concluding *Wild Seed* with a tentative agreement between Doro and Anyanwu, Butler remains rather ambivalent in her treatment of these two characters and their interpersonal struggles, which have been the focus of this novel. Doro has—finally—made some concessions and seems to have let go of a degree of the control he's long wished to exert over Anyanwu and, for her part, Anyanwu has regained a degree of the agency she lost to the powerful and manipulative Doro, yet the very nature of their agreement reveals it to be far from a win-win scenario for these two. The fact that their problems are not fully resolved both sets the stage for *Mind of My Mind* (the next book in the series) and anticipates the conflicts to come. Yet, the unresolved nature of *Wild Seed* also points to the fact that, even when Butler was writing these books in the late 20th century, the legacy of slavery persists, creating very real problems for its (actual and figurative) descendants.

Thus, Butler uses *Wild Seed* to display the emotional and psychological consequences of slavery through Anyanwu's conflicts with Doro. Butler also shows the possibilities of slave agency in Anyanwu's resistance to Doro's control. Therefore, in this respect, Anyanwu and Doro's relationship displays the dynamics of power versus subordination and captivity versus freedom. Yet, in exploring the dynamics and psychological effects of power and enslavement, Butler also reveals patterns of control so common to abusive families. The genre of science fiction—because it permits (oftentimes fantastic) scenarios that just wouldn't be plausible in more realistic works of fiction—allows Butler to comment on both past and present dilemmas through her exploration of the centuries-long relationship between Doro and Anyanwu.

Mind of My Mind (1977) was written prior to *Wild Seed,* but it is considered the second book in the *Patternist* series. This novel picks up where Butler left off in *Wild Seed* by continuing to showcase the problematic relationship between Doro and Anyanwu. There is much overlap between the two novels, for, as Okonkwo observes, "Butler links *Mind of my Mind* and *Wild Seed* through flashbacks, allusions, and other intertextual transitions" (82). *Mind of My Mind,* however, also introduces many never before seen characters and a new conflict: the struggle between Doro and Mary. Mary, a product of Doro's breeding program (and his descendent), has become both his lover and his protégé, but she will ultimately test his power. Meanwhile, Anyanwu has taken another name and set up residence in a new home. Anyanwu, who now goes by the name Emma, relocated "to pre-modern southern California to escape the impending America Civil War," and has lived there since (Okonkwo, 81).

Told from the point of view of Mary and an omniscient narrator, *Mind of My Mind* takes place in California. In this novel, Doro remains intent on creating a race of beings like him to possibly take over the world. His plans have developed much further than when we saw him last (at the end of *Wild Seed*), and, after much risky experimentation, through his breeding program Doro has created some very promising individuals. He fathered a child with a prostitute named Rina, and she, in turn, gives birth to Mary, who will become his lover, protégé, and (eventual) rival. Compared to the many other children being born to Doro and other "latents" (Butler uses the term "latent" to refer to a being with potential abilities), Mary displays a unique ability, which may even surpass Doro's.

Anyanwu/Emma still plays an important role in the novel. As Doro's power grows, he becomes even more ruthless, but because of his long-term relationship with Anyanwu, he will talk—and listen—to her in a way that he won't with anyone else. Even though "their relationship is tense and conflicted," she is "the only person who has any influence over" Doro (Melzer, 230). Also, she remains central to many of the events of this novel because she houses, mentors, and heals a number of the latents, as well as some "actives" (Butler uses the term "active" to refer to an individual who has already gone through the transformation and knows his or her power). A large number of Doro's latent talents do not survive the transition—the period when they transform and come into their abilities—when their minds become "active" and they can control the (oftentimes agonizing) input they routinely pick up. Many of his actives become uncontrollably violent. Anyanwu/Emma, due to her own special abilities and because of the wisdom she's gleaned over her very long life, has a special knack for helping these individuals. Doro has maintained a relationship with her, and he has no qualms about using his power over her to task her with these duties. At one point, he tells her that "even though you don't want it," it's clear that "you need this project" (Butler, 269).

Though Doro continues to use Anyanwu/Emma and her abilities to help transition and protect some of "his" people, his relationship with Mary becomes an important component of *Mind of My Mind*. What complicates Doro's relationship with Mary—and what further paints Butler's depiction of the family in a rather sinister light—is that he has remained a father figure to Mary, but he's also engaged in a sexual relationship with her. Just as troubling—and reminiscent of his dealings with Anyanwu—Doro's interactions with Mary quite often turn violent. Falling back into the pattern of coercion and control that for centuries characterized his relationship with Anyanwu/Emma, Doro physically abuses Mary and manipulates her to bend her to his will. His beatings of Mary are severe. At one point, Mary discloses freely that she "knew from personal experience how bad Doro's beatings could be" (Butler, 353). She further admits that the memory of the severity of his violent assaults on her remain fresh in her mind, even though she hadn't suffered one "for a few years" (Butler, 353). Not only does her relationship with Doro follow this familiar pattern, but Mary also physically resembles Anyanwu/Emma and reminds Doro of her. The combined effect of this is that much of the original conflict between Doro and Anyanwu/Emma gets re-created through Doro's complicated (and incestuous) relationship with Mary.

When Doro finds out just how powerful Mary is, he decides that she must be destroyed (thereby echoing the response he had to Anyanwu so many years ago when he learned the truth about her abilities). By this point in the novel, however, Mary has formed her own community of what she has started to call "Patternists," other beings with special abilities with whom she can communicate (there are over 1500 of them at this point). Through her telepathic abilities, Mary has formed a "pattern" that enables her to regenerate the castoffs of Doro's breeding program. In addition to communicating with them, she can also can draw on their abilities and use them to her own advantage. When six of Doro's most promising "actives" side with Mary, Doro feels provoked and realizes that his power is slipping away.

Doro, feeling usurped from his position as the lead person in control, and finally confronted with the realization that he can no longer control Mary, casts a declaration of war against her. As justification for taking her on, Doro remarks, "I can't afford her unless she can obey me" (Butler, 442). The epic battle between Mary and Doro appears at the end of the book. Though "Doro fought desperately," it was useless (Butler, 451). In the end, all that he can sense is that he's dying. He notes "Mary's amusement" as she "consumed him slowly, drinking in his terror and his life" (Butler, 451). *Mind of My Mind* thus ends with Doro dying at the hands of Mary. Mary then ascends to Patternmaster and sets into motion the world-altering events that will become the focus of the latter two novels of the series. In the Epilogue to *Mind of My Mind,* we learn that Anyanwu/Emma kills herself upon learning of Doro's death.

The ending of this novel, thus, proves to be rather ambivalent, especially in terms of how Butler resolves (or rather, fails to fully resolve) the family conflicts that have been her focus throughout. *Mind of My Mind* offers a degree of closure with respect to the centuries-long conflict between

Anyanwu (Emma) and Doro because the novel ends with both of them dying. On another level, though, so much remains unresolved about these characters and what each represents. Butler presents both of them as immensely powerful beings who take naturally to leadership roles in their communities, but other than these similarities, the two couldn't be more diametrically opposed. Anyanwu's power derives from her ability to heal; her desire to lead people is motivated by love and an inclination to protect and take care of others. Doro's power, in contrast, rests on his willingness to kill—and kill ruthlessly. He feeds off others, and his ability to survive for millennia remains contingent on his taking the lives of others through the bodies he inhabits and then discards (Doro even admits to being a "kind of parasite," thus acknowledging that his power rests on his ability to take lives). Unlike Anyanwu, whose motivations are, in comparison at least, rather benevolent, Doro wants to rule by fear. Through these two characters, Butler explores the consequences of each type of power. Through Anyanwu, she showcases the power of healing. Through Doro, she paints a picture of colonization, racism, and patriarchy as manifestations of dominating, fear-based power.

Anyanwu/Emma manages to outlive Doro, a man who for so long had kept her in thrall to his desires. Through her ability to transform, she has managed to survive even him, something he thought she wasn't capable of doing. Doro has underestimated Anyanwu (Emma), whom Suzanne Bost refers to as an "African heroine" (183). According to Bost, Anyanwu is the type of being who has the rare ability to "escape limiting identity cate-gories—including slave, black, and even human" and this makes her "the ultimate survivor" (183). Yet, though Anywanwu/Emma has managed to outlive Doro, she *chooses* to die. Thus, Butler presents a troubling picture of Anyanwu and what she represents. On the one hand, because Butler depicts her as a powerful and benevolent healer who values human life, she presents us with an alternate understanding of power. Yet, Anyanwu is in no way immune to the brutality of Doro's power, for not only does she live under his rule for centuries, but, when finally presented with her freedom, she chooses suicide over life without him. Anyanwu has come to feel that Doro is such a presence in her life that she cannot imagine life without him. In this respect (and others) Butler presents a rather complicated pic-ture of domestic violence and intimate abuse. Though she's finally "free," Anyanwu has for so long been oppressed by Doro that she continues to see her existence inextricably bound up with his. Sadly, without him around, she sees no reason to continue to live.

Butler also sends mixed messages about who prevails and who is defeated at the end of *Mind of My Mind*. Doro finally sees his breeding program come to its fruition, but the success of his program inevitably leads to his own death. As Hampton puts it, in *Mind of My Mind*, Doro is "made victim to his own creation" (Hampton, 43). Mary has done what no other before could do by defeating Doro and creating "the pattern," but there are violent repercussions to her actions. Those consequences make up much of the conflict of the latter books of the series.

Clay's Ark and Patternmaster

The first two books of the *Patternist* series, *Wild Seed* and *Mind of My Mind,* deal with the complicated relationship between Doro and Anyanwu, and these novels show Doro setting his selective breeding program into motion. Through these novels, Butler offers a retrospective glance of the myriad struggles of African Americans by her depiction of Anyanwu's journey from tribal Africa, across the Atlantic ocean (thus recreating the Middle Passage), to life under the conditions of plantation slavery in the United States, all the way through the American Civil Rights movement, and up to many of the issues that defined much of the late 20th century. By tracing Anyanwu's journey, Butler comments on both past and present problems that have afflicted, and continue to plague, African Americans. *Clay's Ark* and *Patternmaster,* rather than being set in the past and the present (like *Wild Seed* and *Mind of My Mind* are), are instead set in a fantastic future that Butler has created. This new world represents a restructuring of society and a reordering of family—with violent consequences for both. Though the frightening new world fashioned by Butler is clearly the product of a science fiction imagination, it brings to light provocative questions about the state of the family in the 20th century at the same time as it raises concerns about human rights and individual agency.

Mind of My Mind ends with Doro's plan finally coming to fruition, but ironically, seeing his schemes come to pass also means his own death. As Hampton sums it up, "Doro and Anyanwu eventually procreate a new race of people, but the arrival of the first true Patternist results in the destruction of both the mother and father" (Hampton, 43). The arrival of the Patternists ushers in a new era for humanity, and a violent new world is created as they rise to power. In this respect, the latter two books of the series pick up where Butler left off in *Mind of My Mind*. Both *Clay's Ark* and *Patternmaster* represent a point in time after the events in *Mind of My Mind* have played out (and a point in time when both Doro and Anyanwu/Emma have died), and consequently, these novels detail the alarming consequences of Doro and Anyanwu's union.

In *Clay's Ark*, however, Butler introduces a new conflict and many new characters so, in many ways, this novel departs from the story line that Butler began in *Wild Seed* and continued in *Mind of My Mind*. *Clay's Ark* centers on a colony of people who have been mutated by a disease that astronauts brought back to Earth from outer space. The group tries to prevent the disease from spreading by keeping their members isolated from outsiders. Thus, in *Clay's Ark* Butler presents her readers with the beginning of an extraterrestrial epidemic that has the potential to completely wipe out the human race. Though the characters and the conflict that forward the plot of *Clay's Ark*—as well as many of the novel's themes—differ from the previous books in the series, *Clay's Ark* nonetheless remains an important part of the series because it sets the stage for the conflict that will take place in *Patternmaster*, the last book of the series. As Hampton points out, "*Clay's Ark* is an essential component in understanding the relationship of the Patternist and the Clayark races" (55).

Clayarks are the descendants of the victims of an extraterrestrial disease; the Patternists consider them little more than animalistic mutants. Butler introduces them in the novel *Clay's Ark*, a book with a narrative that "presents vital information about the origin of the Clayarks, and begins to explain their conflict with the Patternists" (Hampton, 55). The conflict between these two groups is further explored in *Patternmaster*, where Clayarks make an appearance alongside the Patternists. In *Patternmaster*, Butler portrays a future in which regular humans are dominated by the networked telepaths, who are themselves ruled by the most powerful telepath, known as the Patternmaster. Thus, in addition to showing the conflicts between these two races of beings, the plot of *Patternmaster* also focuses on the aging of the current Patternmaster and the battle among the other powerful telepaths to see who will become his successor.

Considered to be the third book of the *Patternist* series, *Clay's Ark*, the last book of the series to appear in print, was published in 1984. A novel divided into two separate narratives—the "Past" and the "Present"— which eventually converge, *Clay's Ark* tells the story of a new species, the "Clayarks," a "race of beings who continued to push the boundaries of difference" (Hampton, 55). The novel begins when Eli, a geologist and astronaut, returns from a mission to the Alpha Centurion galaxy carrying an alien organism in his body. The organism has changed him at a molecular level: according to his genetic makeup, he is no longer human, but he's not completely inhuman, either. The disease changes Eli physically for, once infected, he becomes faster and stronger than before (his senses are keener now, too). The mutation affects him psychologically, as well, for he must fight an overwhelming compulsion to infect others with the alien life form. After Eli's ship crashes back on Earth, he comes upon a remote compound in the Arizona desert where a family lives isolated from the rest of society. The world Butler portrays here has become frighteningly dystopic; society is full of dangerous people who will fight and kill for resources that are becoming increasingly scarce. Eli has no choice but to infect the inhabitants of this small community. Several years later, a man and his twin daughters are traveling the highway through the desert when Eli's group, who are now all infected with the disease, kidnaps them to add to their growing community.

Through *Clay's Ark,* its characters (such as Eli, who takes center stage for so much of the novel), and the dilemmas they face, Butler highlights a constellation of concerns related to ethics, individual agency, and identity. She also raises thought-provoking questions such as, what does it mean to be human? Is there such a thing as human rights in a post-human world? These are questions that Eli and other characters must wrestle with as they transform into something not-quite-human. Speaking of *Clay's Ark,* Haraway explains that the characters must "struggle to maintain their own areas of choice and self-definition in the face of the disease they have become" (Haraway, 226). Because the mutation quite literally alters their genetic makeup, characters in *Clay's Ark* must struggle to come to terms with what they once were and what they have now become. In this sense, "Butler's constructions take place on a biological level that mediates human experiences through the body" (Melzer, 70). For Eli and the others who are infected, the human condition may no longer apply. Are they, then, to be held to the same standards that we hold ourselves to? Should human laws apply to them? What are their rights and responsibilities—to themselves and to others—now that they've transformed into Clayarks? Indeed, as Melzer points out, by "questioning the category 'human,' especially through mutation in *Clay's Ark,*" Butler "problematizes any pre-given notion we have about our identity and anything about it we might take for granted" (Melzer, 71). These concerns remain paramount throughout the novel—for readers and for the characters themselves.

At numerous points, Eli insists that though he and the others have changed, they nonetheless still have ethics. He similarly protests any characterization of the Clayarks as animals, despite the fact that a young Clayark child bears a striking resemblance to a "baby sphinx" (Butler, 545). Yet, at the same time, Eli concedes that they *have* changed on a fundamental level, admitting to his people, "We've lost part of our humanity" (Butler, 543). In light of their condition, he advises Lori, another character who's been infected and who is new to his community, that she must listen to her urge to infect others. "You need to infect a man and have children and you won't get any peace until you do," he tells her (Butler, 543). But, despite this admonition, he also cautions her, warning that they could "lose more" of their humanity if they forget what they carry and "what it needs" (Butler, 543). Thus, as these and numerous of the novel's other passages make clear, a central concern of *Clay's Ark* remains bound up with ontological questions (questions of being), such as: What makes us human? Are humans really biologically and socially different from the rest of the created world? Butler complicates these questions through her depiction of the Clayarks, for they share so many of the traits that supposedly distinguish us from other species (such as our self-awareness, our free moral agency, our speech and symbolic cognition, and our capacity to imagine, to name just a few).

In contrast to *Clay's Ark,* in *Patternmaster* (1976), the last book of the *Patternist* series, Butler's focus rests not so much on the individual but, instead, on how we interact with others as families and as a society. While *Patternmaster* was the first book Butler published, it is the last in the series' internal chronology. In this novel, Butler depicts a future in which humans are dominated by the descendants of Doro's breeding program. The products of his union with Anyanwu/Emma, networked telepaths control society (and regular humans, who are referred to in the novel as "Mutes"), but they themselves are governed by the Patternmaster, the most powerful among them. The novel begins in medias res with the current Patternmaster's reign coming to an end. The plot revolves around the impending battle among the other powerful telepaths to see who will become his successor. The descendants of the original Clayarks (who were the focus of Butler's novel *Clay's Ark*) make an appearance in this novel, as well. Like she does in *Wild Seed* and *Mind of My Mind,* in *Patternmaster* Butler combines her focus on family violence with contemporary concerns such as race, class, gender, and hierarchy.

Patternmaster is set in a hypothetical distant future. Humanity is divided into three groups: Patternists, those with telepathic abilities; Mutes, normal humans who do not have any special abilities; and Clayarks, genetic mutants, who were the focus of Butler's novel, *Clay's Ark*. Butler sets up the main conflict in the novel's Prologue, where she also introduces the theme of family violence. *Patternmaster* begins by introducing Rayal and Jansee (Rayal's sister and his lead wife), the two most powerful descendants of Doro and Anyanwu to date. In the Prologue, readers are presented with Rayal, the current Patternmaster of Butler's fantastic new world, and Jansee discussing how someday their children will fight and kill each other to take over the Pattern. While Jansee holds out hope that her sons might not face off to the death—"They wouldn't have to kill each other," she considers— Rayal knows that they will do all they can to obtain power (Butler, 628). He reminds Jansee that he himself had to "kill two brothers and a sister to get" to his position, and he harkens back about how powerful Patternists always feel compelled to fight for control of the pattern, even if it means killing one's siblings (Butler, 629). He also reminds her that he would have tried to kill her, too, had she not been "wise enough to ally herself" with him by becoming his "lead wife" (Butler, 629).

The reward for succeeding Rayal is great, for the Patternists' ability to communicate with—as well as to control—one another is tied to this pattern, and whoever controls this psychic link has domain over the other Patternists and their society. Shortly following this exchange between Rayal and Jansee, there is an assassination attempt on Rayal by the Clayarks: "The Clayarks chose that moment to end the year of peace" (Butler, 630). As a result of the attack, Jansee is killed. As Butler describes it, "Their aim was good and they were very lucky. The first shot smashed through the wall of the Patternmaster's private apartment, beheading the Patternmaster's lead wife" (Butler, 630). During this invasion, Rayal himself is mortally wounded and infected with the Clayarks' disease. The narrative then jumps forward approximately twenty years, and the story picks up with Rayal on his deathbed.

His son, Coransee, believes that he is next in line for Patternmaster when his father passes on. However, a conflict arises when he realizes that his brother, Teray, may also have the potential to control the Pattern. Coransee wants the position of Patternmaster and he will stop at nothing to get it. Through a trade with a fellow Patternist, Coransee acquires Teray as his servant (the role he forces his brother into is tantamount to that of a slave). Coransee keeps a close eye on Teray as he serves him in order to prevent him from usurping his power. When he sees how strong Teray is growing, however, he becomes concerned. Coransee decides to offer him freedom and his own house in exchange for his guarantee that he will never make an attempt for the control of the pattern. Teray, not trusting his brother (nor wanting to relinquish his chance for power) flees from Coransee's rule. The conflict between the two brothers remains the focus of the rest of the novel. Indeed, as Hampton summarizes it, in many ways *Patternmaster* is simply a "tale of two brothers seeking to hold the throne of their father, while a wiser and more powerful sister foregoes the claim to the throne in favor of motherhood and freedom" (Hampton, 60).

Patternmaster shares much in common with many of Butler's other novels. For example, like *Wild Seed, Mind of My Mind,* and *Clay's Ark, Patternmaster* features an epic power struggle and shows the difficulty of maintaining autonomy in the face of a powerful rival. In this sense, *Patternmaster* is another example of "Butler's narratives of survival," which pay "close attention to the process of negotiating identities with a powerful opponent" (Melzer, 54). *Patternmaster,* however, also functions as a means for Butler to raise awareness about contemporary problems such as family violence, at the same time as social practices that are common within the novel—such as the system of slavery and subordination that characterizes life for the Patternists—allow her to indict troubling historical practices, such as the institution of slavery and the practice of oppression and discrimination, all of which African Americans have been forced to confront over the centuries.

Butler's focus on the family remains paramount throughout this novel. Through the infighting, violence, and power struggles that define family life for the Patternists, Butler highlights the mechanisms at work in dysfunctional families. Families exist in the Patternist universe for many of the same reasons they exist in ours: for protection, companionship, and so that their members share with each other in order that each member can develop and thrive. A dysfunctional family, by its very nature, either fails to perform those tasks that fulfill the purpose of the family or only manages to perform them by using harmful or counterproductive methods. Such is the case in the Patternist society, where an atmosphere of fear and violence dominates in the home. The Patternist houses, which are intricate family groupings, ostensibly form and stay together for the mutual protection of their members who need to be defended against outsiders (meaning other Patternist families as well as the Clayarks, who prove to be a real threat to Patternists), but the nature of these families is intrinsically violent. Brothers kill brothers to hold onto power. Violence and coercion are the norm for Patternist families, despite any claim to the contrary. As Hampton emphasizes in his examination of *Patternmaster,* though the "children of Doro claim to advocate peace," it becomes clear that their words are meaningless because "familial murder permeate[s] their communities" (xix).

Yet, Butler's attention to dysfunctional family dynamics in this novel does far more than simply indict the nuclear family for, as Donna Haraway contends, the "reinvented families in the fiction of Afro-American SF writer Octavia Butler" serve as "tropes to guide us through the ravages of gender, class, imperialism, racism, and nuclear exterminist culture" that exists (Haraway, 121). Such is indeed the case in *Patternmaster,* where Butler also calls attention to the problems of racism and gender oppression—not to mention the hierarchal structures, which permit both to perpetuate.

Patternmaster confronts racism through the different species of beings. In many ways, the conflicts between the Patternists and the Clayarks, as well as the oppression of the Mutes (the normal humans who have no special abilities) by the more powerful groups serve as powerful metaphors for the race-based system of hierarchy that for so long defined American society. By contrasting these various groups of beings—and the relative power they hold in relation to one another—Butler makes a statement about social class and theories of power, as well.

In *Patternmaster,* Butler also raises awareness about gender oppression and, to a degree, challenges normative notions about gender (as well as gender roles) through her characters. Through characters such as Jansee, Butler highlights the precarious position of (even powerful) women, whose worth and place in society so often depends upon the men women ally themselves with. In Jansee's case, the fact that her role, not to mention her survival, remains inextricably linked to her connection with her brother (who, in this novel, is also her husband!) suggests the patriarchal context in which she must negotiate. Yet, through other female characters, such as the powerful healer Amber, "Butler challenges the seemingly inevitable social order built on sexual difference with her female protagonists who demand new structures," a point Melzer make in her discussion of the novel. As she notes, Amber diverges from the custom by rejecting "marriage, the legitimized form of being together in Patternist society" (Melzer, 84). Through characters such as Amber, Butler shows that there is another possibility for women than the fate Jansee succumbed to. Indeed, the creation of Amber is significant because Butler imagines a different fate for her and, as Margaret Atwood argues in her book *In Other Worlds: SF and the Human Imagination,* "if things can be imagined differently, they can be done differently" (103).

Through the characters, plot, and dilemmas that make up *Pattern-*

master, the last novel of the series, Butler continues her prolonged focus on dysfunctional family dynamics. She also showcases the constant tension between the family and society. Through the lens of science fiction literature, Butler presents a startling image of family violence and its dire consequences. It's significant that Butler presents these problems in this genre because science fiction offers a quality not found in realistic literature since only through science fiction literature can authors go beyond the boundaries of the known and the possible. Science fiction is indeed an invaluable tool for analyzing current problems and envisioning solutions to them.

A significant component of Octavia Butler's project in *Seed to Harvest* is raising awareness about family violence, and through the lens of science fiction, she confronts this timely and provocative issue. As Hampton emphasizes, bringing to light the dysfunction all too common in families is a big part of this series: "Throughout the *Patternist* series, Butler consistently suggests that the family structure of Doro's people of *Wild Seed* is volatile and subject to dysfunction" (Hampton, 102). At the same time, through the novels which make up the *Patternist* series, Butler continues her exploration of themes such as power versus subordination and captivity versus freedom, which are hallmarks of her oeuvre. The combined effect is that, through *Seed to Harvest,* Butler portrays a richly rendered universe which makes us rethink our own world—and the myriad problems we face still today.

Conclusion

Domestic violence has long been a hidden problem—and this is particularly the case in the African American community—but in recent decades a number of black female novelists have begun to weigh in on the issue of domestic abuse. Their novels not only raise awareness about the issue of domestic abuse, but they also open up a space for more public discussion of the issue of domestic abuse to take place. Ultimately, through their literary works, these authors give voice to silenced, oppressed, and abused women.

My goal in writing this book has been to show how African American female novelists portray domestic abuse and to illustrate how their diverse literary representations of domestic violence respond to a variety of cultural and historical forces. The assortment of 20th- and 21st-century novels discussed in this book—Zora Neale Hurston's *Their Eyes Were Watching God*, Gayl Jones' *Corregidora*, Alice Walker's *The Color Purple*, Gloria Naylor's *The Women of Brewster Place* and *Linden Hills*, Octavia Butler's *Seed to Harvest* series, Terry McMillan's *Mama* and *A Day Late and a Dollar Short*, and Toni Morrison's *The Bluest Eye* and *Love*—all do this, and more. They also all reflect, question, and contribute to the ways in which contemporary American society shapes attitudes about, and responds to, the many problems related to domestic abuse.

In the various chapters of this book, I focused on an underexplored dynamic: the relationship between the abuse of individual women and the larger structure of women's oppression. I also examined the various novels in question as cases in point to show the cultural shift taking place in terms of how we, as a society, deal with (or, as is all too often the case, fail to deal with) the complicated problem of domestic abuse. In my chapter on Hurston's 1937 novel, *Their Eyes Were Watching God*, I highlighted the ways Hurston's treatment of domestic violence reflected an earlier era's misunderstanding of the problem at the same time as she showed how a female from that time period was ultimately able to regain her voice amidst those who tried to silence her. In my chapter on Toni Morrison's *The Bluest Eye* (1971), I argued that her characters kept hidden the violence that occurs within the home. I also examined how Morrison brought to light the degree to which society is to blame for the abuse suffered by so many victims of domestic violence.

In my chapter on *Corregidora,* by Gayl Jones, I focused on how Ursa Corregidora, the novel's protagonist, was forced to deal with the abuse she faced personally at the same time as she tried to come to terms with the legacy of abuse passed down to her by her ancestors. In my chapter on Alice Walker's *The Color Purple,* I called attention to how Walker depicts women's precarious position within a patriarchal context by the way she treated Celie's suffering under this system. Yet, Walker also uses her novel to send a hopeful message about survival in the midst of horrific circumstances since its protagonist, Celie—as well as other female characters like Shug and Sofia—endure and, in some situations, triumph, despite the oppression they suffer. My chapter on Gloria Naylor's *The Women of Brewster Place* (1982) and *Linden Hills* (1985) demonstrated the roles played by environment and setting in allowing, if not altogether encouraging, the abuse of women. I also highlighted how, as Naylor's two novels make clear, domestic abuse is an issue that cuts across lines of social class.

My chapter on Terry McMillan's *Mama* (1987) and *A Day Late and a Dollar Short* (2002) exposed the crucial role popular writers—such as McMillan—play in raising awareness about domestic abuse. In my chapter on Toni Morrison's *Love,* I discussed how Morrison uses this novel and the dilemmas faced by so many of its characters to show how far-reaching the effects of abuse can be. Finally, in my chapter on Octavia Butler's *Seed to Harvest* I explored how Butler's use of the science fiction genre—a genre that I argued can be used as a powerful tool for social criticism—allowed her to consider domestic abuse from a different angle than the ones afforded to more traditional genres.

Domestic violence is a significant, controversial, and timely issue, one well worth addressing. Examining how African American female writers depict domestic abuse is likewise important since the literary lens is—and has for some time been—a means through which to investigate the problem of domestic abuse. In the case of all of the authors discussed in this book, their treatment of domestic abuse has for too long remained an underexplored feature of their novels, which makes this project all the more worthwhile. Indeed, a facet of their fiction that deserves attention, their depictions of domestic abuse raise critical awareness of the issue at the same time as they not only reflect but respond to societal views about the too often ignored problem.

One problem that arises when discussing such a timely and provocative issue as domestic abuse is that, since the topic is still being hotly discussed and debated, our legal, psychological, and medical communities still don't know quite what to do about the problem. As a society, we remain similarly in flux in terms of our popular perceptions about the problem of violence in the home. Consequently, although I draw some conclusions about the function of these various literary representations of domestic abuse in this book—and though I illustrate many of the connections between the choices these particular writers make through their texts and broader social problems with real world consequences—in the end, this book may offer more questions than answers.

Part of the difficulty in making definitive pronouncements about family violence derives from the fact that, to date, the problem is one we simply do not have a answer for yet—and, indeed, it may be that there is no "one-size-fits-all" solution. It also stems from the fact that both I and the authors discussed throughout this project are reflecting and responding to problems that are oftentimes current ones. My hope is that my observations in this book will provide, then, a starting-off point which will allow further analysis to be done.

Works Cited

Allen, Anita. "Privacy." *A Companion to Feminist Philosophy*. Ed. Allison M. Jagger and Iris M. Young. Malden, MA: Blackwell, 1998. 456–465. Print.

Allen, Donia Elizabeth. "The Role of the Blues in Gayl Jones' *Corregidora*." *Callaloo* 25.1 (Winter 2002): 257–273. Print.

Althusser, Louis. "Ideology and Ideological State Apparatuses." *Literary Theory: An Anthology*, 2d ed. Ed. Julie Rivkin and Michael Ryan. Malden, MA: Blackwell, 2004. 693–702. Print.

Alwes, Karla. "'The Evil of Fulfillment': Women and Violence in *The Bluest Eye*." *Women and Violence in Literature: An Essay Collection*. Ed. Katherine Anne Ackley. New York: Garland, 1990. 89–104. Print.

Ashford, Tomeiko R. "Gloria Naylor on Black Spirituality: An Interview." *MELUS: The Journal of the Society for the Study of the Multi-Ethnic Literature of the United States* 30.4 (Winter 2005): 73–87. Print.

Atwood, Margaret. *In Other Worlds: SF and the Human Imagination*. New York: Doubleday, 2011. Print.

Awkward, Michael. "Chronicling Everyday Travails and Triumphs." *Callaloo* 36 (Summer 1988): 649–650. Print.

Baldassarro, R. Wolfe. "Banned Books Awareness: *The Color Purple* by Alice Walker." 20 March 2011. *Banned Book Awareness and Reading for Knowledge*. 21 October 2013. Web.

Berg, Christine G. "'Light from a Hill of Carbon Paper Dolls': Gloria Naylor's *Linden Hills* and Dante's Inferno." *Modern Language Studies* 29.2 (Fall 1999): 1–19. Print.

Bobo, Jacqueline. "Sifting Through the Controversy: Reading *The Color Purple*." *Callaloo* 39 (Spring 1989): 332–342. Print.

Bost, Suzanne. *Mulattas and Mestizas: Representing Mixed Identities in the Americas, 1850–2000*. Athens: University of Georgia Press, 2010. Print.

Boulter, Amanda. "Polymorphous Futures: Octavia E. Butler's *Xenogenesis* Trilogy." *American Bodies: Cultural Histories of the Physique*. Ed. Tim Armstrong. New York: New York University Press, 1996. 170–185. Print.

Bouson, J. Brooks. *Quiet as It's Kept: Shame, Trauma, and Race in the Novels of Toni Morrison*. Albany: State University of New York Press, 2000. Print.

_____. "Uncovering 'the Beloved' in the Warring and Lawless Women in Toni Morrison's *Love*." *The Midwest Quarterly* 49.4 (Summer 2008): 358–373. Print.

Branzburg, Judith V. "Seven Women and a Wall: A Review of Gloria Naylor's *The Women of Brewster Place*." *Callaloo* 21 (Spring-Summer 1984): 116–119. Print.

Brown, Tony. *Tony Brown's Journal*. PBS, 6 April 1986. Web.

Buller, David J. *Adapting Minds: Evolu-

tionary Psychology and the Persistent Quest for Human Nature. Boston: Massachusetts Institute of Technology Press, 2005. Print.

Burrows, Stuart. "'You Heard Her, You Ain't Blind': Seeing What's Said in *Their Eyes Were Watching God." Novel: A Forum on Fiction* 34.3 (Summer 2001): 434–452. Print.

Butler, Judith. *Gender Trouble: Feminism and the Subversion of Identity.* New York: Routledge, 1990.

Butler, Octavia E. *Seed to Harvest.* New York: Warner, 2007. Print.

Cadman, Deborah. "When the Back Door Is Closed and the Front Yard Is Dangerous: The Space of Girlhood in Toni Morrison's Fiction." *The Girl: Constructions of the Girl in Contemporary Fiction by Women.* Ed. Ruth O. Saxton. New York: St. Martin's Press, 1998. 57–78. Print.

Carby, Hazel V. "The Politics of Fiction, Anthropology, and the Folk." *New Essays on Their Eyes Were Watching God.* Ed. Michael Awkward. Cambridge: Cambridge University Press, 1990. 71–93. Print.

Carrillo, Ricardo, and Jerry Tello, eds. *Family Violence and Men of Color: Healing the Wounded Male Spirit.* New York: Spring, 2008. Print.

Champion, Laurie, and Rhonda Austin, eds. *Contemporary American Women Fiction Writers: An A-to-Z Guide.* Westport, CT: Greenwood Press, 2002. Print.

Clear, Val, et al., eds. *Marriage and the Family through Science Fiction.* New York: St. Martin's Press, 1976. Print.

Conner, Marc C. *The Aesthetics of Toni Morrison: Speaking the Unspeakable.* Jackson: University Press of Mississippi, 2000.

Crabtree, Claire. "The Confluence of Folklore, Feminism and Black Self-Determination in Zora Neale Hurston's *Their Eyes Were Watching God." Southern Literary Journal* 17 (1985): 54–66. Print.

Curwood, Anastasia Carol. *Stormy Weather: Middle-Class African American Marriages Between the Two Wars.* Chapel Hill: University of North Carolina Press, 2010. Print.

Cutter, Martha J. "Philomela Speaks: Alice Walker's Revisioning of Rape Archetypes in *The Color Purple." MELUS: The Journal of the Society for the Study of the Multi-Ethnic Literature of the United States* 25.3–4 (Autumn-Winter 2000): 161–180. Print.

Dandridge, Rita B. "Debunking the Motherhood Myth in Terry McMillan's *Mama" CLA Journal* 41.4 (June 1998): 405–416. Print.

Daniels, Cynthia R., and Rachelle Brooks. *Feminists Negotiate the State: The Politics of Domestic Violence.* Lanham, MD: University Press of America, 1997. Print.

Davie, Sharon. "Free Mules, Talking Buzzards, and Cracked Plates: The Politics of Dislocation in *Their Eyes Were Watching God." PMLA* 108.3 (May 1993): 446–459. Print.

Davis, Angela Y. *Blues Legacies and Black Feminism: Gertrude "Ma" Rainey, Bessie Smith, and Billie Holliday.* New York: Random House, 1998. Print.

_____. *Women, Race, and Class.* New York: Random House, 1981. Print.

Delashmit, Margaret. "*The Bluest Eye:* An Indictment." *Griot: Official Journal of the Southern Conference on Afro-American Studies* 20.1 (Spring 2001): 12–18. Print.

Drake, Kimberly. "Rape and Resignation: Silencing the Victim in the Novels of Morrison and Wright." *LIT: Literature, Interpretation, Theory* 6.1–2 (April 1995): 63–72. Print.

Ellerby, Janet Mason. "Deposing the Man of the House: Terry McMillan Rewrites the Family." *MELUS: The Journal of the Society for the Study of the Multi-Ethnic Literature of the United States* 22.2 (Spring 1997): 105–117. Print.

Erikson, Kai. "Notes on Trauma and Community." *Trauma: Explorations in*

Memory. Ed. Cathy Caruth. Baltimore: Johns Hopkins University Press, 1995. 183–99. Print.

Eyerman, Ron. *Cultural Trauma: Slavery and the Formation of African American Identity*. New York: Cambridge University Press, 2001. Print.

Fiske, Shanyn. "Piecing the Patchwork Self: A Reading of Walker's *The Color Purple*." *Explicator* 66.3 (2008): 150–153. Print.

Floyd-Thomas, Stacey M., and Laura Gillman. "Subverting Forced Identities, Violent Acts, and the Narrativity of Race: A Diasporic Analysis of Black Women's Radical Subjectivity in Three Novel Acts." *Journal of Black Studies* 32.5 (May 2002): 528–556. Print.

Gates, Henry Louis, Jr. "Zora Neale Hurston: 'A Negro Way of Saying.'" Afterword. *Their Eyes Were Watching God*. New York: Perennial Classics, 1998. 195–205. Print.

_____. "Zora Neale Hurston and the Speakerly Text." *Southern Literature and Literary Theory*. Ed. Jefferson Humphries. Athens: University of Georgia Press, 1990. 142–169. Print.

Gillan, Jennifer. "Focusing on the Wrong Front: Historical Displacement, the Maginot Line, and *The Bluest Eye*." *African American Review* 36.2 (June 2002): 283–298. Print.

Gillespie, Carmen. *Critical Companion to Toni Morrison: A Literary Reference to Her Life and Work*. New York: Facts on File, 2008. Print.

Goldstein, Philip. "Richard Wright's *Native Son*: From Naturalist Protest to Modernist Liberation and Beyond." *New Directions in American Reception Study*. Ed. Philip Goldstein and James L. Machor. New York: Oxford University Press, 2008. 119–138. Print.

Gomez, Jewelle. "Naylor's Inferno: A Review of *Linden Hills*." *The Women's Review of Books* 2.11 (August 1985): 7–8. Print.

Grewal, Gurleen. "'Laundering the Head of Whitewash': Mimicry and Resist-

ance in *The Bluest Eye*." *Approaches to Teaching the Novels of Toni Morrison*. Ed. Nellie Y. McCay and Kathryn Earle. New York: MLA Press, 1997. 118–126. Print.

Griffiths, Jennifer. "Uncanny Spaces: Trauma, Cultural Memory, and the Female Body in Gayl Jones' *Corregidora* and Maxine Hong Kingston's *The Woman Warrior*." *Studies in the Novel* 38.3 (Fall 2006): 353–370. Print.

Hacking, Ian. "The Making and Molding of Child Abuse." *Critical Inquiry* 17.2 (Winter 1991): 253–288. Print.

Hallett, Jill. "New Voices in the Canon." *World Englishes: Problems, Properties, and Prospects: Selected Papers from the 13th IAWE Conference*. 2009. 415–432. Print.

Hampton, Gregory Jerome. *Changing Bodies in the Fiction of Octavia Butler: Slaves, Aliens, and Vampires*. Lanham, MD: Lexington, 2010. Print.

Hampton, Gregory Jerome, and Wanda M. Brooks. "Octavia Butler and Virginia Hamilton: Black Women Writers and Science Fiction." *The English Journal* 92.6 (July 2003): 70–74. Print.

Hampton, Robert, William Oliver, and Lucia Magarian. "Domestic Violence in the African American Community: An Analysis of Social and Structural Factors." *Violence Against Women* 9.5 (May 2003): 533–557. Print.

Haraway, Donna J. *Simians, Cyborgs, and Women: The Reinvention of Nature*. New York: Routledge, 1991.

Harrison, Elizabeth Jane. "Re-Visioning the Southern Land." *The History of Southern Women's Literature*. Baton Rouge: Louisiana State University Press, 2002. 290–295. Print.

Harrison, Rosalie G. "Sci-Fi Visions: An Interview with Octavia Butler." *Equal Forum*. November 1980: 30–34. Print.

Heath, Judith A., and David H. Ciscel. "Patriarchy, Family Structure and the Exploitation of Women's Labor." *Journal of Economic Issues* 22.3 (September 1998): 781–194. Print.

Works Cited

Hine, Darlene Clark. "Rape and the Inner Lives of Black Women in the Middle West." *Signs* 14.4 (Summer 1989): 912–920. Print.

Holloway, Karla F. C. "The Body Politic." *Subjects and Citizens: Nation, Race, and Gender from Oroonoko to Anita Hill.* Ed. Michael Moon and Cathy N. Davidson. Durham: Duke University Press, 1995. 481–496. Print.

Horvitz, Deborah M. *Literary Trauma: Sadism, Memory and Sexual Violence in American Women's Fiction.* Albany: State University of New York Press, 2000. Print.

_____. "'Sadism Demands a Story': Oedipus, Feminism, and Sexuality in Gayl Jones' *Corregidora* and Dorothy Allison's *Bastard out of Carolina.*" *Contemporary Literature* 39.2 (Summer 1998): 238–261. Print.

Hurston, Zora Neale. *Their Eyes Were Watching God.* New York: Perennial Classics, 1998. Print.

Jacobs, Naomi. "Posthuman Bodies and Agency in Octavia Butler's *Xenogenesis.*" *Dark Horizons: Science Fiction and the Dystopian Imagination.* London: Routledge, 2003. 91–111. Print.

James, Deborah. "Resistance, Rebirth, and Renewal in Zora Neale Hurston's *Their Eyes Were Watching God.*" *Bloom's Literary Themes: Rebirth and Renewal.* Ed. Harold Bloom. New York: Infobase, 2009. 229–238. Print.

Jasinski, Jana L., and Linda M. Williams, eds. *Partner Violence: A Comprehensive Review of 20 Years of Research.* Thousand Oaks, CA: Sage, 1998. Print.

Jones, Gayl. *Corregidora.* New York: Beacon, 1975. Print.

Jones, Jacqueline. "Fact and Fiction in Alice Walker's *The Color Purple.*" *The Georgia Historical Quarterly* 72.4 (Winter 1988): 653–669. Print.

Jones, Sharon Lynette. *Critical Companion to Zora Neale Hurston: A Literary Reference to Her Life.* New York: Facts on File, 2009. Print

Kinnear, Karen L. *Childhood Sexual Abuse: A Reference Handbook, Second Edition.* Santa Barbara: ABC-CLIO, 2007. Print.

Klotman, Phyllis. "Dick-and-Jane and the Shirley Temple Sensibility in *The Bluest Eye.*" *Black American Literature Forum* 13.4 (Winter 1979): 123–125. Print.

Langellier, K. M. "Voiceless Bodies, Bodiless Voices: The Future of Personal Narrative Performance." *The Future of Performance Studies: Visions and Revisions.* Ed. S.J. Dailey. Annandale, VA: National Communication Association, 2003. 207–213. Print.

Lew, Mike. *Victims No Longer: Men Recovering from Incest and Other Sexual Abuse.* New York: Nevraumont, 1988. Print.

Lewis, Catherine E. "Serving, Quilting, Knitting: Handicraft and Freedom in *The Color Purple* and *A Women's Story.*" *Literature Film Quarterly* 29.3 (January 2001): 236–245. Print.

Li, Stephanie. "Love and the Trauma of Resistance in Gayl Jones' *Corregidora.*" *Callaloo* 29.1 (Winter 2006): 131–150. Print.

MacKinnon, Catharine A. *Sexual Harassment of Working Women.* New Haven: Yale University Press, 1979. Print.

_____. *Toward a Feminist Theory of State.* Cambridge: Harvard University Press, 1989. Print.

Martin, Kameelah L. *Conjuring Moments in African American Literature: Women, Spirit Work, and Other Such Hoodoo.* New York: Palgrave Macmillan, 2012. Print.

Matus, Jill L. "Dream Deferral and the Closure in *The Women of Brewster Place.*" *Black American Literature Forum* 24.1 (Spring 1990): 49–64. Print.

Mbalia, Doreatha Drummond. *Toni Morrison's Developing Class Consciousness,* 2d ed. Cranbury, NJ: Associated University Press, 2004. Print.

McGlamery , Tom. *Protest and the Body in Melville, Dos Passos, and Hurston.* New York: Routledge, 2004. Print.

McKnight, Maureen. "Discerning Nostalgia in Zora Neale Hurston's *Their Eyes Were Watching God*." *Southern Quarterly* 44.4 (Summer 2007): 83–115. Print.

McMillan, Terry. *A Day Late and a Dollar Short*. New York: New American Library, 2002. Print.

_____. *Mama*. New York: Washington Square, 1987. Print.

_____."McMillan 'Asks' Readers to Empathize with a Family's Problems." *NPR*. 14 September 2013. Web. 13 November 2013.

Melzer, Patricia. *Alien Constructions: Science Fiction and Feminist Thought*. Austin: University of Texas, 2006. Print.

Miller, Laura. "The Last Resort: Rev. of Toni Morrison's *Love*." *New York Times*. 2 November 2003. Web.

Montgomery, Maxine Lavon. "Good Housekeeping: Domestic Ritual in Gloria Naylor's Fiction." *Gloria Naylor's Early Novels*. Ed. Margot Anne Kelley. Gainesville: University of Florida Press, 1999. 40–55. Print.

Moore, John, and Karen Sayer. Introduction. *Science Fiction, Critical Frontiers*. New York: St. Martin's Press, 2000. Xi–Xiii. Print.

Moore, John Noell. "Myth, Fairy Tale, Epic, and Romance: Narrative as Re-Vision in *Linden Hills*." *Callaloo* 23.4 (Fall 2000): 1410–1429. Print.

Morrison, Toni. *The Bluest Eye*. 1970. New York: Plume, 1994. Print.

_____. *Conversations with Toni Morrison*. Ed. Danille Taylor-Guthrie. Jackson: University Press of Mississippi, 1994. Print.

_____. "Interview with Charlie Rose." *Charlie Rose*. PBS. 19 January 1998. Web. 20 June 2008.

_____. *Love*. New York: Random House, 2003. Print.

_____. *Playing in the Dark: Whiteness and the Literary Imagination*. Cambridge: Harvard University Press, 1992. Print.

Mowatt, Rasul A., Bryana H. French, and Dominique A. Malebranche. "Black/Female/Body Hypervisibility and Invisibility: A Black Feminist Augmentation of Feminist Leisure Research." *Journal of Leisure Research* 45.5 (2013): 644–660. Print.

Naylor, Gloria. *Linden Hills*. New York: Ticknor and Fields, 1985. Print.

_____. *The Women of Brewster Place*. New York: Viking, 1982. Print.

Okonkwo, Christopher N. *A Spirit of Dialogue: Incarnations of Ogbanje, the Born-to-Die, in African American Literature*. Knoxville: University of Tennessee Press, 2008. Print.

_____. "Suicide or Messianic Self-Sacrifice? Exhuming Willa's Body in Gloria Naylor's *Linden Hills*." *African American Review* 35.1 (Spring 2001): 117–131. Print.

O'Leary, K. Daniel. "Psychological Abuse: A Variable Deserving Critical Attention in Domestic Violence." *Violence and Victims* 14.1 (1999): 3–23. Print.

Ooms, Theodora. "A Sociologist's Perspective on Domestic Violence: A Conversation with Michael Johnson, Ph.D." *Center for Law and Social Policy* (2006): 1–7. Web.

O'Quinn, Elaine J., and Heather Atwell. "Familiar Aliens: Science Fiction as Social Commentary." *The ALAN Review* 37.3 (Summer 2010). Web.

Penrice, Ronda Racha. "*The Color Purple* 25 Years Later: From Controversy to Classic." 17 December 2010. *MSNBC*. Web. 10 November 2013.

Peoples, Tim. "Meditation and Artistry in *The Bluest Eye* by Toni Morrison and *Their Eyes Were Watching God* by Zora Neale Hurston." *Midwest Quarterly: A Journal of Contemporary Thought* 53.2 (Winter 2012): 177–192. Print.

Petchesky, Rosalind. "Dissolving the Hyphen: A Report on Marxist-Feminist Groups 1–5." *Capitalist Patriarchy and the Case for Social Feminism*. Ed. Zilla R. Eisenstein. New York: Monthly Review Press, 1979. Print.

Pfeiffer, John R. "Octavia Butler Writes

the Bible." *Shaw and Other Matters*. Ed. Susan Rusinko. Selinsgrove, PA: Susquehanna University Press, 1998. 140–152. Print.

Porter, Evette. "My Novel, Myself." *Village Voice*, 21 May 1996: 41–42. Print.

Potter, George. "Forced Domination: Intersections of Sex, Race, and Power in *Light in August* and *The Bluest Eye*" *Proteus: A Journal of Ideas* 21.2 (Fall 2004): 43–48. Print.

Prescott, Peter S. "A Long Road to Liberation." *Newsweek*, 21 June 1982: 67–68. Print.

Proudfit, Charles L. "Celie's Search for Identity: A Psychoanalytic Developmental Reading of Alice Walker's *The Color Purple*." *Contemporary Literature* 32.1 (Spring 1991): 12–37. Print.

Reiss, Albert J., and Jeffrey A. Roth, eds. *Understanding and Preventing Violence: Social Influences*. National Research Council (U.S.) Panel on the Understanding and Control of Violent Behavior, Washington, D.C.: National Academy Press, 1994. Print.

Rich, Adrienne. "Compulsory Heterosexuality and Lesbian Existence (1980)." *Journal of Women's History* 15.3 (Autumn 2003): 11–48. Print.

Richards, Paulette. *Terry McMillan: A Critical Companion*. Westport, CT: Greenwood, 1999. Print.

Ross, Daniel. "Celie in the Looking Glass: The Desire for Selfhood in *The Color Purple*." *Modern Fiction Studies* 34.1 (Spring 1988): 69–84. Print.

Roynon, Tessa. "A New 'Romen' Empire: Toni Morrison's *Love* and the Classics." *Journal of American Studies* 41.1 (April 2007): 31–47. Print.

Rudolphi, María Frías. "Marriage Doesn't Make Love: Zora Neale Hurston's *Their Eyes Were Watching God*." *REDEN: Revista Española de Estudios Norteamericanos* 6.9 (1995): 37–43. Print.

Rushdy, Ashraf H. A. *Neo-Slave Narratives: Studies in the Social Logic of a Literary Form*. New York: Oxford University Press, 1999. Print.

Sathyaraj, V. and G. Neelakantan. "Family and Parenting in Toni Morrison's *Love*." *Notes on Contemporary Literature* 36.4 (September 2006): 9–10. Print.

Sawhill, Ray, Allison Samuels, and Sherry Keene-Osborn. "How Terry Got Her Groove." *Newsweek* 29 April 1996: 76–79. Print.

Schneider-Mayerson, Matthew. "Popular Fiction Studies: The Advantages of a New Field." *Studies in Popular Culture* 33.1 (Fall 2010): 21–35. Print.

Scholl, Diane Gabrielsen. "With Ears to Hear and Eyes to See: Alice Walker's Parable, *The Color Purple*." *Christianity and Literature* 40.3 (Spring 1991): 255–266. Print.

Sharp, Michael D. *Popular Contemporary Writers*. Tarrytown, NY: Marshall Cavendish, 2006. Print.

Smiles, Robin Virginia. "Romance, Race, and Resistance in Best-Selling African American Narrative." Diss., University of Maryland. 2009. Print.

Smith, Dinitia. "Celie, You a Tree." *Nation*, 4 September 1982: 181–183. Print.

Smith, Sidonie. "Identity's Body." *Autobiography and Postmodernism*. Ed. Kathleen Ashley, Leigh Gilmore, et al. Amherst: University of Massachusetts Press, 1994. 263–292. Print.

Sokoloff, Natalie J., and Christina Pratt. *Domestic Violence at the Margins: Readings on Race, Class, Gender, and Culture*. Piscataway: Rutgers University Press, 2006. Print.

Spilka, Mark. *Eight Lessons in Love: A Domestic Violence Reader*. Columbia: University of Missouri Press, 1997. Print.

Spillers, Hortense J. "Mama's Baby, Papa's Maybe: An American Grammar Book (1987)." *African American Literary Theory: A Reader*. Ed. Winston Napier. New York: New York University Press, 2000. 257–279. Print.

Stiles, Melissa M. "Medicine and Society: Witnessing Domestic Violence: The Effect on Children." *American Family Physician* 66.11 (December 2002): 2052–2067. Print.

Szabó, Péter Gaál. "Transparent Space and the Production of the Female Body in Zora Neale Hurston's *Their Eyes Were Watching God* and *Jonah's Gourd Vine*." *Americana* 3.1 (Spring 2007). Web.

Tanner, Laura E. "Reading Rape: *Sanctuary* and *The Women of Brewster Place*." *American Literature* 62.4 (December 1990): 559–582. Print.

Tate, Claudia. "*Corregidora:* Ursa's Blues Medley." *Black American Literature Forum* 13.4 (December 1979): 139–141. Print.

_____, ed. *Black Women Writers at Work.* New York: Continuum, 1986. 89–99. Print.

Varsam, Maria. "Concrete Dystopia: Slavery and Its Others." *Dark Horizons: Science Fiction and the Dystopian Imagination.* Ed. Raffaella Baccolini and Tom Moylan. New York: Routledge, 2003. 203–224. Print.

Walker, Alice. *The Color Purple.* New York: Washington Square, 1982. Print.

Ward, Catherine C. "Gloria Naylor's Linden Hills: A Modern 'Inferno.'" *Contemporary Literature* 28.1 (Spring 1987): 67–81. Print.

Wardi, Anissa Janine. "A Laying on of Hands: Toni Morrison and the Materiality of *Love*." *MELUS: The Journal of the Society for the Study of the Multi-Ethnic Literature of the United States* 30.3 (Fall 2005): 201–18. Print.

Washington, Mary Helen. "Foreword." *Their Eyes Were Watching God* by Zora Neal Hurston. New York: Perennial Classics, 1998. ix–xvii. Print.

Watkins, Mel. "Some Letters Went to God." *New York Times Book Review.* 25 July 1982. Web.

Waxman, Barbara Frey. "Girls into Women: Culture, Nature, and Self-Loathing in Toni Morrison's *The Bluest Eye* (1970)." *Women in Literature: Reading through the Lens of Gender.* Ed. Jerilyn Fischer. Westport, CT: Greenwood, 2003: 47–49. Print.

White, Deborah Gray. *Ar'n't I a Woman? Female Slaves in the Plantation South.* New York: Norton, 1985. Print.

Whitt, Margaret Earley. *Understanding Gloria Naylor.* Columbia: University of South Carolina Press, 1999. Print.

Wilson, Charles E., Jr. *Gloria Naylor: A Critical Companion.* Westport, CT: Greenwood Press, 2001.

Worthington, Pepper. "Writing a Rationale for a Controversial Common Reading Book: Alice Walker's *The Color Purple*." *The English Journal* 74.1 (January 1985): 48–52. Print.

Wright, Richard. "Between Laughter and Tears (Review of *Their Eyes Were Watching God*)." *New Masses,* 5 October 1937. Web. www.etext.lib.virginia.edu.

Wyatt, Jean. "*Love*'s Time and the Reader: Ethical Effects of *Nachtraglichkeit* in Toni Morrison's *Love*." *Narrative* 16.2 (May 2008): 192–221. Print.

Zosky, Diane L. "The Application of Object Relations Theory to Domestic Violence." *Clinical Social Work Journal* 27 (March 1999): 55–69. Print.

Index

abortion 5, 88
accusations 58, 68, 93
adultery 65, 96, 104, 107
Africa 71, 136, 142, 145–147
Afrofuturism 140–141
alcoholism 40, 45, 65, 99, 101, 104, 107–110, 114
alienation 41, 45
aliens 138–140
Allen, Anita 7
Allen, Donia Elizabeth 59
Althusser, Louis 48
American Civil Rights Movement 14, 143, 156
American Civil War 152
American Psychiatric Association 12
archetypes 62
arson 5, 97, 121
assault 28, 33, 44–45, 55, 62, 65, 85–86, 88, 106, 110, 114, 154
Atwell, Heather 138
Alwes, Karla 43, 47
attempted murder 9, 28, 34, 87, 94
Atwood, Margaret 162
Austin, Rhonda 103
awareness 1–16, 23, 37, 63, 67, 77, 118–119, 136, 143, 159, 161–163, 165–167
Awkward, Michael 108–109

Baldassarro, R. Wolfe 64–65
Battered Woman Syndrome (BWS) 11–12
Berg, Christine G. 80
Biblical allusions 146
Bildungsroman 48
Blues 2, 51, 57–60
The Bluest Eye 2–3, 13–14, 16, 22 39–49, 121–122, 165–166
Bobo, Jacqueline 65
Bost, Suzanne 155

Branzburg, Judith V. 81, 86
breeding program 137, 145, 149, 152–156, 159
Brooks, Rachelle 124–125
Brooks, Wanda M. 145
Brown, Chris 1
Brown, Sterling 19–20
Brown, Tony 64–65
Buller, David J. 117
Burrows, Stuart 33
Butler, Judith 1, 55
Butler, Octavia 2–5, 15, 17, 37, 135–163, 165–166

Cadman, Deborah 41
capitalism 6–8, 39, 52, 124, 126, 143
Carby, Hazel V. 20
Carrillo, Ricardo 107
Champion, Laurie 103
childhood 21, 24, 41–43, 67, 104, 106–107, 114–115, 122, 129, 133
Ciscel, David H. 124
Clay's Ark 2, 136–137, 158–161
Clear, Val 138–139
coercion 88, 136–137, 143, 148, 150, 153, 161
The Color Purple (book) 2, 13–16, 61–75, 165–166
The Color Purple (film) 62
coming-of-age 48, 61
commodification 49, 54, 122, 131, 134, 143
Conner, Marc 41
control 30, 70–71, 73–74, 78, 83–91, 94–98, 124, 136, 139, 143, 148–154, 158–161
Corregidora 2, 13–14, 16, 51–60, 165–166
courtroom 12, 34–36, 114
courtship 31–32, 83, 131
Crabtree, Claire 22–23
crime 1, 13–14, 53–54, 59, 115, 118

Curwood, Anastasia Carol 32
Cutter, Martha J. 62, 75

Daniels, Cynthia R. 124–125
Davis, Angela Y. 7, 39, 52, 59
A Day Late and a Dollar Short 2, 13, 15–16, 99, 112–119, 165–166
death 31, 36, 45, 47, 67, 81, 83, 86, 96–97, 112, 115, 119, 121–123, 129, 139, 145, 151, 154, 156, 160, 166
Delashmit, Margaret 44
desire 52, 54–58, 87, 127, 148
dialect 22, 65
divorce 92, 111, 116
domestic labor 6–7, 27, 73, 124
domestic sphere 2–7, 14, 16, 23, 27, 39, 41, 49, 70–72, 77, 121–124, 131, 134
Drake, Kimberly 45
DSM-IV 12
DSM-V 12
dystopia 142, 149

Eatonville, Florida 21–22, 29–32
education 41, 48, 87, 102, 106, 108
Ellerby, Janet Mason 101–102, 119
employment 114
epistolary 2, 61, 66
Erikson, Kai 143
Eyerman, Ron 143

fantasy 141
Federal Writers Project 67
feminism 7–8, 14, 20, 23, 58–59, 65, 124, 139
firearms 86, 134
Fiske, Shanyn 67
Floyd-Thomas, Stacey M. 64, 66
folklore 23
French, Bryana H. 63
gambling 33, 111, 127

Gates, Henry Louis 22, 35
gender roles 8, 27, 73, 102, 145, 162
genre 15, 47–48, 51, 100–101, 135–142, 152, 163, 166
Gillan, Jennifer 45, 47
Gillman, Laura 64, 66
Giovanni, Nikki 1
Goldstein, Philip 20
Gomez, Jewelle 96
Grewal, Gurleen 41
Griffiths, Jennifer 56–57

Hacking, Ian 10
Hallett, Jill 112

Hampton, Gregory Jerome 140, 114–146, 151, 156–157, 161, 163
Hampton, Robert 89–90
Haraway, Donna J. 144, 158, 162
Harrison, Elizabeth Jane 22
Harrison, Rosalie G. 140
Heath, Judith A. 124
heteronormativity 58, 102, 127
heterosexuality 58, 102, 127, 140
Hine, Darlene Clark 11
historical fiction 141
Holden, Bob 13
Hollywood, role of 43
homosexuality 58, 65
Horvitz, Deborah M. 13, 30, 54–55
Hurston, Zora Neale 1–5, 14, 16–17, 19–37, 165

ideological state apparatuses (ISA's) 48
ideology 42, 48, 94, 124
illness 67, 74, 96, 157–158, 160
immortality 145–146
incest 65, 75, 115, 146
Inferno 80, 90, 92, 97
invisibility 42, 63

Jacobs, Harriet 67, 131
James, Deborah 20
Jasinski, Jana L. 78
jealousy 33–35, 58, 74, 93, 104, 107
Jones, Gayl 2–5, 14, 16–17, 37, 39, 51–60, 165–166
Jones, Jacqueline 75
Jones, Sharon Lynette 25

Kinnear, Karen L. 115
Klotman, Phyllis 47–49

Langellier, K. M. 59
Las Vegas, Nevada 99, 112
Lewis, Catherine E. 62, 64, 68, 71, 73
Li, Stephanie 54–55
Linden Hills 2, 13–16, 77–80, 90–98, 165–166
Love 2–3, 13, 15–16, 39, 121–134, 165–166

MacKinnon, Catharine A. 58
Magarian, Lucia 89–90
Malebranche, Dominique A. 63
Mama 2, 13–16, 99–113, 118–119, 165–166
marriage 5, 15, 19–29, 31–33, 36, 40, 46, 53, 63, 68–71, 75, 79, 91–95, 110–112, 114, 127–128, 130–134, 138, 162,

Martin, Kameelah L. 145, 148
Marx, Karl 6
Mary Janes 41–42
masculinity 33, 73, 89–90, 109, 115
maternal body 54–55
Matus, Jill L. 79, 82
Mbalia, Doreatha Drummond 125
McGlamery , Tom 33
McKnight, Maureen 35
McMillan, Terry 2–5, 14–17, 99–119, 165–166
Melzer, Patricia 139–141, 153, 158, 161–162
Middle Passage 149, 156,
Miller, Laura 121
Mind of My Mind 136–137, 144, 152–169
Montgomery, Maxine Lavon 91–92
Moore, John 138
Moore, John Noell 91
mores 47, 73
Morrison, Toni 2–5, 14–17, 19, 37, 39–49, 102, 121–134, 165–166
Mowatt, Rasul A. 63
murder 5, 9, 34, 65, 95, 121–122, 145, 148–151, 155, 159–160, 162

narration 16, 22, 35–36, 39, 104, 128, 131, 133, 153
Naylor, Gloria 2–5, 14–16, 19, 37, 77–98, 102, 165–166
Neelakantan, G. 122
neo-slave narratives 141–142
nostalgia 35

objectification 49, 51–54, 56–57, 63, 122, 131, 134
OED 10
Okonkwo, Christopher N. 92, 96–96, 151–152
O'Leary, K. Daniel 70
Oliver, William 89–90
Ooms, Theodora 88
O'Quinn, Elaine J. 138
otherness 140

paternity 93
pathology 12, 40–41, 64, 70, 93
patriarchy 94, 124–126, 129, 145, 162, 166
Patternmaster 2, 136–137, 141, 145, 154, 156–157, 159–152
pear tree 24
Penrice, Ronda Racha 65
Peoples, Tim 22
Petchesky, Rosalind 6

Pfeiffer, John R. 146
Playing in the Dark: Whiteness and the Literary Imagination 40
police 77, 111, 117–118
politics 3, 52, 124, 141
popular culture 135
popular fiction 99–119
Porter, Evette 103, 113
Potter, George 44, 46
Pratt, Christina 108
pregnancy 25, 67, 84, 87–88
Prescott, Peter S. 66
prison 13
private sphere 2, 7, 8, 12
Proudfit, Charles L. 66–75
public sphere 2, 7–8

race 1–17, 42–44, 52–53, 79, 94, 101, 108–109, 135–136, 140–149, 156–157, 159, 162
rape 5, 8–11, 25–26, 42, 45–48, 62, 65, 67, 75, 81–82, 110, 121, 125
realism 102, 109, 111, 135–138, 141, 152, 163
recognition 4, 41, 140
reconciliation 15, 75
regionalism 19–37
Reiss, Albert J. 124
religion 146
Rich, Adrienne 58
romance 91, 101, 131
Ross, Daniel 63
Roth, Jeffrey A. 124
Roynon, Tessa 123
Rudolphi, María Frías 19, 31
Rushdy, Ashraf H. A. 142

sadism 30
Samuels, Allison 119
Sathyaraj, V. 122
Sawhill, Ray 119
Sayer, Karen 138
Schneider-Mayerson, Matthew 100–101
Scholl, Diane Gabrielsen 75
Schwartzman, Lisa H. 8
science fiction 2, 15, 135–163
Seed to Harvest 2, 13, 17, 135–163, 165–166
self-defense 12–14, 34–36
sentimentalism 20
sexism 39–41, 49, 79, 122, 131, 134
sexual harassment 7, 58
sexuality 45, 87, 133, 140, 143
Shange, Ntozake 1

shape-shifting 145, 147, 150, 153, 155, 158
Sharp, Michael D. 103–104
slave narratives 67, 141–142
slavery 7, 25–26, 51–55, 66–67, 127–128, 131, 136, 141–144, 147–152, 155–156, 160–161
Smiles, Robin Virginia 101–102, 104
Smith, Dinitia 66
social class 7, 14, 45, 49, 80, 98, 108, 162, 166
Sokoloff, Natalie J. 108
Spielberg, Steven 62
Spilka, Mark 20
Spillers, Hortense J. 52–53
The State of Kansas vs. Peggy Stewart 12
stereotypes 41–44
Stiles, Melissa M. 106
suicide 92, 151, 154–155
supernatural 15, 136, 144–145, 149
Survivor 2
Szabó, Péter Gaál 27

taboo 1, 10–11, 65–66
Tate, Claudia 51
Tello, Jerry 108
testimony 51, 53–54, 57–60
time travel 141
Transatlantic slave trade 136, 141–142
trauma 26, 30, 53–54, 62, 67–69, 75, 106–107, 114–119, 125–127, 143–144
Turner, Ike 1
Turner, Tina 1

unemployment 89, 107–108
U.S. Department of Justice 13

Varsam, Maria 142, 149
victimization 8, 11–14, 23, 25, 30, 34–36, 44–47, 62, 66, 70, 73–75, 106–107, 109, 111, 113–119, 125, 143, 156–157, 166
Violence Against Women Office 13

Walker, Alice 1–5, 14–17, 19–20, 61–75, 165–166
Walker, Lenore 12
Wardi, Anissa Janine 127, 129
Washington, Mary Helen 22
Watkins, Mel 65
Whatever Happened to Baby Jane? (film) 130
What's Love Got to Do with It? (film) 1
White, Deborah Gray
Wild Seed 2, 136–137, 141, 144–153, 156–157, 159, 161–163
Williams, Linda M. 78
"With No Immediate Cause" (poem) 1
"Woman" (poem) 1
The Women of Brewster Place 2, 13–15, 77–90, 165–166
workplace 6, 56–58
Worthington, Pepper 65, 72, 75
Wright, Richard 20, 46
Wyatt, Jean 125, 127, 129, 131, 133–134